Praise for *Life, Liberty, and the Pursuit o*

"Sam Crane's new book is a richly rewarding exploration of the ancient Chinese values and insights that have been the focus of his academic research in connection with the deepest questions of personal and public ethics in the modern United States. Every chapter draws from Crane's scholarship but also from his unsparing description of wrenching choices in his own life. Readers who are China specialists will learn more about its traditions; readers who are not will have new tools and concepts with which to understand their own societies, institutions, and creeds."

– James Fallows, of *The Atlantic*, author of *China Airborne*

"Sam Crane has written a lively and insightful guide to China's two key philosophical schools – Confucianism and Daoism – by looking at how they would deal with today's problems in Western countries. Abortion, education, crime, dealing with the mentally challenged: by exploring how China's greatest philosophical schools might have dealt with them, we learn not only about these ancient ways of thought but also take away innovative ways of looking at our own society. Sprinkled with humorous and touching first-person anecdotes, Crane has given us a truly innovative and fascinating book aimed at general readers."

– Ian Johnson, Pulitzer Prize-winning author of *Wild Grass: Three Stories of Change in Modern China*

"This is a book for those who value life in all its combinations. Sam Crane's marriage of ancient Chinese thought and modern American life is filled with profound insights, intimate anecdotes, and something beyond mere humanity. Applying the teachings of Zhuangzi and Confucius to debates about abortion, same-sex marriage, and euthanasia, it will be read and argued-over again and again."

– Jonathan Watts, author of *When a Billion Chinese Jump*

"Sam Crane's erudite writing on ancient Chinese philosophy in the modern era gives us a new window on some of the most hotly discussed issues in American society today, from democracy to sex."

– Edward Wong, China Correspondent, *New York Times*

Blackwell Public Philosophy
Edited by Michael Boylan, Marymount University

In a world of 24-hour news cycles and increasingly specialized knowledge, the Blackwell Public Philosophy series takes seriously the idea that there is a need and demand for engaging and thoughtful discussion of topics of broad public importance. Philosophy itself is historically grounded in the public square, bringing people together to try to understand the various issues that shape their lives and give them meaning. This "love of wisdom" – the essence of philosophy – lies at the heart of the series. Written in an accessible, jargon-free manner by internationally renowned authors, each book is an invitation to the world beyond newsflashes and soundbites and into public wisdom.

1. *Permission to Steal: Revealing the Roots of Corporate Scandal*
   by Lisa H. Newton
2. *Doubting Darwin? Creationist Designs on Evolution*
   by Sahotra Sarkar
3. *The Extinction of Desire: A Tale of Enlightenment*
   by Michael Boylan
4. *Torture and the Ticking Bomb*
   by Bob Brecher
5. *In Defense of Dolphins: The New Moral Frontier*
   by Thomas I. White
6. *Terrorism and Counter-Terrorism: Ethics and Liberal Democracy*
   by Seumas Miller
7. *Who Owns You? The Corporate Gold Rush to Patent Your Genes*
   by David Koepsell
8. *Animalkind: What We Owe to Animals*
   by Jean Kazez
9. *In the Name of God: The Evolutionary Origins of Religious Ethics and Violence*
   by John Teehan
10. *The Secular Outlook: In Defense of Moral and Political Secularism*
    by Paul Cliteur
11. *Freedom of Religion and the Secular State*
    by Russell Blackford
12. *As Free and as Just as Possible: The Theory of Marxian Liberalism*
    by Jeffrey Reiman
13. *Life, Liberty, and the Pursuit of Dao: Ancient Chinese Thought in Modern American Life*
    by Sam Crane

Forthcoming:

Evil On-Line: Explorations of Evil and Wickedness on the Web
by Dean Cocking and Jeroen van den Hoven

For further information about individual titles in the series, supplementary material, and regular updates, visit www.blackwellpublishing.com/publicphilosophy

Life, Liberty, and the Pursuit of Dao

Ancient Chinese Thought in Modern American Life

Sam Crane

WILEY Blackwell

This edition first published 2013
© 2013 John Wiley & Sons Inc.

Wiley-Blackwell is an imprint of John Wiley & Sons, formed by the merger of Wiley's global Scientific, Technical and Medical business with Blackwell Publishing.

Registered Office
John Wiley & Sons Ltd, The Atrium, Southern Gate, Chichester, West Sussex, PO19 8SQ, UK

Editorial Offices
350 Main Street, Malden, MA 02148-5020, USA
9600 Garsington Road, Oxford, OX4 2DQ, UK
The Atrium, Southern Gate, Chichester, West Sussex, PO19 8SQ, UK

For details of our global editorial offices, for customer services, and for information about how to apply for permission to reuse the copyright material in this book please see our website at www.wiley.com/wiley-blackwell.

The right of Sam Crane to be identified as the author of this work has been asserted in accordance with the UK Copyright, Designs and Patents Act 1988.

Library of Congress Cataloging-in-Publication Data
Crane, George T., 1957–
   Life, liberty, and the pursuit of Dao : ancient Chinese thought in modern American life / Sam Crane. – 1 [edition].
      pages cm. – (Blackwell public philosophy ; 13)
   Includes bibliographical references and index.
   ISBN 978-0-470-67477-2 (cloth : alk. paper) – ISBN 978-1-118-65641-9 (pbk. : alk. paper)
1. Philosophy, Confucian. 2. Philosophy, Taoist. 3. United States – Social conditions – 21st century.
4. United States – Politics and government – 21st century. I. Title. II. Title: Ancient Chinese thought in modern American life.
   B127.C65C73 2013
   181'.112 – dc23

                                                                                      2013006640

A catalogue record for this book is available from the British Library.

Cover image: Confucius statue © sinopics / iStockphoto; background © istockphoto
Cover design by www.simonlevy.co.uk

Typeset in 10.5/13pt Minion by Laserwords Private Limited, Chennai, India
Printed in Singapore by Ho Printing Singapore Pte Ltd

1   2013

For Maureen, Maggie, and Aidan

Contents

Acknowledgments

This book has been a long time in the making. It reflects my continuing education in Chinese philosophy, a process still in its rudimentary stage. I have, to paraphrase Confucius (*Analects* 2.4), turned myself to learning, have taken a stand on a few issues, but am very far from having no doubts – which makes me, intellectually, less than forty years old! Many generous colleagues have helped me but there is much I do not yet know about this vast and wonderful field. Whatever mistakes or misinterpretations there are in this text are mine and mine alone. For what I have learned, however, I must express my gratitude to those who have helped me along the way.

A seminar organized in Beijing by Daniel Bell, of Tsinghua University, including Chris Panza, Randy Pereenboom, and several of Daniel's graduate students provided helpful early feedback. Tian Chenshan hosted me for a talk at Beijing Foreign Studies University and shared his insights. I also gained much from a conference on "Confucianism in a Post-Modern World" at Beijing Language and Culture University. The Johns Hopkins–Nanjing University Center gave me an opportunity to present some of my ideas to an audience of intelligent Chinese and American students. In the United States, a lecture at Bennington College, organized by Paul Voice, and a colloquium at the Oakley Center for Humanities and Social Sciences at Williams College brought critical scrutiny to bear on my arguments. Colleagues in the Department of Asian Studies at Williams also read and discussed a chapter, providing constructive criticisms. Most notably, Christopher Nugent has consistently drawn my attention to translation problems, though I fear he will still be dissatisfied with some of my choices. In addition, over the past decade I have shared portions of this work with my own students at Williams. They have been my partners in education: I have learned from them as we have learned together. One of those students, in particular, also served as a summer research assistant: thank you, Ran Bi.

Several other people have helpfully read and commented on chapters. My thanks goes to Kim Gutschow, Leanne Ogasawara, and Tracy Finnegan.

Much of my thinking on Chinese philosophy has evolved through my blog, *The Useless Tree* (http://uselesstree.typepad.com). That forum has brought me into contact with many scholarly and incisive thinkers who have shaped my understanding in myriad ways: Manyul Im, Stephen C. Angle, Stephen Walker, Alexus McLeod, and Bill Haines stand out in this regard. They, and many other serious students of Chinese philosophy can be found at the group blog: *Warp, Weft and Way* (http://warpweftandway .wordpress.com).

An especial note of gratitude is owed to Michael Boylan, who edits for the Public Philosophy series at Wiley-Blackwell. He recognized the potential of my initial manuscript and carefully commented on every chapter, making this a better book in the process. Five anonymous reviewers have provided constructive comments. Thanks also to Jen Bray at Wiley for bringing the volume to fruition.

The time that this project has taken has been time subtracted from familial and social life. My wife and daughter have borne my distraction with good humor and encouragement. Maureen and Maggie are constant reminders of what Confucius means when he tells us that the love of our family is the starting place of our humanity. And, of course, Aidan, my son, has been and continues to be an inspiration for all that I do.

Text acknowledgments

The author and publisher gratefully acknowledge the permission granted to reproduce the copyright material in this book:

From *The Analects of Confucius* by Burton Watson, trans. Copyright © 2007 Columbia University Press. Reprinted with the permission of the publisher.

From *The Complete Works of Chuang Tzu* by Burton Watson. Copyright ©1968 Columbia University Press. Reprinted with the permission of the publisher.

From *Mencius* by Irene Bloom, trans. Copyright © 2009 Columbia University Press. Reprinted with the permission of the publisher.

Introduction

Two black men approach each other on a New York sidewalk. Their steps are deliberate, their expressions resolute but not severe. As they get close enough for speech, they exchange familiar salutations: "What's up?" Each raises his right arm, forearm cocked back and fingers cupped, and then smoothly reaches a hand to the other. They grasp hands at the thumb and close them together into a mutual fist. After a firm squeeze, they open their hands and slowly let their fingers slide across each other. Finally, they curl their right hands into free fists and gently tap them together.

This, or some variation on the theme, is an everyday scene, something recognizable to many Americans. We think of it as uniquely contemporary, something emerging from African-American culture and extending to American culture more broadly in the here and now. What most of us probably do not realize is that it is also a deeply Confucian act.[1]

Yes, Confucian, as in the ancient Chinese philosopher, Confucius. Let me explain.

Confucius believed and taught that ritual action was the glue that holds civilized society together. By "ritual," or *li* in Chinese, he meant not only the grand commemorations of life's defining moments – marriages, births, deaths – but also the meaningful symbolic gestures of everyday life. Good etiquette in greetings and farewells meant a great deal to him, as did recognition of moral achievement. Noble-minded persons, who strive to live a humane life, must take care to show proper respect, "props" in contemporary American terms, to others. And we do this by adhering to established rules of civil conduct rooted in the norms of a particular community.

Life, Liberty, and the Pursuit of Dao: Ancient Chinese Thought in Modern American Life, First Edition. Sam Crane.
© 2013 John Wiley & Sons, Inc. Published 2013 by John Wiley & Sons, Inc.

Everything about the interaction of the two men mentioned above is designed to communicate solidarity and sociability. As with any style of handshake, the actions are ritualized: they are devised to convey a particular message. If that specific manner of greeting were not used in that context, it could signal aloofness, perhaps even hostility. The gestures may appear to be natural and spontaneous but they are, in fact, intentional and deliberate. Indeed, specific elements of the performance vary from time to time and place to place, and keeping up with and understanding the subtleties of such variations is itself a part of the ritual quality of the conduct.

This is not to say that American culture is thoroughly Confucian. Vast differences obviously exist between the cultural landscapes of ancient China and contemporary America. Whatever those differences, however, an awareness of Confucian thought allows us to appreciate the full social significance of a daily activity that we might ordinarily overlook.

And that is my point in writing this book: to illustrate how ancient Chinese philosophy is helpful for understanding and living in a modern American world.

I am not the first person to make this claim. For hundreds of years, at least since the Jesuits started to systematically translate and interpret the classic texts in the sixteenth century, Westerners have learned a great deal from ancient China. In the past few decades, philosophers have redoubled their efforts to build bridges between Chinese and Western thought. But these recent efforts have not fully succeeded in expanding awareness of Chinese philosophy beyond a relatively small number of academic specialists. How many of us, in our daily lives, ever call upon the ideas of Confucius or Zhuangzi? How many of us ever encounter allusions to these authors in our reading or conversations or television viewing or web surfing?

In our popular culture some aspects of ancient China are widely known and practiced, albeit in revised modern forms. *Feng Shui* is now fairly familiar to many Americans, as is acupuncture and other aspects of traditional Chinese medicine. Daoism seems to pop up in all sorts of places, from New Age music to various book titles beginning with "*The Tao of . . .*" This is all for the good and shows how we continually reach back to other times and places to find ideas valuable for our current circumstances. And if we can do this for easily absorbable cultural fragments, then, without too much effort, we should be able to bring more challenging and rewarding texts into our daily lives. That is my goal.

So, I have written this book not for academics, philosophers, and Sinologists. They have other places they can go to deepen their knowledge of the Chinese classics. This volume is for a general audience, people who have an interest in seeing how ancient Chinese thought might cast new light on the present day but who are not yet familiar with the time-honored works.

In order to demonstrate the contemporary relevance of Confucianism and Daoism, I focus on familiar social and ethical debates. After a brief survey of some key concepts of the two philosophies, I apply them to various issues common to modern American experience, questions that emerge across the arc of a human life. Birth is where it all begins, so we start, in Chapter 2, by analyzing several controversies associated with human birth: abortion, *in vitro* fertilization, and fetal stem cell research. From there we move on to childhood, whether it should be treated as a moral status different from adulthood and whether children who break the law should be tried as adults. Career questions come next, followed, in subsequent chapters, by marriage, public and political life, and, finally, end-of-life issues. Along the way we will reflect upon Confucian and Daoist reactions to, among other matters, gay marriage and adoption, work versus family conflicts, and right-to-die claims.

I hope that the book will serve as an introduction to ideas from a different time and place. No assumption is made here of any prior exposure to, or understanding of, these philosophies. The goal is to present different reasons, derived from classical texts, for familiar ethical beliefs. Daoists and Confucians, for example, differ on the question of abortion – Daoism is generally against it, while Confucianism is more accepting – but not for the reasons we often hear in contemporary debates. They each have a unique perspective, which will unfold over the course of this book. Whether Daoist and Confucian reasoning might change someone's mind now is a matter for each reader to decide. My undertaking is simply to bring those ideas, which I believe are coherent and applicable, into the discussion. They are worthy of our consideration and just might persuade us.

The book will also contribute to our understanding of what Daoism and Confucianism can be now. For centuries Chinese writers and thinkers have amended and revised these philosophies. Western scholarship is extensive. There are many, many contending interpretations. We will not review these academic disputes here, nor anywhere in the present volume. Rather, I will simply put forth what I believe are reasonable accounts, drawn from close readings of translated classical texts, of how Daoism and Confucianism would respond to contemporary issues. Of course, not everyone will agree with my interpretations and assertions. There is nothing I would enjoy more than to inspire another author to put forward a contending Confucian account of, say, gay marriage. Bringing the ancient texts into contemporary debates, and debating what these great books might mean in modern contexts, is my primary purpose.

If it succeeds, this book will show the curious reader how something like a greeting between two African-Americans might resonate with Confucian sensibilities of ritual and benevolence. More than that, it may demonstrate how dead Chinese men might actually be able to help us moderns and postmoderns in managing life's worries and sorrows. And it might also serve as a pathway into further reading of the old books themselves.

In the spirit of full disclosure, I should mention that I have a personal stake of sorts in this task. I am a walking endorsement of the contemporary value of ancient Chinese thought.

It happened years ago, when my son, Aidan, was born with profound disabilities. He was our first child and my wife and I had little direct experience to draw upon in those initial confusing days of new parenthood. So, when things went bad on the tenth day of his life, we were cast adrift into every parent's nightmare: doctors solemnly intoning that our baby might die at any time and, if he did live, he would be physically incapacitated and mentally disabled. They turned out to be right in some ways. Aidan was very limited in conventional terms. He could never speak or see or stand or walk. His mental aptitude did not develop beyond that of an infant. He had an intractable seizure disorder, a tube in his stomach and a tracheostomy in his neck. But the doomsayers were wrong on certain fundamental questions. I came to see that Aidan's life, precisely as it was unto itself, was as valuable as any other. The regret and sadness I felt initially subsided to a comfortable acceptance of the fullness of his own existence. When he died, at age fourteen, I grieved not for what he had lacked in his life, but for all that he had brought into the lives of others, now diminished in his absence. And it was Chinese philosophy that helped me see that truth.

I had recourse to classical Chinese texts because they are a part of my professional life. Teaching contemporary Chinese politics is my job. To facilitate that work, I read and speak modern Mandarin. The topics I study have led me into Chinese history and literature and philosophy. So, I had some background, though not a great deal, in certain strains of Chinese thought, especially Daoism, when Aidan was born. As I struggled to make sense of his condition, I found myself drawn back to the *Daodejing* and

Zhuangzi. I read and re-read them, in several English translations, and found some comfort there, especially in *Zhuangzi*, which tells us:

> . . . the real is originally there in things, and the sufficient is originally there in things. There's nothing that is not real and nothing that is not sufficient. Hence, the blade of grass and the pillar, the leper and the ravishing beauty, the noble, the sniveling, the disingenuous, the strange – in Way they all move as one and the same. In difference is the whole; in wholeness is the broken. Once they are neither whole nor broken, all things move freely as one and the same again. (Hinton, 23)

"Way," here means something like the complex totality of all things. Zhuangzi said to me, through this passage, that Aidan had his place in the world. Whatever kinds of assumptions people might have made about who he was and what he could or could not do, he was as much a part of humanity as any other. That, and many other insights, helped bring me along to a fuller understanding of Aidan. It changed me, as a person and as a writer. On the latter score, I gradually moved away from academic writing and took up the telling of Aidan's story and the ways in which it is illuminated by ancient Chinese thought. A book, *Aidan's Way*, came out of that effort.[2]

With this present book, I am continuing along the path that Aidan started me on years ago. After finding consolation in Chinese philosophy then, I have now come to realize that the ancient writings can provide new perspectives on a wide range of contemporary quandaries. This volume is not about expert textual explication, because I am not an expert textual explicator. It is about reading the great books in various English translations, trying to appreciate what they were talking about, and applying that thought to our own, very different, time. And in that way, I believe, we can all give "props" to thinkers of great subtly and grace.

Sources

I will focus here on Confucianism and Daoism. Each of these philosophies has a long history and various forms. We cannot exhaustively review all facets of these rich traditions – that would be a book in itself. So, the question of which come from Confucianism and which come from Daoism must first be settled.

I will focus on certain early, pre-Qin Dynasty (i.e. before 221 BCE), texts. My reason for doing so is, at first, personal. I like the early texts, their wisdom, their poetry, their feeling. They are also obviously important, forming as they do the bases for the different traditions as they stretch forward into time. Within them are the key ideas of each philosophy. But in making this choice, and not including texts and variations that come later, certain results follow.

In the case of Confucianism, I will draw upon the *Analects* and *Mencius*, both of which are included in the classics of Confucian education. These are the most widely cited sources in this tradition. The former was most likely compiled by various followers of Confucius over several decades in about the fifth century BCE; the latter is attributed to students of another Confucian thinker, Mencius, dating from about the third century BCE. Other early texts will not be referenced, for reasons of succinctness: we cannot do everything and the *Analects* and *Mencius* provide a good start for bringing Confucian ideas to bear on modern questions. To wander further afield would complicate the project with various interpretive controversies, which are not necessary to the work at hand. Given its nature, it is best to keep the enterprise focused on key ideas and texts.[3]

Another consequence of the choice of texts is the exclusion of significant adaptations and revisions of Confucianism after the Qin Dynasty. Indeed, most of what we understand as traditional Chinese "Confucianism" was established in the Han Dynasty (206 BCE–220 CE) and afterwards.[4] We will not consider how the philosophy became a state ideology during the Han, nor how it was reinterpreted as "neo-Confucianism" during the Song Dynasty (960–1279) to accommodate the emergence of Chinese Buddhism. We will not dwell on the various efforts in the nineteenth and twentieth centuries to modify Confucian thinking in the face of Western modernization. These are all interesting and important issues, but they are not our concern. This is not a book about the variants of traditional Confucianism, but, rather, about what the oldest sources of the tradition might mean today.

Along these lines, it must be stated clearly that any modern application of Confucian thought must reject its age-old connections to male domination.[5] While it is certainly true historically that Confucianism was used by men to subordinate women, it is also true that the core concepts of the philosophy can be separated from those earlier functions and be expressed as a more universal ethical framework. I concur with those scholars who believe that Confucianism better lives up to its own moral standards when it is gender neutral.

Daoism also must be defined more precisely. In this instance a distinction can be made between philosophical Daoism and religious Daoism.[6] Although the two tendencies have probably always existed side by side – neither can claim clear historical precedence – they represent different sensibilities.

Religious Daoism is rooted in indigenous Chinese spiritual beliefs and devotional practices that stretch far back into history. In the later Han dynasty, roughly the second century CE, identifiable sects emerged. Despite numerous doctrinal and geographic variations, religious Daoists generally recognize a pantheon of deities who are solemnly worshipped, drawing from a repertoire of sacred rituals. But I will not delve into this fascinating world because my interests run more in the direction of philosophical Daoism. No value judgment is intended in this choice; it is simply a matter of personal preference. Religious Daoism may have relevance for modern questions, and the answers it provides will at times be different than those offered by philosophical Daoism, but that is not the object of this book.

Philosophical Daoism is secular; it does not rely upon the invocation of divine beings or gods. Spirits and ghosts make occasional appearances in some texts, but there is no necessity to invest these figures with immortality or omnipotence or omniscience. They are simply a part of "*Dao*," or Way (defined in the next chapter). As theoretical assertions, Daoist ideas can stand or fall by themselves without any claim of sacred significance. This is what I like about philosophical Daoism: we can analyze it, apply it, think about it, and, if it does not seem to work, we can revise or discard it without danger of upsetting established religious dogma.

Some scholars reject the separation of philosophic and religious Daoism, arguing that the two have always been interrelated, and that may be true to a certain degree. But it is also true that there has long been a self-consciously articulated non-religious philosophical Daoism (*daojia*, as opposed to *daojiao*, in Chinese) with an ancient pedigree in Chinese history. We can carry forward this outlook as an authentic form of Daoism. As long as there has been Daoism there have been philosophic Daoists, thinkers who do not make it into a religion.

As for which Daoist volumes will be consulted, we will focus on the two most famous texts: the *Daodejing*, thought to have been originally composed some time in or before the fourth century BCE; and *Zhuangzi*, parts of which were possibly written in the fourth century BCE. There are various interpretive debates surrounding these texts and their authorship but I will mention here only one point of controversy. I tend to agree with those scholars who doubt the historical existence of a single person named "Laozi" who purportedly wrote the *Daodejing*. This puts me at odds with religious Daoists who deify him. I mean no disrespect. My project, applying philosophical Daoist ideas to contemporary American problems, does not rely on the existence or non-existence of "Laozi." What matters are the ideas as found in the extant texts, not the authors. I will not, however, refer to "Laozi" as the author of the *Daodejing*. On the other hand, I do accept the existence of a person named Zhuangzi (or Zhuang Zhou), who may have had a hand in the composition, but was not the sole author, of the book that bears his name.

It should also be noted here that philosophical Daoism is not a singular, unified school of thought. The two texts consulted here can be quite different in some ways: for example, the *Daodejing* engages with political questions more extensively and directly than does *Zhaungzi*. Generally, however, they share a certain sensibility, a common skepticism about human efficacy in the world, and thus can be placed together under the rubric "Daoist." Thus, when I use the terms "Daoism" and "Daoist" here, I do not mean to suggest complete consistency between the two major texts but, rather, a somewhat looser philosophical affinity.

Translations, transliterations, and transpositions

Translating and interpreting classical Chinese, the language of the original texts considered here, is a difficult enterprise. Historically there have been significant debates over the meaning of these works in Chinese, even before translation into other languages. Vast commentarial collections stretch across centuries. Rendering ancient ideas into the vocabulary and grammar of cultural systems vastly different from that of pre-Qin China is fraught with incongruity and ambiguity. But translation is possible, even if imprecise. We can get a sense of what the texts meant in their own time and what they might mean in our time.

Any particular translation of any one of these texts is bound to have certain problems and limitations. Debates rage among scholars about the finer points of translation. Some linguists demand absolute fealty to the Chinese characters on the page; others take some poetic license to craft more pleasing English sentences. While these are important and interesting differences, I do not want to dwell on them here. I believe that differences among translations are not so great as to obstruct the work of this book:

to bring ideas from the ancient texts into contemporary American debates. Indeed, that explicit purpose has informed my decisions about which translation to use for each individual piece cited. For each passage I have consulted several English translations and, when necessary, checked the Chinese text to get a sense of the linguistic challenges.[7] Ultimately, I draw upon the work of several different translators and my choice for any given passage is determined by my perception of how well the English language rendering works for the purposes of this book. I know that not all of my decisions will meet with universal approval among specialists, but that is the nature of translating classical Chinese.

Regarding transliteration, I use the pinyin system, which has become more standard in English language scholarship on China in recent years. Where translations have used other systems of transliteration, I have changed them to pinyin to maintain textual consistency. Some relatively familiar terms are thus a bit different here: instead of "Taoism" and "*Tao,*" I use, respectively, "Daoism" and "*Dao.*" The "*Tao Te Ching*" becomes, in pinyin, the "*Daodejing,*" and "Chuang Tzu" is "Zhuangzi." I have, however, used the Latinized names "Confucius" (pinyin: *Kongzi*) and "Mencius" (pinyin: *Mengzi*) because of their wide usage in English.

Beyond transliteration and translation, which at base are linguistic problems, this book is a work of what we might call cultural transposition. I am taking ideas from one historical time and place and applying them to a very different social and political and economic context. Thus, what "Confucianism" means in this contemporary situation will not be the same as what it meant in pre-Qin China. There will be a core of indispensable ideas but the interpretation of those ideas must vary, as historical circumstance varies. This has always been the case with Confucianism and Daoism: philosophical meanings have changed over the course of Chinese history. The rub comes when we make a somewhat bigger move, from ancient China to modern America. The question naturally arises: how much interpretive change is too much? At what point does the adaptation of ancient ideas render them unrecognizable, no longer true to some fundamental defining characteristics? There may well be a point at which Confucianism and Daoism cannot be contemporaneously revised. I do not think the arguments of this book cross that line but the reader will be the final arbiter of that question.

Along these lines, I will not draw significantly upon the contemporary experience of China. Although Confucianism and Daoism have certainly enjoyed a resurgence there in recent decades, modern Chinese expressions of these philosophies will not necessarily determine interpretive possibilities in the United States.[8] A contemporary American Confucian would not necessarily believe and behave in a manner identical to a Chinese Confucian. Americans, for example, do not have to contend with the one-child policy and the incredibly competitive economic and educational systems in the People's Republic of China, which can influence the social use or non-use of certain Confucian precepts. This is not to say Chinese experience is wholly irrelevant; rather, it is not unconditionally authoritative for American thought and conduct.

Therefore, when I use terms like "modern Confucian" and "contemporary Daoist," I am referring to people like me: a person in an American context who is trying to adapt ideas from classical Confucian and Daoist texts to contemporary problems. Again, my purpose in all of this is to make Confucianism and Daoism useful for modern ethical debates. At first blush, they may seem to be hopelessly dated and irrelevant. That has not been my experience, however. As I have worked through these texts and thought about them in relation to contemporary issues, I have been struck by the freshness of their insights. I hope to convey that sense of significance, perhaps the way that Zhuangzi finds meaning in the tale of the useless tree.

As the story goes, there is a tree, large and old and uncut. Its wood, in the estimation of the skilled carpenter, is too gnarled and brittle for use in furniture or boat making or other useful pursuits. It is, apparently, a useless tree. But, ironically, it grows taller and provides more shade than other "useful" trees, which are cut down or pruned before they can reach their fullest height and girth. The useless thrives in ways the useful cannot. Its longevity is a lesson for Zhuangzi: if we cling too selfishly to our desires and expectations, if we allow ourselves to be consumed with vanity and conceit, we will fail in our aspirations. The useless thus can have a profound utility; it can show us something about our world and ourselves that we might otherwise not see.

I believe this is what ancient Chinese philosophy can do for modern American life.

Notes

1. Herbert Fingarette famously analyzes a handshake, though not of the African-American variety, as ritual in *Confucius, The Secular and the Sacred* (Prospect Heights, IL: Waveland Press, 1998), p. 9.
2. Sam Crane, *Aidan's Way: The Story of a Boy's Life and a Father's Journey* (Naperville, IL: Sourcebooks, 2003).

3. An important pre-Qin Confucian who is not considered here is Xunzi. The text that bears his name offers an alternative to Mencius, but has not had as much impact historically as Mencius. For a good introductory overview of Xunzi see Paul R. Goldin, *Confucianism* (Berkeley, CA: University of California Press, 2011), Chapter 4. And for an application of Xunzi's ideas to an American contexts, see *Boston Confucianism: Portable Tradition in the Later-Modern World* (Albany, NY: State University of New York Press, 2000).
4. Michael Nylan and Thomas Wilson, *Lives of Confucius: Civilization's Greatest Sage Through the Ages* (New York: Random House, 2010).
5. In the twentieth century, Confucianism was widely criticized, by both Chinese reformers and Western observers, for its patriarchal repression of women. In recent decades, academic analysis has painted a more nuanced picture, one that distinguishes between historical practices that employed Confucianism for patriarchal purposes and the ideas in the early Confucian texts themselves, which are not inherently misogynist. See: Chenyang Li, ed., *The Sage and the Second Sex* (Chicago, IL: Open Court Press, 2000); Li-Hsiang Lisa Rosenlee, *Confucianism and Women* (Albany, NY: State University of New York Press, 2006).
6. Scholars debate the utility of drawing a distinction between philosophical and religious forms of Daoism. Feng Yu-lan demands that the two be understood as separate ways of thinking: Feng Yu-lan, *A Short History of Chinese Philosophy* (New York: The Free Press, 1948), p. 3. And this sentiment is reflected in the organization of the more recent *Encyclopedia of Chinese Philosophy* (London: Routledge, 2003) in the sections "Daoism (Taoism): Classical (*Dao Jia, Tao Chia*)" and "Daoism (Taoism) Religious." On the other hand, Isabelle Robinet argues that "... this division has no significance." Isabelle Robinet, *Taoism: Growth of a Religion*, (Stanford, CA: Stanford University Press, 1997), p. 3.
7. For the *Analects* (*Lun Yu*), I use: Roger T. Ames and Henry Rosemont, Jr., *The Analects of Confucius: A Philosophical Translation* (New York: Ballantine Books, 1998); David Hinton, *The Analects* (Washington, DC: Counterpoint, 1998); Burton Watson, *The Analects of Confucius* (New York: Columbia University Press, 2007).

For *Mencius* (*Mengzi*): Irene Bloom, *Mencius* (New York: Columbia University Press, 2009); David Hinton, *Mencius* (Berkeley, CA: Counterpoint, 1998).

For the *Daodejing*: Roger T. Ames and David T. Hall, *Laozi, Dao De Jing: A Philosophical Translation* (New York: Ballantine Books, 2003); David Hinton, *Tao Te Ching* (Berkeley, CA: Counterpoint, 2000); Robert G. Henricks, *Lao Tzu: Tao Te Ching* (New York: Ballantine Books, 1989).

For *Zhuangzi*: David Hinton, *Chuang Tzu* (Berkeley, CA: Counterpoint, 1997); Burton Watson, *The Complete Works of Chuang Tzu* (New York: Columbia University Press, 1968).

In the cases of *Analects*, *Daodejing*, and *Mencius*, I cite specific passage numbers, for easier cross-referencing. For *Zhuangzi*, I cite page numbers for particular translations, because standard passage numbers are less common.

A handy collection of Chinese language texts for all of these works can be found at the website Chinese Text Project: http://ctext.org/ (accessed March 1, 2013).

8. For an in-depth analysis of the revival of Confucianism in contemporary China, see: John Makeham, *Lost Soul: "Confucianism" in Contemporary Chinese Academic Discourse* (Cambridge, MA: Harvard University Press, 2008).

I

Key Concepts of Confucianism and Daoism

Ancient Confucianism and Daoism are distinct streams of thought, their differences stark at times. But they emerge from and flow through a shared cultural context and historical time. Certain common assumptions are to be found in each, and distinguish both from Western ways of thinking. Thus, before we consider the particulars of these two ancient Chinese perspectives, and the ways in which they differ from one another, we should take a moment to note some similarities.

An ancient Chinese sensibility

Historically, the time of the greatest creativity in Chinese philosophy was also a time of political disintegration and strife.[1] From about 770 BCE onward, the feudal Zhou dynasty, which had begun around 1045 BCE, was falling apart. Recognition of the Zhou king was giving way to the emergence of a variety of smaller sovereign states, each vying to strengthen its army, expand its territory, and heighten its power. As individual sovereigns searched for political and military advantage, they looked to employ the best and brightest men as advisors and strategists, undermining older hereditary practices of office-holding. The venerable privileged families were being challenged by clever and, in some cases, ruthless newcomers. In addition, agricultural and commercial transformations were creating the rudiments of a market economy, opening up new avenues of social

Life, Liberty, and the Pursuit of Dao: Ancient Chinese Thought in Modern American Life,
First Edition. Sam Crane.
© 2013 John Wiley & Sons, Inc. Published 2013 by John Wiley & Sons, Inc.

advancement. Everything – the politics, the culture, the economics – was changing, and the changes were accompanied by more and more warfare. The period from 481–221 BCE is referred to by historians as the Warring States period.

This dynamic and competitive context placed a premium on practicality. It is not surprising then that commentators have noted the "this-worldly" quality of much of ancient Chinese thought.[2] Many Chinese writers focused on questions of the here-and-now and offered prescriptive suggestions for the best human action or non-action. Chinese thought thus has a certain concrete and experiential quality about it, lingering on issues of political order, social etiquette, and ethics. This is not to say there was no theoretical speculation but, rather, that pure abstract theory did not hold as high a place in most ancient Chinese minds as more specific ideas for how to live a good life. Even though Daoism was more expansive in its musings than Confucianism, it did not produce the kind of rarefied metaphysics we find in Western thought.[3]

To take one key point of contrast with classical Western thought, and the various writers who look there for wisdom, ancient Chinese thinkers did not concern themselves with the very large question of the origins of the universe. They did not accentuate a creation myth; they had no story of how Order emerged from Chaos, of how the stuff of the cosmos, and ultimately humankind, was made from Nothing.[4] They simply took the universe as given, a continuous, self-generating totality with no beginning and no end. It was, for them, vast and unfathomable, beyond the descriptive capacities of human language.

A certain humility thus infused many ancient Chinese thinkers. They did not search for singular principles that might bring some sort of ultimate and comprehensive order to the natural world, recognizing, instead, that nature was marvelously complex. The natural world, for them, was not structured around immutable laws, but was a more open-ended and fluid process of movement and change, with each particular thing having its own experience unto itself. The whole, referred to as *Dao* – Way – encompasses everything, both being and nonbeing, from cosmos to photon, and heaven, earth, and the "ten thousand things." A kind of unity was to be found in *Dao*, an organic and interactive coincidence of all things, but it was a unison that could not be reduced to abstract principles. The current fascination among physicists with a "super string theory" that might provide an "explanation of everything" would seem absurd for many ancient Chinese. Why would you want to try to find a supposedly solitary explanation of everything, when each thing has a particular quality and place in the organic totality of nature?

Confucians and Daoists alike thus understood things and persons in context. Socially and politically, individual persons were not presumed to have the kind of autonomy and independence that liberal Western theories assert. We are all embedded in social relationships and political structures and natural environments. While some Daoists might have wanted to withdraw from human society, with all of its distractions and diversions, they would still recognize an individual's interdependence with nature. In ancient Chinese thought generally, no man is an island, entire of itself.

When comparing Western philosophy and ancient Chinese thought, we will also notice a marked difference in writing style, especially for the earliest Chinese texts.

When you open the oldest classics of Chinese philosophy, what you often find is a collection, sometimes untidy, of short anecdotes and aphorisms. The long, rigorous exposition of an argument or theory is not the predominant style of the earliest Confucian and Daoist texts.[5] Poetry, as opposed to analysis, is the inspiration for key Chinese thinkers. Confucius repeatedly tells us to return to the *Book of Songs* (*Shi Jing*), a compilation of verse, and his book *Analects* relies on analogy and allusion. The *Daodejing* can be viewed as a series of poems. The suggestive and allusive quality of these and other important works makes them appear, to our modern senses, hardly to be philosophy at all. Some Western critics argue that there is no philosophy to be found in ancient China; it is just a bunch of sketchy thoughts, not worthy of the august title *philosophy*.[6]

I do not want to get bogged down in academic controversies about the meaning of the term "philosophy." Suffice it to say that enough scholarship has been produced in the past several decades to demonstrate the historical significance and sophistication of ancient Chinese thought. We can safely call it philosophy.[7]

And there were great philosophical debates that occurred among various philosophical perspectives. The two, out of many, we will focus on in this book, Confucianism and Daoism, differ with one another on fundamental issues of how we should relate to one another and to the world around us. To get at these differences, and to see what both might be able to tell us about modern issues and problems, we need to examine some basic concepts of each.

Confucianism

Confucius is often associated with the idea of filial piety, the expectation that children will faithfully respect and follow the dictates of their parents and grandparents and elders. That is certainly a part of the Confucian legacy, but it is far from the whole story. Three other concepts are even more essential to Confucian thinking: humanity, duty, and ritual.

Humanity – ren (仁)

For Confucius and Mencius the highest moral goal for any person – man or woman, adult or child – is humanity.[8] In Chinese, the term is *ren* (or *jen*, under a different transliteration) and it has a number of connotations: "benevolence," "humanity," "humaneness," "altruism," "compassion," "goodness." I like the term "humanity" because it suggests many of the other possible translations but crystallizes them around a core aspiration of human character and achievement. While it is an individual moral state that is aspired to, it simultaneously suggests what each individual might realize and what all people collectively can become. This is not a biological concept, but a moral one.

The Chinese character for *ren* tells us something about what Confucius and his followers were striving for when they put forth the idea of humanity:

$$仁$$

It has two parts. On the left hand side the sloping line and the vertical line are a signifier of "person," and on the right the two horizontal lines are the Chinese symbol for "two." Thus, the character suggests that personhood is relational, a process involving at least two, and perhaps more, persons. It's that simple. Humanity, the highest form of benevolence and moral goodness, is to be found in relationships among persons. An individual, alone, cannot achieve it. It is a social, reciprocal, dynamic exercise of finding the best we can be in relation to others. Confucius himself is quite clear about this:

> As for humanity: if you want to make a stand, help others make a stand, and if you want to reach your goal, help others reach their goal. Consider yourself and treat others accordingly: this is the method of humanity. (Hinton, *Analects*, 6.29)

Think about the first part of that passage: you can realize your personal goals – and by this Confucius means moral goals, the plans we have for achieving something good in this world – only through others. To improve ourselves, to make our own lives better, we must offer a helping hand to people around us. He then adds a classic statement of ethical reciprocity: treat others as you would have them treat you. First time readers of Confucius are often surprised to find this reference to the "golden rule," but it is central to his teachings. He is quite direct in other passages:

> Zigong asked, Is there a single word that can guide a person's conduct throughout life?
>
> The Master said, That would be reciprocity, wouldn't it? What you do not want others to do to you, do not do to others? (Watson, *Analects*, 15.24)

This is not a matter of selfishness. We help others not simply to secure our own personal interests, which is a secondary outcome of ethical reciprocity. Confucius would have us do good unto others because it has a higher intrinsic value in and of itself, regardless of whether we materially profit from it or not. Indeed, if we face a choice between humanity and personal profit, humanity clearly wins out, because it is, as Confucius says, " . . . more vital to the common people than even fire and water" (Ames and Rosemont, *Analects*, 15.35).

Ethical reciprocity is impossible in isolation, and Confucius very much emphasizes the social and communal requirements of humanity. Doing right for others is, for him, a positive obligation: we must do it, if we are to live up to our innate moral potential. If we do not do it, we are denying something essential in our human nature.

Confucius is, thus, an optimist. He believes that everyone, at least initially, is born with a capacity for humanity. This notion is expressed only fleetingly in the aphoristic *Analects*:

> The Master said: "We're all the same by nature. It's living that makes us so different." (Hinton, 17.2)

What is the same about us – a benevolent human nature – is more prominently developed by Mencius:

> Suddenly seeing a baby about to fall into a well, anyone would be heart-stricken with pity: heart-stricken not because they wanted to curry favor with the baby's parents, not because they wanted praise of neighbors and friends, and not

because they hated the baby's cries. This is why I say everyone has a heart that can't bear to see others suffer.

And from this we can see that without a heart of compassion we aren't human, without a heart of conscience we aren't human, without a heart of courtesy we aren't human, and without a heart of right and wrong we aren't human. A heart of conscience is the seed of humanity. A heart of conscience is the seed of duty. A heart of courtesy is the seed of ritual. And a heart of right and wrong is the seed of wisdom.

These four seeds are as much a part of us as our four limbs. To possess them and deny their potential – that is to wound yourself... (Hinton, 3.6)[9]

There's a lot in that passage. First, it reiterates the social context of the cultivation of humanness within each individual. In this case it is our interaction with the endangered baby that incites our inherent benevolence, and humanity is thereby generated by the connection between two persons. Second, Mencius also rejects the notion that altruism is inspired by the expectation of profit. We want to help the baby not because it will benefit us personally, but because our natural, innate humanity impels us. That inherent human benevolence is embedded in both our emotions and our rationality. The "heart" that Mencius invokes suggests, in Chinese (*xin*, 心), both heart and mind, a "heart-mind" of sorts. Third, human nature is universally good: *everyone* has a heart that cannot bear to see others suffer; *anyone* would want to save the baby.

Mencius and Confucius may be optimistic about the potential goodness of all persons, but they are not foolishly idealistic. They recognize that some people will either choose or be drawn to immoral actions. That is the "living" that can make us so different. People must be taught and encouraged to do the right thing in order to understand and realize their natural propensity for goodness. Volition, an idea that is not often associated with Confucianism, can lead us astray, but it can also become a powerful motor of morality. As Mencius says:

There's only one way to know if people are good or evil: look at the choices they make. We each contain precious and worthless, great and small. Never injure what is great for the sake of the small, or the precious for the sake of the worthless. Small people nurture what is small in them, great people nurture what is great in them. (Hinton, 11.14)

We must choose to do the right thing; we must willfully assume that responsibility. But what precisely is the right thing? Humanity is a general goal of ethical reciprocity. Duty (*yi*) is the more concrete definition of our moral obligations.

Duty – yi (乂 (義))

This term has been translated as "rightness," "appropriateness," "righteousness," and "meaning" as well as "duty." Its range of associations overlaps with the previous concept – *ren*, humanity – as well as the next idea – *li*, ritual. Indeed, it is difficult to linguistically isolate these key Confucian tenets, forming as they do an interlinked foundation for the central imperative to do the right thing. My preferred approach is to view "humanity" as the most general understanding of achieved moral goodness. "Duty" (*yi*), by contrast, can be taken as somewhat more specific, the particular obligations that attach to an individual within a certain social context. It is *what* should be done. And "ritual" (*li*), which itself presumes "duty" (*yi*), calls our attention to action. It is the actual *doing* of what should be done in the best manner possible. This distinction between "duty" and "ritual" is suggested in a couple of passages in the *Analects*:

> The Master said: "The noble-minded make Duty their very nature. They put it into practice through Ritual; they make it shine through humility; and standing by their words, they perfect it. Then they are noble-minded indeed." (Hinton, 15.18)

The notion here that our social and familial obligations are rooted in our very nature is echoed in Chapter 6A (or Chapter 11 in some editions) of Mencius. There, Mencius famously argues that "duty is internal" (義內也) (Hinton, 11.5) and suggests that our propensity to fulfill our obligations is something like an appetite: we have a natural craving to do the right thing. Of course, we still have to actually go out and do it, which is sometimes obstructed by other human inclinations. In the *Analects*, a disciple of Confucius encounters a hermit, perhaps a Daoist, who by his actions seeks enlightenment in social isolation. The Confucian is not convinced:

> "To refuse office is to ignore Duty," pronounced Adept Lu. "The obligations of youth and age cannot be abandoned. And the Duty of rulers and officials – what would happen if that were abandoned? In such devotion to self-purification, the great bonds of human community are thrown into confusion. The noble-minded put Duty into practice: they serve in office, though they know full well this world will never put the Way into practice." (Hinton, 18.7)

We have certain duties by dint of our social locations. The young and old have particular sorts of obligations pertaining to their stations in life. The noble-minded, those who have conscientiously progressed toward humaneness, have a duty to take public office in order to facilitate others in their pursuit of doing the right thing. To abandon duty, as the hermit does, is immoral. Yet moral abandonment is possible: people can and do choose to ignore their obligations. That is what distinguishes the noble-minded person: he or she "puts Duty into practice" (行其義也). Exemplary individuals sate the inner moral appetite, duty, through carefully considered ethical action. They do their duty.

For Confucius, the best place to start doing good unto others is with those who are closest to you. Our primary duties, in Confucianism, are familial. Our most pressing obligations are those we owe to our immediate family members. The instruction most often mentioned in the *Analects* is "respect your elders," especially your parents. This is a tangible expression of humanity. One of Confucius's followers is quoted as saying:

> Master, You said, A man filial to his parents, a good brother, yet apt to go against his superiors – few are like that! The man who doesn't like to go against his superiors but likes to plot rebellion – no such kind exists! The gentleman operates at the root. When the root is firm, then the Way may proceed. Filial and brotherly conduct – these are the root of humaneness, are they not? (Watson, *Analects*, 1.2)

We will encounter the term "Way" (*Dao*), when we consider Daoism. For Confucians the term means an organic social order in which each person is fulfilling his or her particular duties. When families are sound in this fashion, a harmonious community and stable political system arises. If we attend to our immediate familial obligation to honor our elders and parents, and if everyone does the same, the world will be a better place. If we take care of those closest to us, larger, seemingly more remote, moral goals will ultimately be secured. It is in this manner that Confucianism creates a hierarchy of duties: our family obligations come first, followed by our responsibilities to friends and colleagues, acquaintances and neighbors. The closer the social relationship, the greater the duty.

Elders may have pride of place in Confucian ethics, but they are not alone. When asked what he most wants to do, Confucius replies: " . . . to bring peace and contentment to the aged, to share relationships of trust and confidence with my friends, and to love and protect the young" (Ames and Rosemont, *Analects*, 5.26).

It is important to note the Confucian duty that parents have toward children, if only because we hear most often about the deference children owe parents.[10] In building a moral community from the inside out, from one's closest family relationships outward to an ever-broadening social network, caring for children is essential. Here it is given equal ethical significance as respecting elders by Mencius:

> By treating the elders in one's family as elders should be treated and extending this to the elders of other families, and by treating the young of one's own family as the young ought to be treated and extending this to the young of other people's families, the empire can be turned around in the palm of one's hand. (Bloom, 1A7)

In caring for their children, fathers must live up to their duties as fathers, or they may not be worthy of the title "father."[11] Mencius recounts the story of super-filial Shun, a legendary sage-king of antiquity. Shun's father was depraved, so much so that he tried on at least two occasions to kill his son. Clearly, the man was no father. Shun, however, was so good that he continued to be respectful of his father, even when the father did not deserve that respect. Mencius uses this tale to show how Shun, through infinite patience and wisdom, was, in the words of one translator (Hinton), "a son to no father," a truly extraordinary accomplishment. For the rest of us mortals, Mencius understands that we can be justifiably resentful toward a failing parent:

> If you don't resent a parent's fault when it's serious, you're treating parents like strangers. And if you resent a parent's fault when it's slight, you're treating parents with abandon. Treating them like strangers, treating them with abandon – either is no way for a child to honor parents. (Hinton, 12.3)

This puts a great deal of responsibility on children: they have to be respectful of their parents even when they can see that the parents are at fault. But there is another message here as well. If parents fail in their duties to children, they risk sowing resentment, dissention, and, ultimately, they contribute to social disorder – people may, as Confucius warns in *Analects* 2.20, forget how to be loyal and reverent. There is a high price to pay for not cherishing the young.

Duties toward friends, too, are important. A disciple of Confucius puts it this way:

> Master Tseng said: "The noble-minded use cultivation to assemble friends, and friends to sustain their humanity." (Hinton, *Analects*, 12.24)

A collection of friends becomes another forum in which ethical reciprocity, humanity, is enacted. We make promises to friends, we do things for them, and they do things for us, not for reasons of personal profit, but because of the imperative to do right by those closest to us. We find our own humanity there.

Duties, then, are socially determined and constructed. Sometimes Confucian obligations are summarized by the "five relationships," which Mencius enumerates as:

> . . . between parents and children there is affection; between ruler and minister, rightness; between husband and wife, separate functions; between older and younger, proper order; and between friends, faithfulness. (Bloom, 3A4)

Of course, the particular demands and limits of these relationships change with social and historical development. We do not today accept male domination of women; we reject parental abuse of children; and we expect a certain openness from political leaders. These modern norms do not render Confucian duties meaningless, however. What a contemporary Confucianism can do is raise particular ethical questions: Are you attending to your family obligations? Should you think more about how your friends and acquaintances might react to what you are about to do? Are you limiting your selfish desires in recognition of the social context of your humanity?

One last thing to consider here is our duty toward strangers. Does Confucianism recognize any such obligation? Other moral philosophies and religions that emphasize universal equality would tell us that we must afford strangers the same respect and, under certain circumstances, the same treatment that we give to our family members. On the face of it, the ethical particularism of Confucianism, and its imperative that we attend to our family obligations first, suggests that we do not really have much in the way of duties to strangers. But a closer reading leads to a different conclusion.

Confucius himself was kind to strangers. When he encountered a person in mourning, made obvious by clothing and demeanor, "the Master would stand or humbly step aside" (Hinton, *Analects*, 9.10). He paid respect when respect was due, even to someone he did not know. Although he famously approved of fathers and sons shielding each other from the law when one stole a sheep (*Analects*, 13.18), suggesting a relativistic ethics, his followers discerned a universal aspect to his notion of humanity:

> Sima Niu lamented, "Everyone has brothers except for me."
> Zixia said to him, "I have heard it said:
>> Life and death are a matter of one's lot;
>> Wealth and honor lie with tian [heaven].
> Since exemplary persons are respectful and impeccable in their conduct, are deferential to others and observe ritual propriety, everyone in the world is their brother. Why would exemplary persons worry over having no brothers?"
> (Ames and Rosemont, *Analects*, 12.5)

When the noble-minded exemplary person is doing the right thing, and that means, first and foremost, carrying out their family responsibilities, then he or she will naturally be kind toward others as well. All men are brothers: no strangers there, especially when ritual (*li*) is working smoothly.

Ritual – li (礼)

This may be the Confucian principle that is most difficult to transport into a modern context. It is translated as "rites," "etiquette," "propriety," and "worship," as well as "ritual." I would like to emphasize here the sense of action or performance included in this field of meaning. In English, the word "ritual" often has a negative connotation, an image of mindlessly going through the motions of some formal obligation. In an era that values self-expression and creativity, "ritual" can seem an outmoded attachment to past practices. Although much of our modern life has a ritualistic quality to it – the way we participate in politics or follow sports or watch television – many of us would want to deny that our lives are shaped by ritual, or, perhaps, wish that those rituals that we do practice were more meaningful.

Confucius, too, rejects the idea of ritual as thoughtless imitation of supposedly authoritative action. He teaches us to perform our morality, live our duties, through our daily behavior. Words are insufficient in and of themselves to secure good outcomes; we must continually strive to cultivate our humanity. For this, commitment is essential. If you are not whole-heartedly engaged in what you have to do, your actions are literally meaningless. Intention and dedication matter for Confucius. He scoffs at people who put on an act of doing the right thing without really meaning it:

> The Master said: "What could I see in a person who in holding a position of influence is not tolerant, who in observing ritual propriety is not respectful, and who in overseeing the mourning rites does not grieve?" (Ames and Rosemont, *Analects*, 3.26)

And he castigates children who make light of their duties toward parents:

> Ziyou asked about filial conduct. The Master replied: "Those today who are filial are considered so because they are able to provide for their parents. But even dogs and horses are given that much care. If you do not respect your parents, what is the difference?" (Ames and Rosemont, *Analects*, 2.7)

Ritual, for him, is the fully considered performance of our vital moral responsibilities. To do it right, you have to be totally absorbed in it all of the time. Conscientious ritual is not simply a matter of big, public occasions, such as weddings and births and funerals, though those are important. More immediately, ritual is the thoughtful enactment of our daily obligations, putting our hearts and minds into the mundane tasks that our family relationships, and other social connections, demand of us. Small things are as ritually important as large events. When his favorite student, Yen Hui, asked about ritual, Confucius spoke to its pervasiveness:

> Yen Yuan [Hui] asked about humaneness. The Master said: To master the self and return to ritual is to be humane. For one day master the self and return to ritual, and the whole world will become humane. Being humane proceeds from you yourself. How could it proceed from others?
>
> Yen Yuan said: May I ask how to go about this?
>
> The Master said: If it is contrary to ritual, don't look at it. If it is contrary to ritual, don't listen to it. If it is contrary to ritual, don't utter it. If it is contrary to ritual, don't do it.
>
> Yen Yuan said: Lacking in cleverness though I am, I would like, if I may, to honor these words. (Watson, *Analects*, 12.1)

Ritual, in other words, always demands our attention, wherever we are, whatever we are doing. Notice, too, how Confucius urges us to find the humane impetus for ritual first in our personal selves. The commitment to thoughtful action must come from the inside out; it is not simply a response to external social demands, but an internal dedication to doing the right thing in the world.

But how do we know what the right action is? Once again, contrary to the idea of rote imitation, Confucius understands that specific definitions of proper action depend upon particular circumstances. The noble-minded person, one who is striving to achieve humanity by fulfilling duty through ritual, must carefully observe and discern the right course in each social context encountered. This requires a certain creativity and flexibility, a certain vision and panache. David L. Hall and Roger T. Ames, masterful interpreters of the *Analects*, show how, through his appreciation of music, especially in relation to ritual, Confucius was a virtuoso of sorts, ingeniously orchestrating his actions and his social setting.[12] This passage suggests as much:

> The Master said: "The use of a hemp cap is prescribed in the observance of ritual propriety. Nowadays, that a silk cap is used instead is a matter of frugality. I would follow accepted practice on this. A subject kowtowing on entering the hall is prescribed in the observance of ritual propriety. Nowadays that one kowtows only after ascending the hall is a matter of hubris. Although it goes against accepted practice, I still kowtow on entering the hall." (Ames and Rosemont, *Analects*, 9.3)

He knows what traditional ritual calls for, but he weighs this against the common contemporary practice and then makes a personal decision based upon the meaning he is trying to express. It is an art, not a science.

To be a bit more precise: in devising proper action at any given moment, we can start with reflection upon our duties. We know, generally, that we should honor our parents, cherish the young, and trust our friends. And we should continually return to these duties. But what they mean in any particular circumstance requires an inventive dedication. There is no universal formula, just a well-intentioned engagement:

> The Master said, with regard to worldly affairs, the gentleman has no strong likes and no strong dislikes – he sides with what is right [*yi*]. (Watson, *Analects*, 4.10)

We should not go into a social situation with our minds already made up about what we need to do. Rather, we must attune ourselves to the surroundings, absorb the whole moment, think about our duties, and constantly try to see and do the right thing. That is ritual awareness and action.

These, then, are three key concepts of Confucianism: humanity, duty, ritual. The Confucian worldview, of course, includes many other ideas and principles but these offer a starting point. In the chapters that follow, we will apply these ideas, these aspirations, to modern ethical issues and, with the addition of other Confucian ideas added along the way, construct a modern American Confucian perspective. But before we do that, we must now turn to some key concepts of Daoism.

Daoism

It is famously difficult to describe the main ideas of Daoism.[13] The first lines of the *Daodejing*, a foundational text, say that the *Dao*, or "Way," that can be spoken or made manifest is not really the *Dao*. Since Way is a central concept of the philosophy, that makes my job a bit harder – but not impossible. Recognizing Daoism's playful ambiguity, and thus the imprecision of our definitions, we can begin discussing three concepts as an introduction: Way (*Dao*), integrity (*de*), and non-action (*wuwei*).

Way – Dao (道)

In relation to Daoism, and to other schools of ancient Chinese thought, the term *Dao* (*Tao*) is most often translated as "Way." The character implies both a thing – a road or path or way – and a process – moving along a road or path or way. It also has normative implications, suggesting what should be, or what should be done. Additional definitions include: "method," "principle," "to say or speak," "to think or suppose." Its broad field of meaning is the thing we should notice, if we are to understand its philosophical connotations.

For Daoists, Way suggests totality, the simultaneous existence and unfolding of all things now. It is vast, beyond human comprehension, and its unity cannot be captured by any singular image or idea. The Daoist Way is not God in a monotheistic sense, though theologians have projected God into Way.[14] There is no one face of Way, only an infinite number of particular expressions. There is no one controlling principle or power, only a profusion of unique occurrences, each following their own Ways as they create a coincidentally complete Way. The term is used in both of these senses: the specific experience of a single thing or person and the entirety of all such experiences. I have my own personal Way which exists within the totality of Way.

Totality, therefore, is to be found within each thing, as each thing is a part of totality. There is no outside of Way, no beginning, no end, no moment of creation, no prophecy of apocalypse. All of these are impossible because Way is everything, whatever happens. It encompasses both being and nonbeing and, thus, is timeless.

Passage 34 from the *Daodejing* speaks to the nature of Way:

> Way is vast, a flood
> so utterly vast it's flowing everywhere.
>
> The ten thousand things depend on it:
> giving them life and never leaving them
> it performs wonders but remains nameless.
>
> Feeding and clothing the ten thousand things
> without ruling over them,
> perennially that free of desire,
> it's small in name.
> And being what the ten thousand things return to
> without ruling over them,
> it's vast in name.
>
> It never makes itself vast
> And so becomes utterly vast.
>
> (Hinton)

The "ten thousand things" refers to earthly material objects. They are, collectively, something less than Way – they do not include "Heaven," which represents a realm of energy and time, fate and destiny. Passage 34, then, is a partial observation of Way, discerning only its worldly presence. Even from this limited perspective, however, Way is everywhere. It nurtures each and every material thing around us, yet it does not control or "rule over" anything. Both vast and small, Way reflects the totality of all things while it is expressed in each thing. It is both the provider of life – in the sense that context provides meaning – and the condition to which all things return, which suggests a lastingness beyond the limits of time. If everything, all the ten thousand things, disappeared tomorrow, there would still be Way.

But so what? What does it matter that various ancient Chinese thinkers put forth a vague and paradoxical notion of totality that they named "Way"? What use is it?

The idea of Way is invoked by Daoists to remind us of the limits of our presence in the cosmos, indeed the smallness of all things in comparison to the immensity of Way. Confucians have a more focused definition of Way: the network of organic interpersonal relations emanating from family ties and radiating outward to a harmonious social order that orients us toward our duties. Daoists have a grander vision, one that zooms out to the widest of all big pictures, in which social relationships are submerged in an endless field of things and events and possibilities. This is meant to have a humbling effect. We should not expect to have all that much of an impact on Way when we are such an infinitesimal part of it. Duties lose their urgency and ritual its necessity in the vastness of the Daoist Way. Even humanity seems less important since Way includes so many other things besides social relationships.

Daoism thus posits an ethics quite different from Confucianism, and that difference has much to do with the more expansive understanding of Way. Where Confucians counsel responsible action, Daoists urge cautious inaction, as will be discussed below.

The two philosophies also differ on questions of knowledge and behavior, what we can know of the world and what we can do in it. This passage from *Zhuangzi* suggests some of these differences:

> The Dao [Way] has its own nature and its own reliability: it does nothing and it has no form. It can be passed on, but never received and held. You can master it, but you can't see it. Its own source, its own root – it was there before heaven and earth, firm and constant from ancient times. It makes gods and demons sacred, gives birth to heaven and earth. It's above the absolute pole, but is not high. It's below the six directions, but is not deep. It predates the birth of heaven and earth, but is not ancient. It precedes high antiquity, but is not old. (Hinton, 87)

Way cannot be known by conventional intellectual means because it is invisible and formless. A person can "master it," orient one's life to Way and move along with it, but cannot hold it. From this follows a profound Daoist skepticism of human knowledge, so much of which is divorced from the subtleties of Way. As the *Daodejing* tells us: "the knowing are never learned, and the learned never knowing." (Hinton, 81) – the "learned" being those who have filled themselves with humanly created ideas and images. To know Way is to "give up learning" (Hinton, 20). To which Zhuangzi adds, "dwell in the ordinary" (Hinton, 23). Don't search for comprehensive theoretical explanations of nature, all of which must fail to capture the enormity and complexity of Way. It cannot be "received and held." Just absorb what is around you, for in each microsecond of experience, the whole is present. It is not high nor deep nor ancient. It's right here.

Integrity – de (德)

The relationship between the totality of Way and each of its innumerable parts is captured in the concept of integrity, the "*de*" of the *Daodejing*. This character is variously translated as "virtue," "integrity," "potency" "power," "efficacy," and "excellence." To my understanding, however, these are all effects of a thing being complete unto itself and integrated into Way; that's why I prefer "integrity."

Integrity defines the individual nature or quality of each particular thing in Way. It is something like potential, a person's inborn disposition and possibility. All persons have a unique *de* to fulfill, as do all animals and minerals and vegetables. When we act in accordance with our *de*, we are following our particular *Dao*. And that gives us a certain virtue and potency: we are living in accordance with Way, realizing our inherent capacities, attaining our personal integrity.

Zhuangzi speaks to this idea here without directly invoking *de*:

> . . . the real is originally there in things, and the sufficient is originally there in things. There's nothing that is not real, and nothing that is not sufficient.
>
> Hence, the blade of grass and the pillar, the leper and the ravishing Xi Shi, the noble, the sniveling, the disingenuous, the strange – in Dao they all move as one and the same. In difference is the whole, in wholeness is the broken. Once they are neither whole nor broken, all things move freely as one and the same again. (Hinton, 23)

All things are real and complete unto themselves; and, in this regard, all things are essentially equal. Each element of Way, however grand or small, has its place, its integrity, and accordingly all are the same. There is a radical egalitarianism here. No person can claim to be superior to any other because each is simply living out his or her own integrity. And no one can be marked as inferior. Since each is unfolding according to its own particular character, no thing can be regarded as better or worse. Daoism, therefore, accepts a kind of moral relativism. If each thing has its own specific integrity, then we cannot use the circumstances of one to judge another. No universal law of nature or morality can be applied to all things.

This may seem paradoxical – all things are essentially the same but each thing is unique unto itself – but Daoism revels in paradox. How else can we understand this excerpt from passage 38 of the *Daodejing*?

> High Integrity never has Integrity
> and so is indeed Integrity.
> Low Integrity never loses Integrity
> and so is not at all Integrity.
>   (Hinton)

This is a slap at Confucianism, which puts forth a set of general social practices and conventions that everyone should apply to their own individual circumstances. For Confucius, "integrity" is associated with duty and ritual and humanity, all of which the *Daodejing* is here rejecting as "low integrity." The Daoist message is: if you strive for integrity by following someone else's standards, you will ultimately undermine your own character and efficacy. It is in that sense that "high integrity," that which is quietly true to itself and does not aspire to an ersatz Confucian "integrity," is more genuinely integrity.

Daoists, then, would accept the Shakespearean dictum: "To thine ownself be true." And they would embrace the biblical teaching, "judge not, lest ye be judged," without further reference to a higher divine law.

Yet this raises a disturbing possibility: what happens if someone is naturally bad, if his or her inherent character produces a hurtful and evil "integrity"? How can we respond to injustice and harm if there is no universal standard of morality to call upon?

Daoism does not deny the existence of evil; nor does it hold out the hope of a perfectly good world. Instead, it recognizes a human tendency to do wrong willfully. Some of this is inescapable:

> The way of tian [heaven] is also to let some go where there is excess
> And to augment where there is not enough.
>
> The way of human beings on the other hand is not like this at all.
> It is instead to take away from those who do not have enough
> In order to give more to those who already have too much.
>   (Ames and Hall)

This excerpt from passage 77 of the *Daodejing* suggests that people can naturally tend toward greed and callousness, the roots of violence and injury. This is not to say that everyone will always be bad. Unlike Mencius, Daoism does not put forth a notion of "human nature" in general. "Way," when applied to "human beings" here, is more indefinite and open ended. It implies that humans can and will act selfishly and harm others, but they are not inevitably destined to do so. Zhuangzi goes so far as to contend that a person can be "without the essentials of man"[15] — can escape the entrapment of doing right or wrong – if he or she simply abides in the natural unfolding of Way.

Indeed, the physical existence of the *Daodejing* and *Zhuangzi* texts, lovingly written and reproduced, can be seen as active appeals to the better angels of our nature. The authors are saying, in the very act of writing, that we may have something bad in us, but we are also capable of cooperation and moderation, as the continuation of passage 77 of the *Daodejing* indicates:

> Only a master of the Way
> can give abundance to all beneath heaven.
> Such a sage acts without presumption
> and never dwells on success:
> great worth has no need to be seen.
>
> (Hinton)

A "sage" can master Way, which means follow Way, and conform to the natural unfolding of things. He or she can thus provide abundance to all. This requires a refusal to be distracted by the temptations of wealth and power and fame, all of which prey upon the ignoble aspect of our character. We are not captives of an essentially bad human nature. The ideal of sageliness holds out the possibility of a liberating integrity:

> You have the audacity to take on human form and you are delighted. But the human form has ten thousand changes that never come to an end. Your joys, then, must be uncountable. Therefore, the sage wanders in the realm where things cannot get away from him, and all are preserved. He delights in early death; he delights in old age; he delights in the beginning; he delights in the end. If he can serve as a model for men, how much more so that which the ten thousand things are tied to and all changes alike wait upon! (Watson, *Zhuangzi*, 81)

And that something that all wait upon is, of course, Way, where all of us live out our integrity.

Non-actions – wuwei (无为 (無爲))

To follow Way, and express our integrity, we should, Daoism tells us, *wuwei* – "do nothing," The term *wuwei* is among the most cryptic in the Daoist lexicon. It can mean "not doing," or, to reverse the order of the characters, "doing nothing." But the "nothing" – *wu* – comes before the "doing" – *wei* – so the compound suggests "nothing doing." That implies a certain productivity in nothingness. "Nothing" is active and creative; it is doing. That's the key. My favorite translation, therefore, is David Hinton's: "nothing's own doing."

To clarify: if Way is beyond our control, if it unfolds as it will, regardless of our efforts, in all of its complexity, then our attempts to affect it, to take meaningful action in the world, are bound to fall short of our expectations and desires. Better to do nothing than try to do something and have it blow up in our faces:

> Longing to take hold of all under heaven and improve it . . .
> I've seen such dreams invariably fail.
> All beneath heaven is a sacred vessel, something beyond all improvement.
> Try to improve it and you ruin it.
> Try to hold it and you lose it.
>
> For things sometimes lead and sometimes follow,
> sometimes sigh and sometimes storm,
> sometimes strengthen and sometimes weaken,
> sometimes kill and sometimes die.
>
> And so the sage steers clear of extremes,
> clear of extravagance,
> clear of exaltation.

(Hinton, 29)

There is a certain fatalism here, and that is central to Daoism. But fate, in this instance, is not predetermined; it is spontaneous and flowing – things will move and strengthen and weaken of their own accord. It is Way unfolding. The sensibility of "nothing's own doing," therefore, is not so much submissive obedience as it is liberated acceptance. Way is boundless and uncontrollable, and, as the passage above tells us, it has a perfection all of its own, regardless of our wishes or plans. If we embrace that understanding and marvel at its fullness and beauty, relinquishing our desire to channel and dominate it, we will find peace and joy:

> Life, death, preservation, loss, failure, success, poverty, riches, worthiness, unworthiness, slander, fame, hunger, thirst, cold, hot – these are the alterations of the world, the workings of fate. Day and night they change place before us and wisdom cannot spy out their source. Therefore, they should not be enough to destroy your harmony; they should not be allowed to enter the Spirit Storehouse [mind]. If you can harmonize and delight in them, master them and never be at a loss for joy, if you can do this day and night without break and make it Spring with everything, mingling with all and creating the moment within your own mind – this is what I call being whole in power.
> (Watson, *Zhuangzi*, 73–74)

Not forcing ourselves on Way brings liberation: even in the face of death we will not lose our joy.

"Nothing's own doing" does not, then, have to be taken as a strict command to take no action at all. The image of the Daoist hermit, isolating himself from the world in an extreme form of inaction, is an enduring one in history. Some people fervently believe that the texts tell them to remove themselves from the world as much as possible. It is a reasonable interpretation, but not a necessary one. Some level of activity is obviously required for human life: food has to be grown and prepared, shelter secured, children raised. Daoism does not tell us to return to some primitive animal state. It urges, rather, that we do not get caught up in the human creations, both material and intellectual, that might distract us from the natural unfolding of Way.

It is difficult, perhaps impossible, to know what exactly is natural and what is not, especially when talking about human passions and personalities. Daoism, however, does not demand absolute precision. Instead of an unbending moral standard, it offers a supple appreciation of restraint and humility.

> In yielding is completion.
> In bent is straight.
> In hollow is full.
> In exhaustion is renewal.
> In little is contentment.
> In much is confusion.
> (Hinton, *Daodejing*, 22)

The trick is to perceive how to do nothing, sensing when some action is in keeping with Way and when something else might be too much. We have to find how nothing and doing fit together. There is no absolute formula, no guidebook, only intuition and instinct. Intellect cannot tell us because Way is beyond our logical capacities. We have to open ourselves to our surroundings, let go of our preconceptions, and feel what can and should be done.

These three concepts – Way, integrity, and doing nothing – get us started on Daoism. We will expand upon these ideas, and add others, as we consider how Daoism might speak to modern issues.

One final point of contrast between Daoism and Confucianism needs to be made, however. The more radical particularism of Daoism – its notion that each thing, while embedded in Way, is unique unto itself – makes it more difficult to use as a basis for ethical judgment. If we cannot refer to the experience of one thing to understand and assess the experience of another, then we do not have a general set of expectations and standards that might function as moral principles. Confucians would agree that particular circumstances might require that guidelines be modified in practice. But Daoism goes further. It denies the possibility of any general statement, such as "respect your elders," as relevant for regulating the behavior of most individuals.

Is it impossible, then, to apply Daoism to modern social and ethical questions? I think we can use it, if we remember that Daoist prescriptions are particular and personal. They are suggestions to individuals, not public doctrines that might be anticipated to suit most people, most of the time. In a sense, Daoism is not playing the same moral game as Confucianism. It is not striving for regulation of society; rather, it seeks something like the liberation of individuals. And that is a project that is certainly pertinent to modern debates.

Notes

1. For a general historical overview of early China, see Michael Loewe and Edward L. Shaughnessy, eds, *The Cambridge History of Ancient China: From the Origins of Civilization to 221 B.C.* (Cambridge: Cambridge University Press, 1999).

2. Frederick W. Mote, *Intellectual Foundations of China* (New York: McGraw-Hill, 1989), Chapter 2; David L. Hall. and Roger T. Ames "Chinese philosophy," in E. Craig, ed., *Routledge Encyclopedia of Philosophy* (London: Routledge, 1998).

3. Joseph Needham mentions Daoism's "characteristic distaste for metaphysics" in *Science and Civilisation in China*, vol. 2 (Cambridge: Cambridge University Press, 1956), p. 40.

4. Derk Bodde, "Myths of Ancient China," in Samuel N. Kramer, ed., *Mythologies of the Ancient World* (Garden City, NY: Quadrangle Books, 1961). For a fuller philosophical discussion of the contrast of Greek and Chinese thinking, see David L. Hall and Roger T. Ames, *Anticipating China: Thinking through the Narratives of Chinese and Western Cultures* (Albany, NY: State University of New York Press, 1995).

5. Among the earliest writers, *Mozi*, is a notable stylistic exception, with longer and more analytic chapters. And that textual form becomes more influential into the third century BCE, as seen most prominently in *Xunzi*.

6. Hegel argued, to significant historical effect, that ancient Chinese thought was not "philosophy": Young Kun Kim, "Hegel's Criticism of Chinese Philosophy," *Philosophy East and West*, 28 (2) (April 1978), pp. 173–180. See also Amy Olberding, ed., *APA Newsletter on Asian and Asian-American Philosophers and Philosophies*, 8 (1) (Fall 2008).

7. Bryan W. Van Norden, *Introduction to Chinese Philosophy* (Indianapolis: Hackett Publishing Company, 2011); A.C. Graham, *Disputers of the Dao* (Chicago, IL: Open Court Publishers, 1989); Benjamin Schwartz, *The World of Thought in Ancient China* (Manoa, HA: Belknap Press, 1985).

8. Tu Wei-ming, "The Creative Tension Between *Jen [Ren]* and *Li*," in Tu Wei-ming, ed., *Humanity and Self-Cultivation: Essays in Confucian Thought* (Berkeley, CA: Asian Humanities Press, 1979), pp. 5–16; Shirong Luo, "Is Yi more basic than Ren in the teachings of Confucius?" *Journal of Chinese Philosophy*, 38 (3) (September 2011), pp. 427–443.

9. Hinton uses a different numbering system than Bloom in organizing the *Mencius* text. I use the system particular to each translator in citations of his or her work.

10. Karyn Lai makes note of parental duties toward children in *Learning from Chinese Philosophies: Ethics of Interdependent and Contextualized Self* (Burlington, VT: Ashgate, 2006), pp. 25–26.

11. The notion that "names," whether they connote social roles or political offices, bring with them certain moral imperatives is famously expressed in the "rectification of names" reference in *Analects* 13.3. This idea is returned to in Chapter 5.

12. My understanding of Confucius is influenced by their key text, *Thinking Through Confucius* (Albany, NY: State University of New York Press, 1987). Their discussion of the sage as virtuoso can be found there on pp. 275–283.

13. Good starting points are: Hall and Ames's "Philosophical Introduction," in Roger T. Ames and David L. Hall, *Dao De Jing: A Philosophical Translation*

(New York: Ballantine Books, 2003); Burton Watson's "Introduction," in his translation, *The Complete Works of Chuang Tzu* (New York: Columbia University Press, 1968).

14.   Thomas Merton, the contemplative Trappist monk who was drawn to Zhuangzi, resists this temptation, noting that he did not write a book: " . . . in which Christian rabbits will suddenly appear by magic out of a Daoist hat." Thomas Merton, *The Way of Zhuangzi* (New York: New Directions, 1965), p. 10.

15.   A.C. Graham, trans., *Chuang-Tzu: The Inner Chapters* (Indianapolis: Hackett Publishing Company, 2001), p. 82.

2

Birth

> Modern Daoists would not recognize conception as the beginning of human life but would generally oppose abortion, in vitro *fertilization and stem cell research. Modern Confucians would permit abortion,* in vitro *fertilization and stem cell research under certain conditions but would not base their arguments on individual and privacy rights.*

When my wife, Maureen, was pregnant with our second child the doctors suggested an extra-powerful sonogram at sixteen weeks. They did so because our first child, Aidan, had been born with significant brain abnormalities which had left him profoundly disabled for life. We were, obviously, anxious about what might happen the second time around. Our neurologist had assured us that Aidan's condition was not likely to be repeated in subsequent pregnancies, but genetic counselors were not so sure: they told us that there could be as much as a 25 percent chance that a second child would be similarly disabled.

All that was said, when the sonogram was proposed, was that it would allow them to see whether the fetus's brain was developing normally. They would be able to tell if we were going down the same path as Aidan's. The unspoken question was: what would we do if history was repeating itself? No one elaborated on the choices; everyone understood the possibilities. Maureen let me know that, whatever happened, she would continue with the birth.

As it turned out, we did not have to do anything. The sonogram revealed a typical brain and all was well. But the choice had been laid before us.

Life, Liberty, and the Pursuit of Dao: Ancient Chinese Thought in Modern American Life,
First Edition. Sam Crane.
© 2013 John Wiley & Sons, Inc. Published 2013 by John Wiley & Sons, Inc.

If things were not as we had hoped, we had the authority and power to prevent birth. We did not have to, but the fact that we could have, and that society would have supported, even encouraged, a decision to abort, was a sobering reality.

* * *

Today, we can control birth as never before in human history. If we want to stop a pregnancy we can. We may select for the sex of our child-to-be and we routinely abort fetuses with certain disabilities. If we are having trouble conceiving, a host of technological alternatives is available to help get things started. And those interventions produce even more choices: sperm and egg donors can be screened for many particular characteristics. "Designer babies" were a thing of science fiction for my parents; now they are sitting next to me in the coffee shop.[1]

We can also harness the fertile potential of birth for other human purposes. Embryonic stem cell research suggests that the life-giving powers of procreation can be used to fight life-threatening diseases. There are obvious benefits to such work, but new complexities are created. How can we procure or produce embryonic tissue and what do we do with it when we are done?

It seems, then, the more that we try to control birth, the more unwieldy it becomes. So many questions, so many issues.

But the big question lurking behind all of these issues is the same: should we?

In the United States, answers to that big question are often linked to contending definitions of human life.[2] One common line of argument opposes abortion and stem cell research on the grounds that human life begins at the moment of conception. If a fetus is defined as a complete human, it is then entitled to all of the moral consideration that any person receives and should not be aborted or experimented upon. Conversely, a familiar defense of abortion rights maintains that human life does not begin until the fetus is viable outside the mother's body. Thus, an early term fetus is not the same as a fully formed person and can therefore be treated differently.

The anti-abortion position is extended by some, most prominently the Catholic Church, to a prohibition in of *in vitro* fertilization (IVF) and embryonic stem cell research.[3] Yet this view is not shared by all who oppose abortion. The wide acceptance of IVF techniques in the United States suggests that many people view medical intervention to create life as ethically more tolerable than procedures that end life, as they define it. Maybe some people sympathize with childless couples and are thus willing to let doctors "play God" to facilitate birth. Of course, the question of disposal of left-over embryos returns us to the abortion issue – is it tantamount to killing? We should, however, notice the qualification of the standard anti-abortion argument that allows some to accept IVF while opposing stem cell research, which from this perspective is considered abortion of sorts.[4]

There is less disparity among those who accept the moral argument in favor of abortion when it comes to IVF. While all would agree that care must be taken, since we are talking about *potential* human beings, there is no apparent reason why a person who believes human life begins at viability would oppose procedures that create or act upon embryos before viability.

For the most part, therefore, the public debate about birth-related issues in the United States tends to crystallize into two camps. The position of abortion opponents is generally consistent, except for the variation on IVF. And the stance of abortion defenders is also fairly well set, bolstered as it is by invocations of a woman's right to control her body. Indeed, public disputes, as important as they are, often lapse into a predictable pattern. Little new is ever added to the well-worn scripts of the public and political discourse of both sides: conception versus viability; the interests of the fetus versus the rights of the mother.

Insights from Confucianism and Daoism, however, disrupt this usual conversation in productive ways.[5] While they ultimately come down for or against abortion and other related issues, they do so for reasons other than those usually put forward in conventional American debates.

Confucianism on the beginning of life and abortion

For Confucians, human life is irreducibly social. A person alone cannot move toward humanity. Isolation is morally empty and aimless; it is, in effect, inhumane. If we cannot, or do not, perform our social roles, we cannot realize our human hearts, and without that realization we are not fulfilling our human potential. Confucius is too optimistic about moral improvement to brand the lone misanthrope as "less than human," but he attaches a sense of failure and inferiority to those who shun their duties: they are petty "little people."

> The Master said: "The noble-minded are clear about duty. Little people are clear about profit." (Hinton, *Analects*, 4.16)

Profit, here, encompasses more than material gain; it also includes personal interest and selfish advantage, all of which push against the essential sociality of humanity. To be human is to live with and through others.

Human life, then, is something more than biology. Although shaped by chemistry and physiology and ecology, we become fully human through the cultivation of our closest loving relationships. That is what separates us, as humans, from other biological entities. Animals may be social, but human social behavior is, for Confucians, the means by which we create a moral life. It is how we humanize ourselves. We use all of our faculties, especially our "heart-mind," consciously to orchestrate proper relations with other persons. Duty and ritual provide ideals of right and wrong, which are our path to humanity. When we fail in those duties and act selfishly for the sake of narrowly defined personal profit, we allow our humanity to atrophy and we become "little people."

Biological conception, by these lights, is clearly not enough to define a human person. It produces a biological basis for life, but it does not tell us what it means to be "human."

Instead of inquiring about the beginning of biological life, therefore, Confucianism would ask about the beginning of social life. When do meaningful social relationships set in motion a process that produces a human?

The first and most tangible answer is birth itself, the moment when a baby leaves the womb and is placed in her mother's arms for all to see. Those of us who have experienced the physical drama of birth know that moment; we have felt the palpable transformation of a circle of people as a new life is made present. Social interactions begin immediately: the mother's touch, the family's embrace, the reciprocal effect of the child on parents and siblings and relatives. Even at rest and with eyes closed, the infant causes those around her to re-examine themselves, who they are and what is important for them in their lives.

But the act of birth is not an absolute starting point of social life. Expectations of a child-to-be, while the fetus is still in the womb, can, in and of themselves, create meaningful social interactions. When we know that a baby is coming, and we want that baby to come, we can attach ourselves genuinely and intensely to the imminent person. Our behavior changes. We go to the store and buy various and sundry baby gear, or pull what we already have from closets and basements. As the news seeps out, friends and family relate to us differently. We see ourselves in a new light; we calculate, however imperfectly, the impact the new child will have on our closest relationships. All of this is the stuff of social life inspired by a child not yet born.

Modern technology makes the presence of the enwombed fetus even more tangible. How many of us now hang the first fuzzy sonogram image, the shadowy figure in the wedge-shaped field, on our refrigerators, expectant, perhaps, of kindergarten drawings to come? The little one is there with us, even before she is physically born.

Confucians would thus accept that, under certain conditions, the social processes that define a human life can begin before biological birth.

This leaves a further question: what conditions allow for the start of social humanization of the fetus?

As suggested above, parental acceptance is a key element in the social status of the impending child. This may seem rather unreliable to those searching for definite answers, but it is true, in practice, presently in the United States: if the creators of the fetus want to bring it to term and miscarriage does not occur, then, it will most probably reach the stage of biological viability and be born. Conversely, if parents do not want a child, they can, and do, seek out an abortion in those locations where the procedure is available, since US law does not recognize the humanity or rights of a first trimester fetus. Realizing the potential person is, in effect, a function of the parents' preferences.

Confucianism provides more of a philosophical basis for this position. Parental acceptance, in the first instance, is the beginning of social interaction, the process by which we all become human. This is not simply an effect of a legal definition of viability and rights; rather, it is the very foundation of Confucian moral personhood. When we "love and protect the young," as Confucius tells us (*Analects*, 5.26), we are not only making ourselves and our children better, we are making the world better. Confucians, then, would be generally predisposed to bring to delivery any given pregnancy, since raising children creates another forum for the enactment of humanity. Most fetuses would be presumed to be persons.

But not all fetuses. If parents do not want a child, Confucians would then acknowledge that the fetus had no social import. The humanizing process would not have begun; so, the fetus, while it may possess biological life, lacks an essential human characteristic: sociality. The motivations and intentions and actions of parents, from this perspective, determine the human possibilities of their offspring.

Modern Confucianism would impose certain conditions on parental choice, however. Selfish motives would be disallowed as insufficient moral grounds for withholding parental recognition of the potential humanity of a fetus. If the parents were concerned only with maintaining a rollicking, hedonistic lifestyle without the burdens of child-rearing, a Confucian would disapprove. Such people would be undermining their own humanity by making bad choices in their own lives. And they would be extending those bad choices to thwart the humanity of the fetus. The moral isolation of selfishness should not be projected and prolonged by abortions of this sort. In such a case, Confucians might encourage the couple (yes, fathers would be held responsible for the sperm they contribute to the pregnancy) to reconsider and keep the child so that the new family unit could contribute to their own and the world's humanity. Alternatively, delivery and adoption could be a solution. Better, for a Confucian, to allow the child to participate in the humanizing practices of another social network than to accept the loss of a latent human for bad, selfish reasons.

There are reasons a Confucian would accept abortion. If the parents' existing social duties to living family members and relations would be fundamentally obstructed by the responsibilities a new child brings, then terminating the biological life of the fetus would be acceptable. The claims of the living trump the claims of the not yet socially alive. This position can be derived from Confucius's views of life and death. Although he generally did not talk about death and the afterlife, being more concerned with the problems of the living, he responds to a direct question:

> Jilu asked how one should serve the gods and spirits. The master said, When you don't yet know how to serve human beings, how can you serve the spirits?
> Jilu said, May I venture to ask about death? The Master said, When you don't understand life, how can you understand death? (Watson, *Analects*, 11.12)

The key here is the notion of "serve human beings," which implies the daily living commitment to cultivating social relationships, starting first with family and moving then to friends and acquaintances and even strangers. "Life" is the process of serving the living. Our duties toward those now living around us are more important than worries about death. Although we have obligations to remember the dead, to venerate the ancestors, we do so because they have already lived and provided for us the social interactions that nurtured our humanity. This is different from the not yet living, who have not begun humanizing themselves by adding to the humanization of others around them.

Confucianism, then, is not absolute on either the beginning of life or abortion. Whether a fetus is a "human life" or an abortion is justified depend upon the social circumstances of each particular case. What matters most is social context defined first by parental intentions and motivations and actions, but also including the experiences of siblings and aunts and uncles and grandparents, extended family members, and the community at large.

Determining motives is, of course, difficult. How can we know if the duties entailed by a new child truly and significantly weaken a person's capacity to fulfill extant responsibilities to living family and relations? How do we know that such a claim is not simply an excuse to continue a profit-seeking and irresponsible lifestyle? Although it might be easier to come up with some universal standard, such as the physical moment of birth as the beginning of human life, Confucian ethics eschew rigid doctrines:

> The Master said, The gentleman is fair-minded and not partisan. The petty person is partisan and not fair-minded. (Watson, *Analects*, 2.14).

The rightness or wrongness of each case must be determined individually, based on specific conditions. Thus, Confucians would resist overarching laws that would outlaw all abortions regardless of circumstances. Indeed, Confucianism would generally be "pro-choice," in that individuals faced with these sorts of difficult decisions should have the opportunity to determine the best outcome in light of their specific situation. Generalized rules enforced by state power could obstruct fair-mindedness and non-partisanship.

A further complicating factor is this: the social significance of any particular new child cannot be fully understood until after the physical act of birth itself. Even with modern ultrasound and other imaging technologies, we cannot know a child's social potential until he has come through labor and delivery. In a variety of ways and for various reasons, potential children can die before or during or just after birth. They are mourned as fully human persons. More challenging, from an ethical point of view, are those instances where a child is born with unexpected characteristics which might lead parents to reject the child's potential humanity.

I raise this possibility because, historically, infanticide was practiced in ancient China. The custom is nowhere condoned, or even mentioned, in the *Analects* or *Mencius*, but it seems that social and political interpretations of Confucianism in early China did not impede the killing of unwanted infants. We cannot know if Confucius personally approved of it, but the ways in which his thought was understood and applied did not stop it.

What we can say is that two historically asserted reasons for infanticide – the rejection of girls and the disabled – would have to be disallowed by a modern Confucianism. These characteristics, without any other conditions that might justify ending biological life, are, in and of themselves, insufficient to deny the human potential of a fetus or newborn infant. A modernized Confucianism *must* reject these grounds because to accept them would be to accept an inflexible, categorical approach to humanity that contradicts the non-dogmatic, all-encompassing orientation of the noble-minded person. These points should also be rejected because, under conditions of modern society, they do not carry with them the meaning and consequences they might have had in ancient times.

The gender issue is straightforward. Today, it is widely understood that women contribute as much to the moral processes of humanity as do men. Indeed, given the Confucian emphasis on the cultivation of social relationships, it could be said that women do more to create and reproduce humanity, on average, than do men. Women take on most of the care of children and elders, the foundations of Confucian morality. If humanity is the highest moral goal, how, then, could we possibly justify aborting a female fetus, or killing a female infant, only because she is female?

In ancient China, the primary justification for female infanticide was the perceived filial duty to carry on the family name, which was traditionally limited to the father's surname continued by his sons. Women married out of the father's family, and their surnames were not registered as part of the lineage they married into. Confucius tells us to honor our parents, both parents, not just our fathers. But, in practice, fathers and sons clearly had a greater moral value since they sustained the line. A female child, especially one born after a son or two were already present, could have been viewed as more of a burden than a moral agent, and she might then be killed.

Traditional female infanticide thus rested on a moral calculation that gave greater weight to the continuation of the father's name than the humanity-creating potential of women.

The overemphasis on male lineage is unnecessary for modern Confucian morality and must be jettisoned.[6] It is true that the historical practices of Confucianism, the ways in which it was interpreted and put in to practice by innumerable people over the centuries, were thoroughly infused with patriarchal social and political customs. But it is also true that male domination limited the moral possibilities of traditional Confucianism. The philosophy could not live up to its full ethical potential because one possible expression of filiality, the son's continuation of the father's name, blocked many other possible expressions of filiality, the many ways in which women care for their elders and others. The increased social, political, and economic status of women in modern times makes the moral disparity of this tradeoff obvious. We lose more humanity than we gain when we kill a female infant. Thus, selecting for the sex of a child-to-be, in anticipation of male children being more valuable than females, as a reason for abortion would also be rejected by a contemporary Confucian.

Much the same can be said for disabled infants, though this issue is more complex in light of the wide range of physical conditions encompassed by the term "disabled."

My reasoning here has been shaped by my personal experience.

We had no inkling that Aidan, our first born child, would be profoundly disabled. The sonogram for his pregnancy revealed nothing amiss. His birth was fairly normal – a long labor that ultimately gave way to a caesarian delivery – and his initial medical exam was fine. Ten days later, however, he stopped breathing, due to a seizure, and we were cast into a maelstrom of pediatric intensive care units, neurology consultations, physical therapies, and scrambled expectations for years to come. It was indefinably painful and demanding. Yet it was through the process of caring for Aidan that I came to learn what Confucius meant by humanity.[7]

If someone had asked me before the fact whether I would choose to have a profoundly disabled child, I would have likely responded, "no." I almost certainly would have accepted abortion of a fetus so identified. It seemed so hard, so unnecessary: why take the time to bathe and diaper and lift a child who could not see or speak or walk, whose cognitive capacities would never progress beyond the infant stage, and who would obviously never be able to care for himself or contribute "productively" to society? It was only as I experienced Aidan's care, as I was forced by circumstance to surrender my desires and preconceptions of child-rearing, that I came to realize that it was the care itself, not the possible material or psychological consequences of the care, but the process of nurturing this boy, my son, that was making me more human.

From that experience, I now believe that caring for disabled family members is as much a "root of humanity" as caring for elders. The two activities are essentially the same. Thus, a modern Confucian orientation cannot accept a blanket denial of the humanity-creating potential of disabled fetuses or children. Since through caring for them we perform and extend our moral personhood, we should fully embrace and sincerely fulfill our duties toward them.

There is one, rather significant, qualification, however. The care of a profoundly disabled child takes an extraordinary amount of time and energy. If it is to be done well, it must take priority over other obligations. In our case, my job as a college teacher and my wife's profession as a registered nurse allowed us to coordinate and organize our working hours so that we could spend the time necessary for Aidan's care. Even with that flexibility, and the relatively good health insurance benefits we had, we regularly faced conflicting obligations: time with Aidan versus time with other family members; time with Aidan versus household duties; time with Aidan versus the everyday demands of modern life. There was little time for ourselves. We witnessed other families fall apart under the stresses and strains, unable to find time to do everything that had to be done. Social services and extra help that we paid for ourselves were insufficient. We did the best we could but always felt more could be done.

The demands of caring for a disabled child can, therefore, frustrate the fulfillment other equally important Confucian duties. Time and attention given to the child is time and attention that cannot be given to elders or siblings or spouses or other relations. These sorts of conflicts would not justify a universal rejection of all disabled fetuses. Rather, Confucianism would allow for abortion in those cases where it could be reasonably determined that the parents in question did not have the social and material resources required to balance the needs of a disabled child against their other familial duties. This is not simply a matter of disrupting personal lifestyles but a question of fulfilling other social obligations. Serving selfish interests is not, for Confucians, an acceptable reason for an abortion; serving the interests of others may be a sufficient justification for rejecting a disabled fetus.

However much I loved Aidan, and was positively transformed by his presence, I cannot assume that everyone will find themselves in the circumstances that allowed me and my wife to give him the time he needed.

But would a modern Confucian accept the killing of a newly born disabled infant in those instances where the family was unable to fulfill its various social duties? I think not. Although there may be no inherent distinction between abortion and infanticide in Confucian thinking – since in each case what matters is not the biological condition but the social context – the recognition that birth confers a certain human status is now so widely accepted, in the United States and China and elsewhere, that Confucians would also embrace that standard. Confucianism would resist and reject much about modern society, but sympathy for the living and optimism about the possibilities of human improvement, notions dearly held by Confucius, would translate into a general agreement that the process of humanization begins at birth. Only in the most extreme and egregious circumstances might infanticide be tolerated.

A Confucian confronted with the question of disability would first encourage parents to take up the care necessary, because through that care they would realize their own humanity. If the parents could demonstrate that their duties to their existing children, their parents, or other significant social relations would be undermined by their obligations toward a yet-to-be-born disabled child, then aborting a disabled fetus would be allowed. But if the disabled infant was already born, Confucians would require significant government intervention, in the form of readily available therapies and medical treatment and respite care, to help the family nurture the child; or, adoption, with all necessary support, would be encouraged.

In sum, Confucianism does not recognize conception as an absolute starting point of "human life." The focus on the creation of humanity through the conscientious cultivation of social relationships permits abortion when the introduction of a new child would significantly limit the family's ability to fulfill its existing duties.[8] Gender and disability, in and of themselves, without reference to a broader social context, are insufficient grounds for abortion. And infanticide is generally ruled out.

Daoism on the beginning of life and abortion

Daoists would be puzzled by the notion of the beginning of a human life. Way is vast, and any effort to impose analytic distinctions and categories upon its fullness, even separating being from nonbeing, is futile. There is much about birth in Daoism but nothing about a definitive determination of the beginning of life.

In the *Daodejing* we encounter a resistance to a clear notion of beginnings of any sort. Way, it is said, "precedes gods and creators." (Hinton, 4) At the same time, Way is the origin of all things, it is the source or mother of all beneath heaven (Hinton, 52). Yet it does not provide for us a simple, identifiable beginning of the universe. There is no decisive Big Bang, no discrete evolutionary moment when man separated from the apes, and no precise demarcation of the start of any particular human life. As passage 2 of the *Daodejing* suggests, there is no sure beginning or end to anything within Way:

> All beneath heaven know beauty is beauty
> only because there's ugliness,

and knows good is good
only because there's evil.

Being and nonbeing give birth to one another,
difficult and easy complete one another,
long and short measure one another,
high and low fill one another,
music and noise harmonize one another,
before and after follow one another;
that's why a sage abides in the realm of nothing's own doing,
living out that wordless teaching.

The ten thousand things arise without beginnings there,
abide without waiting there,
come to perfection without dwelling there.

Without dwelling there: that's the one way you'll never lose it.

(Hinton)

All things "arise without beginnings there." Where? In the "realm of nothing's own doing." In other words, origins are not actions; they are processes of non-action. Entities do not have clear-cut starting points. What seem to be distinct beginnings are simply moments in a continuous process of reproduction beyond human perception or understanding.

The various opposites set forth in passage 2 above, including being and nonbeing, are not discrete qualities that merely complement one another. They are integrally interrelated aspects of a broader cosmic unity. Good can only be understood in relation to evil, it cannot be analytically or conceptually separated from evil, nor long from short, high from low. Another translation of this passage, by Robert G. Henricks, suggests the indivisibility of existence and nonexistence: "the mutual production of being and nonbeing." Both are always present and each relies upon the other for its re-creation.

In human terms, the interdependence of being and nonbeing is not self-evident. We are alive and we know there is a state of death: they seem quite separable and distinct. We can observe all sorts of natural processes and mark a fairly definite boundary between life and death and, in that sense, being and nonbeing. Daoism asks us to let go of that humanly created demarcation, to take a broader perspective that would show us that the physical stuff of our body, for example, does not simply disappear upon our death. There is a slow and gradual process of decomposition during which the body is broken down and, if allowed to, absorbed into the earth. Bones may remain, but even they will dissolve with time. Marking a completion of that transformation is impossible.

We assume we lose consciousness upon death and that might be a clear break with life. But why, Daoism asks, should we reduce being to consciousness? Awareness obviously adds much to existence, but being is always something more than consciousness. It is in this sense, then, that our conventional expectation of a stark distinction between life and death, being and nonbeing, is challenged by Daoism. If we think in terms of broader organic processes, why should the moment we lose consciousness be taken as a unique transformation? There are many more transformations the body will experience. At what point are all of those processes finished? Never, really. The physical stuff of our bodies is swept up into other organic currents. The sensibility here is something like the Christian prayer notion of "ashes to ashes, dust to dust." Or, as the book of Genesis has it: "for dust thou art, and unto dust shalt thou return."

These ideas about death help us understand the Daoist notion of birth. Zhuangzi describes the body coming together:

> The hundred joints, the nine holes, the six organs – they just came together in this body's life. So which am I closest to? All of them? Or is one more me than the others? But they're all servants, nothing more, and servants cannot govern themselves. And how could they take turns being ruler and servant? There's something that rules. If we go looking for its nature, there's nothing to find. But that doesn't make its truth any more perfect, or any more ruined. (Hinton, 20)

There is a sense of randomness here: the various parts of the body "just came together." The dust from which we all emerge swirled haphazardly into a particular form; it could have been some other body but, by chance, settled into this shape. In other passages, *Zhuangzi* repeats this sense of fortuitous beginnings: "Once we happen into the form of this body…" (Hinton, 20); "If you follow the realized mind you've happened into…" (Hinton, 21). Moreover, no one part of the developing body is more important than any other. This can be understood as a swipe at Mencius, who tells us that the heart, or "heart-mind," is most essential. By contrast, Zhuangzi suggests all elements are equal in their dependence on one another. This implies that a fetus is no more important than an egg or a sperm or a gametocyte or any other part, or collection of parts, of the human body at any particular time. The thing that "rules," for a Daoist, is Way, which we cannot comprehend. Thus, the process of creation of a human body disappears into the vastness of the cosmos.

This infers that conception, the fertilization of egg by sperm, carries no special moral meaning. Just as there is no concrete end of the organic processes involved in and around a human body, so too there is no definitive beginning.

Surprisingly, the Daoist position has a bit of resonance with that of the Catholic Church. Of course, Catholics *do* attach great moral significance to conception, which is, for them, a clear beginning of human life. But Catholic teaching also recognizes the potential humanity of the precursors of the fetus: egg and sperm and procreative processes more generally. It is for that reason that the church opposes many forms of birth control. To interfere in the natural processes of human reproduction, even those stages of it that occur before conception, is to disrupt God's plan. Although they make no references to God or a divine plan, Daoists also couch their understanding of human birth within a broader natural context, understood as Way, that extends beyond the moment of conception. Daoism, however, views the cosmic environment of Way as so vast and incomprehensible that discrete beginnings and endings are indecipherable.

Though that difference is important, Daoists would generally agree with Catholics that abortion should be discouraged. They would not invoke "conception is the beginning of life" or "sanctity of life" arguments, but they would be uncomfortable with medical interventions to stop the natural process of reproduction.

For Daoists, human life is not sacred because there is no divine source to impart sanctity. If there is no God, and for philosophical Daoists there is none, then life is not God-given and thus not sanctified. There is a recognition of the uniqueness of each thing in and of itself and the beauty of all things existing together; and there is an appreciation of an essential similarity of all things, insofar as they are all elements of a larger Way. But there is no special status given to human life, as opposed to other forms of life, nor to any particular human life. Each individual develops and lives according to his or her own inherent integrity (*de*) and context-dependent circumstances (*Dao*); the experience of one cannot be used to judge the experience of another.

Without a universal standard of sacred life or human rights, how then can a Daoist oppose abortion? If conditions seem to warrant medical intervention to stop a pregnancy, on what grounds would Daoism reject it?

It is here that the "do nothing" injunction would come into play. Although it is not a strict command, the idea of doing nothing is rooted in a skepticism about our ability to control our fate in Way. Why should we intervene in the process of human reproduction? The initial Daoist response would be that we should not because it is, on the face of it, an effort to stop the tendency of Way. The Daoist position would not be hard and fast. Immediate circumstances would be taken into consideration.

In those cases where an abortion seems necessary because the lifestyles of the potential parents would be diminished by the costs in time and money of a new baby, a Daoist would generally argue against the procedure. This is especially true in those instances where middle-class career paths are in danger of disruption. If a modest existence is possible, if food and shelter and clothing and basic medical care can be provided, then there is really no reason, for a Daoist, to reject the child. Our desires and expectations about professions or possessions are pointless since accomplishments wither with time and wealth distorts our lives, as expressed in passage 9 of the *Daodejing*:

> Forcing it fuller and fuller
> can't compare to just enough,
> and honed sharper and sharper
> means it won't keep for long.
>
> Once it's full of jade and gold
> your house will never be safe.
> Proud of wealth and renown
> you bring on your own ruin.
>
> Just do what you do, and then leave:
> such is the Way of heaven.
>
> (Hinton)

Notice there is a sense of doing here – Daoism does not require complete non-action. But doing is minimized; it should not be aimed at filling up our bank accounts or sharpening our reputations. If we reach for too much, we are destined to fall short. Although nothing like abortion is mentioned here, the passage suggests that we should not justify those actions we do take on economic or social grounds. A limitation on income, above some practical minimum, or an interruption of career plans are not sufficient justification for any sort of significant action, abortion included.

Quite to the contrary, a Daoist would counsel acceptance. When our circumstances shift unexpectedly, we should embrace the change and follow where Way is leading: "in yielding is completion" (Hinton, 22).

It should be noted here that the Confucian rationale, which could, under certain circumstances, accept an abortion, would be rejected by Daoists. Social responsibilities and duties to family members do not figure prominently in either the *Daodejing* or *Zhuangzi*. While it may be true that a parent's love for a child, and a child's for a parent, is a natural aspect of the Way of humankind, the hardening of those innate sentiments into a firmly established set of duties and rituals is not a Daoist notion. In this regard, Daoism is more relativistic than Confucianism: there is no prior assumption that, generally, duties to living family members should outweigh deference to evolving circumstance.

There are, of course, other, more dire circumstances which could be invoked to justify abortion. In those cases where the consequences of having a new baby are truly devastating economically for the mother and extant family, when not merely a comfortable lifestyle or social duties are at stake but survival, a Daoist might be open to the possibility of abortion. Such an action, however, would not be seen as a solution but as a symptom of larger social problems. A Daoist would ask how it is that conditions have developed to such a point that people feel they have to intervene to stop pregnancies. Stark differences in economic life, where some people have much more than they need while others struggle with very little, are not in keeping with Way:

> Were I to have the least bit of knowledge, in walking on a Great Way, it's only going astray that I would fear.
> The Great Way is very level;
> But people greatly delight in tortuous paths.
>
> The courts are swept clean;
> While the fields are full of weeds;
> And the granaries are all empty;
> Their clothing – richly embroidered and colored;
> While at their waists they carry sharp swords.

They gorge themselves on food, and of possessions and goods they have plenty.

This is called thievery!
And thievery certainly isn't the Way

(Henricks, *Daodejing*, 53)

This passage expresses a paradox of human nature. On the one hand, it is natural for humans to exercise their free will in ways that might be hurtful to others. People adore "tortuous paths" that lead to inequality and injustice. Yet, on the other hand, this natural tendency produces unnatural outcomes, which "certainly isn't the Way." If Way encompasses everything – good and bad alike – then it should follow that the bad effects of willful human behavior are an integral element of Way. But this passage suggests that through our volition we can choose to violate Way and that some portion of our bad behavior is "not the Way." This does not mean that humans are somehow outside of Way (which is impossible) but, rather, that the human condition, unlike perhaps anything else in Way, can uniquely defy the natural unfolding of Way.

All of this suggests that extreme inequality – economic and social and political – is unnatural, the result of un-Way-like human actions. If these sorts of conditions were invoked to defend a particular abortion, a Daoist would hold that ending the pregnancy is simply an extension of these prior aberrant circumstances. Although there would be sympathy for the immediate plight of the potential parents, and thus perhaps some tolerance for an abortion, the Daoist would maintain a general aversion to, though not an absolute rejection of, the procedure.

In those cases where there was a clear threat to the mother's life, abortion would probably be tolerated by Daoists. Zhuangzi tells us to accept death as simply another of the countless transformations that happen constantly to everything in Way. Yet, at the same time, we can find in his book a clear sense of self-preservation. In accepting our inevitable death we liberate ourselves from it, perhaps even living longer in the process. An apparently useless tree, ignored by carpenters because its wood is knotted and splintery, outlasts other more beautiful and functional varieties. It preserves itself in its uselessness. Zhuangzi makes the point even more directly:

Follow the middle; go by what is constant, and you can stay in one piece, keep yourself alive, look after your parents, and live out your years. (Watson, 50)

There is a Confucian ring to the idea of a "middle," or prudent, approach to life, but Zhuangzi here is pointing to something inherent in the integrity (*de*) of many people, maybe all: the impulse to protect and preserve ourselves. Daoists would counsel that we not hold on too tightly to our worldly lives but they would not rule out all actions aimed at self-preservation. We can accept the cosmic inevitability of death but still step out of the way of the bus as it approaches us.

If, when confronted with a choice of her own death or an abortion, a woman chose an abortion, a Daoist would not stop her and would understand that her decision may well be driven by a natural instinct for survival that is in keeping with Way.

While such extreme threats might justify an abortion to a Daoist, actions taken primarily on the basis of gender or disability would be rejected.

As to gender, Daoism would find no basis whatsoever in claims that a male child is somehow more valuable than a female child. The *Daodejing* venerates "female" values.[9] Although we might not want to take this as a proto-feminist text (it was, after all, written by men and primarily for men), we can safely conclude that, at the very least, it grants females the same status in Way as males. Sex-selected abortions would be seen, then, as unwarranted interference in the unfolding of Way.

Disability, too, is a normal element of Way. Zhuangzi invokes many images of disability – people who have had a foot cut off; a crippled man; a person experiencing a disfiguring demise. These figures are used to illustrate the fundamental equality of all things and the value and worth of the apparently broken or unwhole. Disability is not something to be shunned or avoided or feared. It is simply another of the myriad expressions of humanity in Way. A Daoist would, therefore, reject arguments favoring abortion of disabled fetuses, except perhaps in those cases where delivery would threaten the physical life of the mother.

Finally, Daoism would caution against infanticide. Killing is generally avoided by Daoists: we should not take action to stop a life because by doing so we are obstructing that life's unique development in Way. Passage 74 of the *Daodejing* tells us, in part:

> Now, killing people in place of the one in charge of executions,
> this is like cutting wood in place of the head carpenter.
> And those who cut wood in place of the head carpenter,
> very few do not hurt their hands!
>
> (Henricks)

The "one in charge of executions" is generally understood to be Way, the natural rise and fall of all life forms. Nothing good comes of intervening in those organic forces. Killing will likely create results you did not intend.

Infanticide would also be shunned because infants, in all of their innocence and purity, are closer to Way than adults, whose minds are filled with all sorts of humanly created expectations and desires that lead toward "tortuous paths." Again, the *Daodejing* tells us:

> One who is vital in character (*de*)
> Can be compared with a newborn baby.
>
> Wasps and scorpions will not sting a baby,
> Snakes and vipers will not bite him,
> And birds of prey and ferocious beasts will not snatch him up.
> Though his bones are soft and his sinews supple
> His grip is firm.
>
> (Ames and Hall, 55)

The various threats cannot hurt the child because she has not yet taken on adult beliefs and fears and plans. Her engagement with, and perception of, Way are full and clear and unblocked. For a Daoist, an infant is not a problem or complication but, rather, a valuable model representing how adults can follow Way, and obviously should not be killed.

Daoists would resist systematizing and hardening their positions on infanticide, abortion, and the beginning of life. They are, after all, relativistic in their ethics and outlook. Proper action in any particular case is determined completely by the immediate circumstances of that specific case. Generalizations of any sort are neither sought nor proffered. The overarching aversion to intervention into the affairs of others, the social aspect of "doing nothing," greatly limits the reach of Daoist advice. All of the points made above should be taken as suggestions or guidelines or inclinations. They would best be employed by individuals in their own personal lives as they seek to find the right thing to do in their unique conditions. Daoists would hesitate long before telling someone else what he or she should do.

Confucianism and Daoism on in vitro fertilization

Positions on the ethics of *in vitro* fertilization are often related to arguments about abortion. If you believe that human life beings with viability, then you are likely to have few qualms about creating not-yet-fully human embryos in laboratory conditions. Conversely, if you believe that human life begins at conception and is divinely sanctioned, then you may, though not necessarily, believe that "artificial" means of creating life unduly interfere with God's work. Confucianism and Daoism, similarly, maintain a certain consistency between their attitudes on abortion and IVF.

Confucians would generally accept IVF, especially in those cases where a child was being conceived in order to extend the practices of humanity within the family. Caring for children is a moral counterpart to caring for elders, which is, in the *Analects*, referred to as the "root of humanity." It is right, then, for young adults to want to have children, since parenting provides them with a vital venue for the performance of humanizing duties and rituals. Child care is not the only way to perform our morality, but it is one of the most significant ways.

The possible moral costs of IVF, especially the disposal of embryonic tissue, would not trouble a Confucian. Such biological matter, if it has not yet entered into meaningful and reciprocal social relationships, has not yet begun the humanizing process and, so, can be discarded without scruple.

There is one IVF issue that would concern Confucians: the possibility that selecting specific characteristics for a child-to-be, through screening of egg and sperm donors, is driven by vanity and material gain. Potential parents can get caught up in designing perfect babies; they want just the right set of physical and mental abilities for their children. Companies now advertise their intelligent and beautiful and talented providers, promising an increased likelihood (it is a probabilistic enterprise, after all) that these sorts of traits will be passed on to your child. All of this distracts from the fundamental Confucian purpose of having a child. It is not about engineering flawless progeny, bound to be popular and successful in fleetingly fashionable and materialistic ways; it is about creating a social context where duties are defined and performed in a manner that makes all involved morally better. The child's hair color or putative IQ or athletic ability really do not matter. What matters is that parents inculcate children with a sense of social obligation and ritual awareness, and that children learn to reciprocate that parental inheritance with respect for elders, care for family members, and civility toward others.

The commercialization of IVF, the flip side of the vanity problem, would also bother modern Confucians. At present, IVF is a business, open to all the economic pressures and problems of any business. Profit motives drive IVF companies, pushing them to cut costs and increase prices. With price differentials for eggs and sperm of varying quality comes the possibility that materialistic calculations will seep into subsequent parent–child relations. Will parents resent children who do not live up to the expectations of their genetic plans? Might parents feel that the increasingly large sums of money for IVF services are not "worth it" if their kids do not turn out as they intended? Mencius worries about profit infecting human relationships:

> If you, sir, use profit to persuade the kings of Qin and Chu, and if the kings of Qin and Chu, being amenable to the idea of profit, stop their armies, the personnel of those armies will be delighted with the cessation of hostilities and amenable to profit. Ministers serving their rulers will be preoccupied with profit; sons serving their parents will be preoccupied with profit; and younger brothers serving older brothers will be preoccupied by profit. Finally, rulers, ministers, parents, children, and older and younger brothers will abandon humaneness and righteousness and encounter one another based on a preoccupation with profit. Whenever this has happened, loss has always ensued. (Bloom, 6B4)

Extending this idea, fathers should not serve their children according to profit, either. If creating a child is seen as a materialistic investment with an expected payoff in the future, then humanity has been lost. To the extent that profit seeking defines child-rearing through the commercialization of conception, IVF business contributes to the corrosion of family morality.

Although these are serious concerns for Confucians, ultimately they would be favorably disposed toward IVF. Even if a child is conceived for reasons of personal vanity or profit, there is still a good possibility that parents will be transformed in the process. What started out as a selfish act could become, through the demands of selfless care-giving a child creates, a morally life-altering event. How many of us have marveled at the unexpected ways in which our children have changed us for the better? While some parents may fail in their duties, such failures are not necessarily tied to IVF in particular. "Natural" parents may fail just as often and just as badly as IVF parents. Thus, the promise of humanization that comes with any child would be extended, by Confucians, to IVF children, and that promise would outweigh the potential pitfalls.

Daoists, on the other hand, would be wary of IVF. It is, like abortion, a human action that seeks to push Way in seemingly unnatural directions. If a person, for whatever biological or social reasons, cannot have a child, there is no need to create one artificially. A Daoist would not have the Confucian's anxiety about performing humanity. Although infants may be closer to Way than adults, child-rearing is not the only, or even the best, means of living out one's integrity in Way. We can come to appreciate Way through our ordinary, daily experiences, with or without children. Should a person realize that it is an indelible element of his or her integrity to care for a child, alternatives to IVF are readily available – adoption most obviously. Or, if that is not possible, there are a wide variety of professions that would allow for the expression of that side of one's integrity: pediatric medicine; teaching; day care; social work; and the like. Creating fetuses in laboratories, with all the science and technology that entails, is not necessary.

There is, however, an interesting possibility for Daoist acceptance of IVF (and this might apply to stem cell research as well), in passage 64 of the *Daodejing*:

It's easy to embrace the tranquil
and easy to prevent trouble before omens appear.
It's easy for the trifling to melt away
and easy for the slight to scatter away.

Work at things before they've begun
and establish order before confusion sets in,
for a tree you can barely reach around
grows from the tiniest rootlet,
a nine-tiered tower
starts as a basket of dirt,
a thousand mile journey
begins with a single step.

Work at things and you ruin them;
cling to things and you lose them.
That's why a sage does nothing
and so ruins nothing,
clings to nothing
and so loses nothing.

When people devote themselves to something
they always ruin it on the verge of success.

Finish with the same care you took in the beginning
and you'll avoid ruining things.

This is why a sage desires without desire,
never longing for rare treasures,
learns without learning,
always returning to what people have passed by,
helps the ten thousand things occur of themselves
by never presuming to work at them.

(Hinton)

The tension in this passage between doing and not doing is palpable. At one point the idea is to "work at things before they've begun," which suggests that early intervention in subtle but significant ways is justified. Yet the text shifts back to "work at things and you ruin them," seemingly warding us off any sort of purposive and persistent action. Then it tells us that finishing with the same care with which we began will keep us from ruining things, another guidance for how to act, albeit carefully. We should not take the last line as some sort of definitive resolution. Even though helping the ten thousand things "occur of themselves" might point to a rationale for all sorts of medical procedures, those understood as facilitating the inherent development of things, the overall sense of the passage is a struggle over whether or not to act.

But that struggle, in and of itself, suggests that some actions, especially those that happen early in a process of change, are wise. IVF occurs in the opening stages of human life and, as such, might be taken as an instance of working at things before they've begun. The manipulation of a small number of cells could be understood as a subtle yet straightforward act. Doctors are merely putting the sperms and eggs together and giving them a place to grow. They are only helping along what nature might have accomplished itself, under different circumstances. It may take certain high-tech skills and machines, but the idea itself is rather simple, so simple that a Daoist might go along with it.

In the end, however, Daoist skepticism of scientific efforts to "··· take hold of all beneath heaven and improve it" (Hinton, *Daodejing*, 29) would, in the case of IVF, likely outweigh the possibility of working at things "before they have begun." There is just too much doing and planning and desiring associated with IVF to make it comfortable for Daoists, who would find it best to simply accept Way as it is and learn to live without a birth child.

Confucianism and Daoism on stem cell research

As mentioned above, ethical questions regarding stem cell research are related to those involved with abortion and IVF. Those who define a fetus as morally human reject the use of embryonic stem cells for research, while those who define human life in terms of viability or sociability generally accept it.

Confucians would, therefore, allow embryonic stem cell research, for the same reasons they would accept IVF: the biological material involved has not yet been humanized through social relationships and thus can rightly be used for scientific purposes. Similarly, disposal of extraneous embryonic tissue would not really be an issue. In fact, a modern Confucian would likely encourage and support this sort of research since the results could improve existing social relationships. Serious disease and illness can destabilize families and undermine friendships. The prospect of maintaining and strengthening social bonds, the venue of humanity, through good health is very appealing from a Confucian point of view.

Of course, it could be said that the most meaningful social relationships are those forged in adversity. We perform our most significant acts of humanity when we must give up selfish pursuits to care for loved ones. And if that is true, then we should not place such a high value on relieving the suffering of sickness, since it is precisely that distress that calls us to our highest human purpose.

This, however, would not be enough to turn a Confucian against embryonic stem cell research. There are many threats to our social relationships, many types of adversity that demand our dedication to family and friends: war, natural disaster, economic decline, unexpected turns of fate and fortune. By contrast, the promise of stem cell research is rather modest; it can aspire to cure only a limited number of illnesses and disabilities, addressing only a fraction of the total of human miseries. The gains would be positive – some lives and social networks would be better off – but marginal from the perspective of all people everywhere. Hardship would not disappear, but still be very much present to test our commitments and inspire our performance of humanity. And some people would be better able to respect their elders, cherish the young, and delight in their friends. There is no real hazard here that the social good of stem cell research might somehow become a social deficit.

The only potential downside to stem cell research, from a Confucian perspective, is the vanity issue. Obviously, this sort of work should not be done to produce body parts for cosmetic surgeries or transitory fashions. Serious scientific endeavors should be oriented to improving the social context of humanity, not the personal profit or interest – which here include obsessions with beauty and appearance – of narcissistic individuals. Regeneration of human limbs? Perhaps, if it was a matter of permitting a person to better carry out his social duties. Replacement of wrinkled skin on an aging woman's face? No, if it is merely a matter of pride and conceit. Cure of Parkinson's disease? Absolutely, if it facilitated the continuing enactment of humanity, duty, and ritual.

Daoists would, however, shy away from stem cell research, just as they would be uncomfortable with IVF and abortion. They might ask: Why do we think we have to do this? To relief human suffering? As if that were possible. In the vastness and caprice of Way, a person cured of affliction at one moment could be besieged by some other tragedy in the flash of an eye. Nothing, no accumulation of science or engineering or human effort, can change that. While it is true that some lives would be improved for some period of time, a Daoist would warn us not to make stem cell research, or any medical procedure, into a panacea it can never really be.

Philosophical Daoist objections would not be based on claims of the sanctity of embryonic life, since there is no source of transcendent sacredness. A more mundane aversion to deliberate and systematized action, *wuwei*, would cause hesitation. We cannot know, with any certainty, just how much action or precisely what sort of action might be in keeping with "nothing's own doing." On the face of it, however, embryonic stem cell research is a significant and artificial intrusion into the free flow of Way. Cells that would otherwise develop into human beings are either synthetically created or abnormally "harvested" and then manipulated and made to serve uncharacteristic purposes. The social benefits might be positive, but Daoists would not accept apparently good effects as justification for regulating Way. It is not for us to determine what is good and bad in Way, but only to follow along where it takes us. That might sound like a prescription for helplessness – and that is precisely what Daoism would suggest. We cannot control our fate in Way, and when try we can never escape our human predicament, even if we gain better health for some period of time. Better to make the most of the moment we are in and not worry about living longer or stronger. The Daoist writer Liezi tells us:

> That which is born is that which in principle must come to an end. Whatever ends cannot escape its end, just as whatever is born cannot escape birth; and to wish to live forever, and have no more of ending, is to be deluded about our lot.[10]

Daoism would not necessarily reject all medical research. But the more elaborate the procedure, the less accepting a Daoist would be. To the extent that stem cell research requires a great deal of prior theoretical knowledge, large amounts of capital, and very high expectations for improved health, it would likely be seen as beyond the pale.

Yet Daoism is a fluid enough philosophy to allow for an alternative interpretation. Stem cell research might be seen as a simpler process of working at things before they've begun, and that could open the way for Daoist acceptance. To a degree, it is an extension of the human presence in Way, another of the many seemingly contradictory but still organic aspects of human integrity. People want to alleviate physical suffering and they will work within Way, and at times push against Way, to achieve that. While we ultimately have to accept death, we can still take plain and simple actions to preserve life.

Indeed, in its religious expressions, Daoism is deeply involved in various life-extending practices and procedures. The bases of Chinese medicine – herbs, acupuncture, and the like – were shaped by ancient seekers of immortality who found inspiration in Daoist texts. Even though this might fly in the face of the ideas of acceptance of death and yielding to fate that pervades philosophical Daoism, it must be recognized as a part of the historical practice and legacy of Daoism more generally.

It seems to me, however, that the more consistent Daoist position, consistent at least with the philosophical spirit of *Zhuangzi* and the *Daodejing*, is that which would avoid embryonic stem cell research. Assertions that the procedure is simple and subtle do not ring true. There is just too much involved and too much at stake. And that would give a Daoist pause, at least on a personal level. If it were a matter of telling someone else what they should or should not do, however, a Daoist would not intervene. We each have to find our own way in Way.

Notes

1. Liza Mundy, *Everything Conceivable: How Assisted Reproduction is Changing Our World* (New York: Knopf, 2007); Debora L. Spar, *The Baby Business: How Money, Science, and Politics Drive the Commerce of Conception* (Boston, MA: Harvard Business School Publishing, 2006).
2. A rigorous review of various arguments can be found in David Boonin, *A Defense of Abortion* (Cambridge: Cambridge University Press, 2003).
3. "*Dignitas Personae* (The Dignity of a Person)," United States Conference of Catholic Bishops, December, 2008. Available at: http://old.usccb.org/comm /archives/2008/08-196.shtml, accessed March 3, 2013.
4. This view was represented in The President's Council on Bioethics, "Reproduction and Responsibility: the Regulation of New Biotechnologies," (Washington, DC: The President's Council on Bioethics, 2004). Available at: http://bioethics.georgetown.edu/pcbe/reports/reproductionandresponsibility /_pcbe_final_reproduction_and_responsibility.pdf, accessed March 3, 2013.
5. Fan Ruiping, "A Confucian Perspective," in Moira Stephens *et al.*, "Religious Perspectives on Abortion and a Secular Response," *Journal of Religion and Health*, 49 (4) (2010), pp. 513–535; Philip J. Ivanhoe, "A Confucian Perspective on Abortion," *Dao*, 9 (1) (2010), pp. 37–51; Geling Shang, "Excess, Lack, and Harmony: Some Confucian and Taoist Approaches to Family Planning and Population Management – Tradition and the Modern Challenge," in Daniel C. Maguire, ed., *Sacred Rights: The Case for Contraception and Abortion in World Religions* (New York: Oxford University Press, 2003), pp. 217–236.
6. Thus, a modern Confucian would be sharply critical of practices of female infanticide, sex-selected abortion, and neglect of girls in contemporary China and India. See Amartya Sen, "More than 100 Million Women are Missing," *New York Review of Books*, 37 (20) (December 20, 1990).
7. Sam Crane, "Confucius Speaks," *Newsday*, February 15, 2004; Sam Crane, "Productive in His Own Way," *New York Times*, November 30, 1998; Sam Crane, "Aidan's Gift," *Commonweal*, 125 (16) (September 25, 1998).
8. For an argument similar to this, drawn from Western sources, see Michael Boylan, "The Abortion Debate in the 21st Century," in Michael Boylan, ed., *Medical Ethics* (Upper Saddle River, NJ: Prentice Hall, 2000), pp. 289–304.
9. Karyn Lai, "The *Daodejing*: Resources for Contemporary Feminist Thinking," *Journal of Chinese Philosophy*, 27 (2) (June 2000), pp. 131–153.
10. A.C. Graham, *The Book of Lieh-tzu: A Classic of Tao* (New York: Columbia University Press, 1990), p. 23.

3

Childhood

Confucians recognize childhood as a moral status distinct from adulthood; children, therefore, should not be treated as adults under the law, even when they commit horrendous crimes. Daoists do not draw such a clear distinction between children and adults. Infants and young children, in their naivety and purity, are closer to Way, and are, for Daoists, models of what adults should be.

Aidan could never have been an adult. His disabilities kept him a child for all of his short life. Never would he gain the mental capacities that allow for mature cognition and communication. He could not develop into an autonomous individual, free to make responsible and considered ethical choices. This was, of course, a painful, and therefore unvoiced, realization for my wife and me. We took care of him, we spoke for him, made decisions for him, and we did that willingly and with all of our hearts. But he could never be an adult.

His forever-childhood made me think about the lines we draw between supposedly clear moral states. At one point we are children, not fully responsible for ourselves; at another we cross over into adulthood, when we are expected to bear the costs as well as enjoy the benefits of our actions. When is that point, really? Is it ever all that clear?

And that made me wonder about personal autonomy. Aidan would never have it, not in the sense of a capacity to exercise, and be held accountable for, his free will. I, a mature adult who makes myriad decisions every day, seem to be secure in it. But how independent am I, or any of us, actually? We

Life, Liberty, and the Pursuit of Dao: Ancient Chinese Thought in Modern American Life,
First Edition. Sam Crane.

are all forever embedded in dense networks of social relations. On a daily basis we rely on scores of other people, many of them unseen, to secure our needs and wants. I go into the coffee shop in the morning, where someone has made that drink I enjoy; I go to the store to buy food that others have grown and processed and packaged. I go online and surf for news and ideas, drawing on the work – literary, analytic, and technical – of all sorts of people in every corner of the world. My knowledge, which underwrites my understanding of myself, the definition of who I am, is produced by my constant interaction with others. And, of course, I am nurtured and supported by my closest loved ones.

If we are all bound up together, and none of us is completely independent, then Aidan's obvious childhood dependency may have been more of a mirror of my own adult condition than I ever realized.

* * *

Every society has its own ways of marking the transition from childhood to adulthood. Rites of passage are common, even in mundane modern forms. In contemporary America, we permit children to drive cars when they reach fifteen or sixteen years old, in recognition of their emerging capacity for good judgment. At eighteen they can vote and join the military (though this latter option is possible at seventeen with parental permission), taking on civic duties of great import. And at twenty-one they can legally buy and consume alcohol. This last threshold is delayed because we are as yet uncertain that the young will drink responsibly, especially when driving is involved. Each of these points in time – sixteen, eighteen, and twenty-one – is a culturally acknowledged and legally defined step on the road to adulthood.

Other countries and cultures have their own ways of socially and lawfully recognizing the move from youth to maturity. But all such affirmations are based on the same assumption: that children are something less, morally, than adults.

Perhaps "less" is the wrong word here, though it does get to the heart of the matter. Children are generally viewed as partial moral beings. They are endowed with certain basic human rights: as persons they should not be exploited or harmed or killed.[1] Yet their immaturity limits their responsibility for their own actions. If they do something wrong, they cannot be held fully accountable because they may not realize the ethical context or implications of their conduct. Morality must be taught to them and they must gradually acquire a sense of right and wrong, and thus eventually be granted ethical autonomy and responsibility. Before that time, however, they cannot act independently. They are not fully fledged moral agents, and so must be restricted and directed in their behavior.

All of this, of course, is subject to qualification. Everyone knows individual children who come to understand and exercise personal responsibility at an early age. Indeed, they may be more conscientious in their social behavior than some adults. Simple age markers, then, are obviously inadequate to determine whether a person should be considered an adult or a child ethically. It is quite easy to conceive of a perceptive fourteen-year-old with a more fully developed moral sensibility than a dissolute forty-year-old.

Societies and legal systems, however, cannot operate on a case-by-case basis. Cultural understanding, social organization and political institutions require more general criteria. And so we create age-specific points of reference, times of life when we expect most individuals to have refined some aspect of their moral selves: sixteen for driving, eighteen for voting, twenty-one for drinking. Outside of the realm of secular law, some religious traditions also define and perform a universal passage to adulthood, as in the Jewish Bar (Bat) Mitzvah, which sets thirteen as the age of moral responsibility for an individual.

These sorts of systematic definitions of the end of childhood, both secular and religious, only make sense, however, if they are accompanied by some program of moral education. Otherwise, they are simply meaningless external facades, disconnected from the interior moral life of the individual. We must teach children how to do the right thing, how to nurture a conscience. Childhood is, thus, a time of moral learning.[2] Humans may have an innate moral sense – some philosophers and psychologists suggest that we are born moral – but that capacity has to be cultivated and honed. It must be given particular meaning in specific social and cultural contexts. It has to be enacted and revised and perfected. Children need to learn how to act ethically in order for them to grow into adulthood.

Education, then, is central to childhood experience.[3] Early on, parents play a key role in this regard, explicitly instructing children in principles of right and wrong and implicitly modeling good and, perhaps unwittingly, bad behavior. Their lessons may often be ignored, and their efforts deflected, but mothers and fathers have continuing, lifelong effects on the moral education of their children.

Formal schooling also shapes the ethical lives of children. When we finish high school or college we hold "commencement" ceremonies, which mark the beginning of autonomous adulthood and the end of childhood. Our juvenile education is done and we are ready to start life as non-children, something more morally complete. Although modern education has been infused with many other purposes – the acquisition of technical knowledge, the development of analytic skill – we still expect moral progress. In public school settings in the United States, "character education" is now commonly taught, an explicit effort to emphasize moral edification in a secular and technical educational environment. Families and churches and other groups also play a role in ethical learning, perhaps more important than public institutions, all of which illustrates the social importance of childhood moral development.

Our assumptions about childhood are most obvious when they fail, when children commit horrendous crimes that shock the conscience, that seem so adult in their depravity. We want to say, as we often do with children, that they don't know any better. And if that is true, if they are not fully aware of the moral ramifications of their actions, then they are obviously not adults, and should not be treated as adults under the law. But when faced with terrible scenes of murder or violence, a significant number of political leaders have demanded that young persons, who under most definitions would not be considered adults, be tried as adults in US courts. From this point of view, the perpetrators are children who are not child-like, adult in their immorality but juvenile in their morality; they don't know any better but they should have.

In the United States, it is now commonplace that children who commit serious violent crimes are tried as adults. Twenty-seven states allow pre-adolescent children to be tried as adults for certain crimes.[4] There is, of course, a counterargument that children are not adults, in either cognition or conscience, and thus should never be tried as adults, however terrible the crime.

These sorts of cases raise fundamental questions about childhood: Are children really morally different from adults? At what point and by what process does a person move from childhood to adulthood? And what should we do with children who commit appallingly violent crimes?

Confucian childhood

Confucius and Mencius do not directly discuss young children very much at all. Of course, they have much to say about the obligation of all children to honor and support their parents – the filial pillar of Confucian ethics. But this duty applies to adult children as well as juveniles. Our obligations to our parents extend throughout the entire course of our lives; they do not end when our childhood ends.

We can, however, derive a Confucian understanding of childhood from a number of passages and ideas in the *Analects* and *Mencius*. And what we find is quite familiar to our modern sensibilities: children are morally distinct from adults and should be treated differently.

Perhaps the best place to start a consideration of Confucian childhood is with a famous passage from the *Analects*:

> The Master said: "From fifteen, my heart-and-mind was set upon learning; from thirty I took my stance; from forty I was no longer doubtful; from fifty I realized the propensities of tian [heaven]; from sixty my ear was attuned; from seventy I could give my heart-and-mind free rein without overstepping the boundaries." (Ames and Rosemont, 2.4)

This is Confucius's famous statement about ageing, how we mature morally as we grow older. There is a clear sense of progression here, a purposive effort to acquire and develop an ethical sensibility. The first move comes, in his case, at fifteen, when he turned himself to learning. We can take this as the beginning of a lifelong process of self-cultivation. Before that age, he was not fully engaged with questions of right and wrong; thus, he was not yet an adult but a protected and limited child. At fifteen he took it upon himself, perhaps after exposure to the exemplary behavior of his parents or other adults, to learn how to be good. And he did not reach the first point of mature moral conviction until he was thirty. His twenties, then, were a period of still undeveloped ethical understanding. He was not yet certain of his positions, but neither was he a naive and untutored child.

For Confucius, from birth to fifteen can be taken as a pre-moral period. Morality is a function of learning, and before fifteen this kind of self-conscious and engaged instruction had yet to take place. This is Confucian childhood: the period of life before moral understanding has taken hold and, therefore, also before personal responsibility can be assigned. We cannot hold someone responsible for ethical issues they cannot yet understand. By extension, the years from fifteen to thirty can be taken as a Confucian moral adolescence of sorts. Ethical learning has begun, and so responsibility can be borne, but mistakes are probable.

Confucius expects children, perhaps those ten to fifteen years of age, to be aware of their moral status as juveniles and not to act as if they were adults:

> A youth from Que village would carry messages for the Master. Someone asked Confucius, "Is he making any progress?" The Master replied, "I have seen him sitting in places reserved for his seniors, and have seen him walking side by side with his elders. This is someone intent on growing up quickly rather than making progress." (Ames and Rosemont, 14.44)

Moral development, "progress," cannot be rushed. It comes in due course, as a child grows and eventually comes to realize that he or she must "set upon learning," must make a self-conscious decision to understand and do the right thing. Conversely, adults should not presume that children are morally capable of being adults: if they cannot sit and walk among us, we should not invite them or allow them to do so.

Children, in the eyes of Confucius, are morally and materially dependent upon their parents. Indeed, it is precisely because of the total dependence of infancy and earliest childhood that all children owe their parents a three year mourning period after they die. When confronted by a man, Zaiwo, who argued against that long a formal bereavement, Confucius replied:

> It is only after being tended by his parents for three years that an infant can finally leave their bosom. The ritual of a three-year mourning period for one's parents is practiced throughout the empire. Certainly Zaiwo received this three years of loving care from his parents. (Ames and Rosemont, 17.20)

Our dependence lasts for much longer, over a decade at least; so, it would seem that three years of mourning is the very least a child could do in symbolic repayment of that parental love and care, from a Confucian perspective.

The tricky question is: When, exactly, does our dependence on our parents end? At what point are we able to care for ourselves, and at what point are we able to make fully informed and judicious ethical decisions? Although Confucians believe that our obligations to our parents go on for ever, our actual dependence upon them ceases when we become adults.

There is no universal demarcation between childhood and adulthood for a Confucian. It is an individual process. For Confucius himself, fifteen was a key moment, the time when he became morally self-reflective. Not everyone, however, will have the same experience. Some may turn to learning at thirteen; some may never, though all should. At some age – we could arbitrarily say eighteen or twenty-one – a person is expected to behave morally like an adult, and will have to accept the full consequences of bad behavior. Such stages need to be established for legal purposes, but they are insufficient indicators of the moral development of all individuals.

A Confucian approach to the question, however, might return to ritual, with its emphasis on public declaration and enactment of moral commitment. The Jewish Bar (Bat) Mitzvah does this explicitly in a manner that would be quite pleasing to a modern-day Confucius. Indeed, the term "Bar Mitzvah" connotes: "one to whom the commandments apply." The young person has studied the Torah, is expected to understand it, and will now be held responsible for living up to its moral precepts. All of this is done, moreover, through ritual performance before the congregation. The actions of the ceremony mark the beginning of an adult life of what should be careful and considered ethical behavior. It is not just words, but action.

In contemporary America there is really no secular analogue for the Bar Mitzvah. The closest comparison might be high school graduation: it involves an educational process; it is publicly performed; and it brings with it the social expectation of a certain maturity. Although many people may graduate at eighteen, age itself is not the determining factor. Each person must fulfill certain educational requirements and should demonstrate personal and social responsibility in doing so (even if this is not always evident). Some may graduate at fifteen, some at nineteen or twenty; the specific age matters less than the presumed accomplishment. It is an imperfect model, and would need considerable improvement to better fulfill Confucian goals, but high school provides a context for moral maturation, a process of transition to adulthood.

Not everyone graduates high school and for those who do not, the process of moral learning would have to occur by other means. Graduation itself is less important than the learning that can take place in whatever fraction of high school a student experiences. But if a student leaves formal schooling, parents would have to play a heightened role in his or her moral education. For Confucians, parents generally bear significant, but not exclusive, responsibility for a child's ethical development. Before a son or daughter enters school, parents must introduce him or her to notions of right and wrong, good and bad. When children are in school, and a wider circle of social actors comes to participate in their moral learning, parents continue to play an important role: modeling good behavior, reinforcing

lessons learned elsewhere, and offering general guidelines. Confucius himself never considered himself his son's school teacher – others had that
responsibility – but he did encourage the youngster to study ritual and
the *Book of Songs*, a classic text which he understood as crucial to moral
maturity (*Analects*, 17.9, 16.13).

Confucians also recognize that teaching children is a difficult process
and requires teachers outside the immediate family. Parents can provide
general moral guidelines and model good behavior, but they should not
take on daily teaching duties. Mencius explains:

> Gongsun Chou said, "Why is it that a gentleman does not instruct his
> own son?"
> Mencius said, "The circumstances do not allow it. Instruction necessarily
> involves correction, and when the correction is not effective, the next thing is
> that they become angry. When they become angry, then, paradoxically, they
> hurt one another." The son says, 'My master instructs me in what is correct,
> but my master himself does not display correct behavior.' This is when father
> and son hurt one another, and for a father and son to hurt one another is a
> terrible thing.
> "In ancient times people exchanged sons and taught one another's sons.
> Between fathers and sons there should be no carping about goodness, because
> when there is carping about goodness, there is disaffection, and nothing could
> be more unfortunate than disaffection." (Bloom, 4A18)

No parent will be perfect all of the time, and children are very much
attuned to hypocrisies when parents do not live up to their own moral
instruction. Preserving the parent–child bond is paramount for Mencius
and Confucius; thus, the lion's share of teaching needs to occur outside
the home. Mencius, in fact, discusses various forms of schools, and their
common function of clarifying "human relations" (Bloom, 3A3). This
suggests that Confucians would support "character education" in schools,
designed to instill courtesy, respect, filiality, and other virtues.

If a child has left formal schooling, then parents will have to work harder
to find a means of engendering ethical understanding. As a juvenile grows,
getting closer to the age at which Confucius assumed responsibility for his
own moral learning, the obligation of discerning right from wrong gradually
shifts away from parents to the child. There is a Confucian presumption,
based on the story of Shun (the young man who knew how to be good even
though his father was bad), that children have a certain accountability for
their personal moral development. However, before the age of fifteen or

so, a child needs moral exemplars. Parents should always play this role but social institutions – schools, churches, government – are also important sources of proper behavior and right action. When those social institutions are not getting the job done, parents must take up the slack.

Ultimately, Confucians would expect high school drop outs to come to moral maturity at about the same time as high school graduates. The sources and pattern of ethical learning would be different for non-graduates but it should still occur. If it has not, then Confucians would take this into consideration when determining a person's responsibility for bad behavior. Although all individuals must take on the duty of learning how to be good, if social institutions and family circumstances have fundamentally failed a child, then some understanding of that flawed childhood should be included in any judgment of unethical conduct when that child becomes an adult.

To summarize: for Confucians, childhood is a time of moral naivety. It ends gradually through learning and the assumption of adult responsibilities, a process that continues throughout life. The beginning of the end of childhood varies by individual circumstance. For many, the educational experience symbolized by high school graduation can be taken as the opening phase of adulthood. For others, some combination of parental oversight and social learning should instill adult ethical sensibilities. What matters most, in any event, is the process, not the specific age. In practical terms, however, we are talking about the teenage years: Confucian childhood would generally end somewhere between thirteen and nineteen.

Mencius adds two points to these ideas: although not morally mature, children possess an inherent moral intuition embedded in their human nature; and environmental factors, which can be overcome through education, are the primary cause of moral breakdown. Both of these notions are captured in this passage:

> Mencius said, "In years of abundance, most of the young people have the wherewithal to be good, while in years of adversity, most of them become violent. This is not a matter of a difference in the native capacities sent down by Heaven but rather of what overwhelms their minds."
>
> "Now, let barley be sown and covered with earth; the ground being the same, and the time of planting also the same, it grows rapidly, and in due course of time, it all ripens. Though there may be differences in yield, this is because the fertility of the soil, the nourishment of the rain and dew, and the human effort invested are not the same."
>
> "Things of the same kind are thus like one another. Why is it that we should doubt this only when it comes to human beings?" (Bloom, 6A7)

Although it is not clear how young the "young people" might be – are they rowdy twenty-somethings? – the imagery of sprouting barley is applicable to early childhood. We all start off with the same, innately good, human nature, and our moral maturation then depends upon the conditions surrounding our growth and development. Mencius expresses this idea even more directly:

> Human nature is inherently good, just like water flows inherently downhill. There's no such thing as a person who isn't good, just as there's no water that doesn't flow downhill. (Hinton, 11.2)

It is all about shaping, through principled education, the ethical sensibilities of a person:

> Think about water: if you slap it, you can make it jump over your head; and if you push and shove, you can make it stay on a mountain. But what does this have to do with the nature of water? It's only responding to the forces around it. It's like that for people too: you can make them evil, but that says nothing about human nature. (Hinton, 11.2)

Children can be made bad, but they can also be made good. Confucius himself was forgiving and optimistic about the possibility of human perfection:

> The Master said, "The young should be held in high esteem. After all, how do we know that those yet to come will not surpass our contemporaries? It is only when one reaches forty or fifty years of age and yet had done nothing of note that we should withhold our esteem." (Ames and Rosemont, *Analects*, 9.23)

This, of course, doesn't mean that childhood can or should last until forty or fifty. Rather, it is a sign of Confucian tolerance, not for the persistence of purposive bad behavior, which should be punished, but for the possibility of human improvement and rehabilitation. In terms of childhood, this suggests that children who do bad should be given ever more instruction on how to do good.

Daoist childhood

Daoists have a very different notion of childhood. In a sense, they reverse the relationship asserted by Confucians: children are not morally imperfect adults-in-training but, rather, adults, if they want to get closer to Way, need to learn from the simple purity of children. Children should not become adults; adults should become children.

As we grow and reach adulthood, Daoism informs us, human-created concerns draw us away from the authenticity and spontaneity of Way. Zhuangzi paints a rather bleak picture:

> Once we happen into the form of this body, we cannot forget it. And so it is that we await out the end. Grappling and tangling with things, we rush headlong toward the end, and there's no stopping it. It's sad, isn't it? We slave our lives away and never get anywhere, work ourselves ragged and never find our way home. How could it be anything but sorrow? (Hinton, 20)

The things we get tangled in are our beliefs that we can "take hold of all under heaven and improve it," as passage 29 of the *Daodejing* tells us. We think we can intervene in Way and guide it and shape it to our purposes. And we throw ourselves into such efforts so completely and blindly that we cannot see that we are simply rushing toward our own deaths, without ever stopping to see and appreciate and follow where Way goes by itself, regardless of our actions. Contrary to Zhuangzi in the passage above, however, there is a stop to it and that would be abandonment of the desire to control Way and fate. This is, essentially, a rejection of adult purposes and capacities.

Children are presented in Daoist texts as being more in tune with Way. They have yet to take on adult apprehensions of ends and means; they are unabashedly dependent on the ebb and flow of circumstance, unable to control events as they unfold. Infants, in particular, are small and weak and incapable of acting effectively. They are thus embodiments of doing nothing or nothing's own doing. Their preferences are immediate and simple: food, warmth, bodily comfort. No grandiose plans to change the world, no expectations of future achievements or possessions cloud their perception and engagement with the world. A security of sorts is thus ensured, as the previously quoted passage 55 of the *Daodejing* suggests:

> One who is vital in character (*de*)
> Can be compared with a newborn baby.
>
> Wasps and scorpions will not sting a baby,
> Snakes and vipers will not bite him,
> And birds of prey and ferocious beasts will not snatch him up.
> Though his bones are soft and his sinews supple
> His grip is firm.
>
> (Ames and Hall)

The hurtful things of life, the hornets and vipers of disappointment and disapproval, cannot injure the one who has no great goals and aspirations. If you live plainly, if you "dwell in the ordinary," as *Zhuangzi* elsewhere says (Hinton, 23), then there will be fewer regrets and losses in life. Infants can, of course, suffer physical harm, but that is not the "ferocious beasts" or "birds of prey" of the passage. It is about keeping ourselves from getting tangled up in intellectual and social and material things and setting ourselves up for failure and remorse.

In the *Daodejing*, meditation provides a model for letting go of the yearnings and expectations of adult life. When a person sits and centers his breathing and empties his mind, he focuses his attention on being in the moment. This kind of practice can serve as a more general Daoist symbol of how to live closer to Way. We cannot always be in a meditative state, but we can release, or at least relax, our attachments to ideas of how we think the world ought to be, and simply open ourselves and accept the world as it is. And the infant figures here as an exemplar:

> In carrying about your more spiritual and more physical aspects
> and embracing their oneness,
> Are you able to keep them from separating?
> In concentrating your *qi* and making it pliant,
> Are you able to become the newborn babe?
>
> (Ames and Hall, *Daodejing*, 10)

Qi is the ancient Chinese notion of life force, the energy we absorb from the environment and which shapes our fate. It has the physical connotation of ether, and the spiritual implication of destiny. The ancients believed that we take in *qi* and we act upon *qi* as we move through space and time. Regulating our breath, and thus the flow of *qi*, is central to meditation. It is also something that comes naturally to the infant. Her *qi* is not obstructed and deflected by worries about status or wealth or accomplishment. She naturally focuses her *qi* in a manner that allows for more direct connection with Way.

Contrast these images of infancy with the *Daodejing*'s advice, in passage 22, for how adults should go about their cultivation of self:

> He does not show himself off; therefore he becomes prominent.
> He does not put himself on display; therefore he brightly shines.
> He does not brag about himself; therefore he receives credit.
> He does not praise his own deeds; therefore he can long endure.

It is only because he does not compete that, therefore, no one is able to compete with him.

(Henricks)

Intentional constructions of the self are precisely what infants and young children do not possess or even try to create. They have to learn how to engage in self-reflection, self-definition, self-promotion, and self-esteem. And it is precisely that kind of deliberate learning that Daoists say we must reject if we are to open ourselves to Way. If a person stops trying to forge a purposeful "self," he will discover a true self, the reflection of his innate integrity (*de*). And when we embody our integrity, or character, we are like the vibrant child.

What, then, of morality? If good behavior must be learned and cultivated into one's self-awareness, as both Confucians and modern Westerners generally believe, and if Daoism wards us off the pursuit of adult consciousness, then how, in Daoist thought, can morality be constituted and passed on to children?

Zhuangzi is quite direct on this point: morality is not something that is explicit and reducible to simple rules or principles. It is intuitive and particular and complex. Morality is neither inherent to the human condition, nor is it generalizable beyond individual circumstance:

Huizi said to Zhuangzi:	"Can a man really be without feelings?"
Zhuangzi:	"Yes."
Huizi:	"But a man who has no feelings – how can you call him a man?"
Zhuangzi:	"The Way gave him a face; Heaven gave him a form – why can't you call him a man?"
Huizi:	"But if you've already called him a man, how can he be without feelings?"
Zhuangzi:	"That's not what I mean by feelings. When I talk about having no feelings, I mean that a man doesn't allow likes or dislikes to get in and do him harm. He just lets things be the way they are and doesn't try to help life along."

(Watson, 75–76)

Zhuangzi is here rejecting the Mencian assertion of a universal and innately good human nature. One can be human, but have no "feelings." The latter notion he links to preferences, which for a Confucian would imply morality, since we should like the good and dislike the bad. But for a Daoist, human-created principles of right and wrong, the centerpiece of moral education, are the basis for likes and dislikes that can "get in and do him harm," distorting an individual's integrity. To be genuinely human, to be more consistent with the shape and form provided by Way and destiny, we have to give up the preferences constructed by conscious moral learning.

This sounds extreme and dangerous. Without moral learning how can good behavior be encouraged and bad behavior limited? Isn't this a recipe for anarchy and chaos and raw domination of power over right? *The Lord of the Flies* run amok?

Daoists do not see it that way because, at heart, they are optimists. While there is no universal Daoist moral code applicable to all individuals, there is a sensibility that comes from following Way. Daoism generally rejects killing and embraces a certain tolerance for the value and existence of all things in Way. If one is close to Way and is behaving in a "Way-like" manner, then he or she will generally not kill or infringe upon the life and development of others. To do otherwise is to violate the unity and flow of Way. Humanly created rules of good conduct, whether secular or religious, can fail, and sometimes fail horrendously – think of mass killing inspired by religious belief or nationalist commitments. "Human nature," therefore, is unreliable in terms of protecting the integrity of things in Way. Better to let things be, let people come to discover the possibilities of non-violence and tolerance for themselves in their own particular circumstances. It is in that sense, then, in the belief that it is possible for such realization to arise from immediate daily experience without strict moral education or government guidance, that Daoists are ultimately optimistic.

Daoist optimism is embodied in young children. In their naivety, they are human but not yet caught up in the demands of "human nature." And it is from them that we can begin to appreciate Way, as Zhuangzi suggests in a passage about the transmission of Way awareness:

> "Where did you hear about Dao?" asked Adept Sunflower.
> "I heard it from Inkstain's child," replied Dame Crookback. "Inkstain's child heard it from Bookworm's grandchild . . . " (Hinton, 90)

We hear about it from children. The word "learn" cannot really be used in this regard, because that would suggest a process like deliberate moral learning. That's not how Way comes to be known. It is apprehended, it is sensed, it is enacted. It unfolds before us, and we can see it and hear it if we open ourselves to it. And if we do, we will, as Zhuangzi says, see that children are as morally whole as adults:

> In all beneath heaven there's nothing bigger than the tip of an autumn hair, and Tai Mountain is tiny. No one lives longer than a child who dies young, and the seven-hundred-year-old Peng Zu died an infant. (Hinton, 26)

Confucian and Daoist parenting

Parents shape their children's lives, both consciously and unconsciously. For Confucians, they play a an important though not exclusive role in moral education, while for Daoists they can, if they are not too overbearing, facilitate a child's unadulterated development in Way.

The *Analects* and *Mencius* do not explicitly discuss child-rearing but the logic of Confucianism suggests that caring for and educating children is the starting point of the broader process of creating and reproducing humaneness in the world. Children must learn to be filial and parents are the ones best situated to oversee that learning. Confucius suggests as much in *Analects* 5.27 (Ames and Rosemont). When asked what he most wants to do, Confucius replies: " . . . to bring peace and contentment to the aged, to share relationships of trust and confidence with my friends, and to love and protect the young."

He wants to love and protect the young. And, for Confucius, loving and protecting suggest cultivating their ethical sensibilities and behavior. We can love better and protect better when children are good. Extending this idea to parental duties, it would follow that these would include the responsibility for the moral education of their kids. Although, as Mencius tells us, all humans are born with an inherent capacity for goodness, specific instruction is required to bring young people to moral maturity. Let's recall this passage, which we considered earlier:

> Think about water: if you slap it, you can make it jump over your head; and if you push and shove, you can make it stay on a mountain. But what does this have to do with the nature of water? It's only responding to the forces around it. It's like that for people too: you can make them evil, but that says nothing about human nature. (Hinton, 11.2)

Viewed from a parent's perspective, this is a starting point for child-rearing. Mencius is advising us that we can and should channel our children toward their better possibilities. Notice how he raises the negative example: "you can make them evil." The natural tendency is toward goodness but, if you do not raise them properly, sons and daughters can turn out bad. Parents thus have a certain responsibility for their children. Their care is not the only factor that shapes the moral character of juveniles, who can be influenced by other people and teachers and society at large, but parents should take their responsibility seriously.

Confucianism also suggests a particular approach for instilling ethical understanding in children, one that emphasizes positive inducements over negative punishments, carrots over sticks. This may seem inconsistent with the familiar association of Confucianism and strict, rule-bound, penalty-laden parenting. But, once again, the historical uses of "Confucianism," or whatever set of ideas and practices that might be attached to that label, are not always in keeping with the ideals expressed in Confucian texts. Take this passage from Mencius, for example:

> It is the way of human beings that when they have sufficient food, warm clothing, and comfortable dwellings, but are without education, they become little more than birds and beasts. It was the part of the sage [Shun] to grieve anxiously over this. He appointed Xie minister of education in order to teach people about human relations: that between parents and children there is affection; between ruler and minister, rightness; between husband and wife, separate functions; between older and younger, proper order; and between friends, faithfulness. Fangxun [Yao] said:
>> Encourage them, lead them,
>> Reform them, correct them,
>> Assist them, give them wings,
>> Let them "get it for themselves,"
>> Then follow by inspiring them to Virtue (*de*).
> (Bloom, 3A4)

Here, once more, we see the importance of moral education: people, and certainly this includes children, will, if materially comfortable, tend toward sloth and idleness, "little more than birds and beasts." They must be taught how to perform the obligations of the "five relationships." (father and son; sovereign and subject; husband and wife; young and old; friend and friend). And the exemplary sage-king Yao offers a method for this work. To bring people to moral understanding we must "encourage them, lead them, reform them, correct them." It is a message more of support and guidance, then of punishment and control. Contrary to the old biblical injunction, Mencius, following Yao, suggests here that we spare the rod in order to improve the child.

A kinder and gentler approach to parenting, one that generally avoids corporeal punishment, is in keeping with other Confucian principles. Confucius himself prefers leading by example as opposed to coercion, as in this famous *Analects* excerpt:

> The noble-minded have the integrity of wind, and little people the integrity of grass. When the wind sweeps over the grass, it bends. (Hinton, 12.19)

The sheer beauty and power of right action should be enough to impress and educate the morally immature. Indeed, in dealings with his own son, Confucius exercised a light hand:

> Chen Gang (Ziqin) questioned [Confucius's son] Boyu, saying, As a son, have you received any special instructions?
> No, replied Boyu. But once, when my father was standing by himself and I hurried across the courtyard, he said, Have you studied the *Odes* [*Book of Songs*]? Not yet, I replied. He said, If you don't study the *Odes*, you won't know how to speak properly! So after that I studied the *Odes*. Another day, when he was standing by himself and I hurried across the courtyard, he said, Have you studied the rites? Not yet, I replied. He said, If you don't study the rites, you won't have any basis to stand on. So after that I studied the rites. He gave me these two pieces of instruction.
> Afterward Chen Gang, delighted, said, I asked one question and learned three things. I learned about the *Odes*, I learned about the rites, and I learned that the gentleman maintains a certain distance in relations with his son. (Watson, *Analects*, 16.13)

All the father is doing here is making broad suggestions for moral improvement: read the *Odes* (an ancient text of poems and lyrics) and study ritual, the daily conscientious effort to discover and do the right thing. Confucius is also teaching his son by his own example, his own commitment and enactment of his family and social obligations. Not much else seems necessary. There is no mention of spanking or punishment or coercion. It's all about modeling proper behavior and promoting ethical literacy.

That last phrase, a "gentleman maintains a certain distance in relations with his son," sounds rather cold and disinterested. It is anything but. The "distance" mentioned here is more like a balance, a careful calibration of encouragement and correction. In the passage above, Confucius gently admonishes Boyu, pointing out his error of not yet being familiar with the *Odes* or ritual. A parent should point out the error of the child's ways, but without harshness or anger or force. Tact is required in order to preserve the core value of the father–son (and this can be expanded to parent–child) relationship: affection. Mencius makes this clear when he states why a parent should not be a child's school teacher:

> The ancients taught each other's children. That way father and son never demand perfect virtue of one another. If they demand perfect virtue of one another, they grow distant. And nothing is more ominous than fathers and sons grown distant from one another. (Hinton, 7.18)

Here "distant" refers to emotional detachment, obviously a bad thing. In order to maintain affection, to avoid estrangement, a different kind of distance is required, a behavioral distance that takes the parent out of a child's daily educational routine. Parents need to set certain standards, create positive incentives, and then get out of the way. Children will make mistakes; they will fall short of expectations at times. Other teachers can be called upon to demand "perfect virtue." Parents cannot personally respond to every stumble a child may take. Some parental interventions will be necessary but they must be occasional and strategic, not constant and nagging.

It's a delicate thing, Confucian parenting. It requires careful attention to adult behavior as a model for a child's moral education. A parent cannot simply tell a child how to act properly but must constantly attend to his or her own proper actions. Furthermore, exacting consideration must be given to when and how a child is corrected. Coming on too strong and forceful will undermine affection; but not intervening when necessary might allow a child to learn the wrong thing.

Daoist parents are more hands-off. Moral education is unnecessary because "morality," for a Daoist, is a humanly created convention that can never capture the fullness of Way and can distract us from our natural human instincts. Parents must take on the physical care of their newborns, something a Daoist would assume to be intuitive. Mothers do not have to be told when their infant is hungry or cold. Of course, some parents will be more attentive and some might be negligent. Such variation, from a Daoist perspective, is just the Way of humankind, something that occurs even in the most highly regulated and diligent societies. Daoists would not create a child welfare agency but would have faith that, for the most part, sufficient care will happen. The larger question for Daoist mothers and fathers is, as children grow and come to care for themselves, what is there for a parent to do?

Passage 18 of the *Daodejing* gives us some sense of the limits of parenthood:

> When the great Way is abandoned
> we're faced with humanity and duty.
>
> When clever wisdom appears
> we're faced with duplicity.
>
> When familial harmony ends
> we're faced with obedience and kindness.
>
> And when chaos engulfs the nation
> we're faced with trustworthy ministers.
>
> (Hinton)

In each couplet, the second line is an effect of the first: conscious efforts to construct "humanity" and "duty" emerge only after the natural balance and order of Way have been disrupted. Duplicity arises only after notions of "wisdom" have created possibilities for sophistry and pretense. Deliberate parental inculcation of basic values like "obedience" and "kindness" is necessary only after instinctual family harmony has deteriorated. And the ersatz trustworthiness of ministers is produced only after the county has been pitched into disorder. In each case, the ostensibly "good" thing – obedience, kindness, humanity, duty – are merely signs of a more fundamental breakdown, a loss of Way. Filial obligation, in other words, is not a means to family harmony, but an indication that family harmony has already been lost.

To press a bit further, the passage suggests that it is only when we lose our innate human impulses, provided to us by Way, that we need to create artificial notions of morality. The implication here is that a natural life, with its share of good and bad, pleasure and pain, joy and sorrow, cannot be improved upon by universal ethical codes. Each individual will find what is good in his or her life, and suffer what is bad. There is, then, no real need for parental moral education of children. There is nothing, really, to teach them. Each child will discover, for his or her self, the possibilities of Way. The experience of the adult cannot be used to guide the unique life of the child.

The *Daodejing*'s passage 51 provides more insight into Daoism's faith in the spontaneous and unadulterated development of individual juvenile character:

> Way gives birth to them
> and integrity nurtures them.
> Matter shapes them
> and conditions complete them.
>
> That is why the ten thousand things always
> honor Way and treasure integrity.
>
> Honoring Way and treasuring integrity
> isn't obedience to command,
> it's occurrence perennially appearing of itself.
>
> Way gives birth to them
> and integrity nurtures them:
> it fosters and sustains them,
> harbors and succors them,
> nourishes and shelters them.
>
> Giving birth without possessing,
> animating without subjecting,
> fostering without dominating:
>
> that is called dark-enigma integrity.
>
> (Hinton)

The focus on integrity (*de*) here calls attention to the distinctive quality of each individual thing in Way. Allowing each child to develop as he or she will, "treasuring integrity," requires a surrender to fate and context, "occurrence perennially appearing of itself." It's not about obedience to, and control by, parents. Rather, it is an acceptance of our fundamental lack of control over not only the circumstances of our own lives but also the possibilities of our children's lives. This may sound preposterous: how can we just let go of our children like that? But, again, there is a certain faith here that the kids will be all right. They will, by themselves, find nurturance and sustenance and succor and shelter. Indeed, our inability to readily accept this radically minimized definition of parenting is what makes it "dark-enigma integrity." It is hard for us to grasp, difficult to embrace, enigmatic to our minds. Daoists, however, would ask us to believe in the efficacy of unadulterated childhood.

If there were to be a slogan for Daoist parents, it might be that penultimate stanza:

> Giving birth without possessing,
> animating without subjecting,
> fostering without dominating

But can we really do that (or, not do that, as the case may be)? In our real, twenty-first century lives, surrounded by legal obligations and social conventions and political forces that powerfully establish familial responsibilities much more extensive than Daoism would acknowledge, we cannot be the effortless parents of the *Daodejing*. We cannot ignore our children's moral and social development because we will be held accountable for their transgressions. But that reality does not render Daoist notions of parenting completely meaningless. Although absolute non-interference may be impractical and illegal, we can take from Daoism the idea of scaling back intrusions into our children's lives. Parenting can be subtler and more indirect, more unobtrusive than the Confucian ideal. We can love and care for our children without possessing or dominating them.

When children do bad

From these different conceptions of childhood and parenting we can now extrapolate Confucian and Daoists answers to the question of whether children who commit terrible crimes should be treated, under the law, as adults.

Confucians would say "no." But this response would be qualified by the specific circumstances of the individual involved. Is the person truly a child? Is he or she receiving an adequate moral education? Age alone would not be sufficient to answer these kinds of questions. An investigation and determination of a perpetrator's moral status would be necessary.

Some rules of thumb have already been suggested above. If the person has completed high school, there would then be a presumption of the beginning of adulthood. He or she has experienced an educational process that attempts, however imperfectly, to instill a sense of adult responsibility. Most people under the age of eighteen would thus be considered children. Some older than eighteen, if they were still involved in a high school education, could also be considered children. Persons as young as fourteen or fifteen would generally not be considered adults.

Teenagers who have dropped out of high school would require some further consideration. The nature and quality of their moral education would have to be established: Have their parents provided them with sufficient ethical understanding? Have they "turned to learning" of their own accord? The answers to these sorts of questions would contribute to an understanding of whether a particular person should be considered an adult or not. There would be no prior assumption that age alone defines adult status: the individual circumstances of each person would have to be judged.

If an individual is found to be a child – that is, a person with still immature moral sensibilities – then Confucians would hold that he or she should not be treated as an adult. The severity of the crime would not be sufficient to change this. If they are not yet morally mature and independent, then they cannot be held responsible for their actions in the same manner that an adult can. Appropriate punishment could be determined, but it should not be premised on the moral maturity that applies to an adult.

What if it could be shown that a child, say sixteen years old and still in high school, intentionally killed another person? Premeditation and planning make it appear like an adult at work. The perpetrator knew what he was doing, knew, at some level, that it was wrong, but did it anyway. Shouldn't such a young perpetrator, who seems to be acting like a willful adult, be treated like an adult?

Confucians would stick to their guns and say "no." If a child has not experienced enough of a moral education, a process that takes time and attention, then he or she cannot exercise the intentionality of an adult. Children may have a portion of adult ethicality, they may know for example that killing others is wrong, but they have not yet had the chance to cultivate mature moral judgment. They may not be able to see beyond their immediate passions and interests; they may not fully understand all of the consequences and ramifications of their actions. Some adults may fail in the same manner but, Confucians would assume, time and experience and education should make adults know better. Children do not know better, even if they know something about good and bad.

Confucians, therefore, would support a juvenile justice system – one that has courts and procedures that are different than those for adults and that has different detention and incarceration facilities. The worst possible outcome would be to take a child who has committed a terrible crime and jail him in a prison filled with adult offenders. This would act as a school of sorts, teaching all of the wrong lessons.

Punishment for children should, from this perspective, have a substantial educational component. In keeping with the Confucian notion of innately good human nature and the capacity of all people to improve themselves, judicial sentences, for adults as well as children, should all encourage rehabilitation. But juvenile corrections should especially emphasize schooling and moral learning. As Mencius tells us, the "water" of a child's innate goodness, even for a child who has behaved badly, can be channeled in the right direction; the "barley" of the juvenile heart-mind can thrive if provided the best growing conditions. Ideally, the child who commits a serious crime would be subjected to closely monitored intellectual and ethical education. Mencius supplies a vision statement of sorts for a juvenile reform school:

> We change and grow only when we make mistakes. We realize what to do only when we work through worry and confusion. And we gain people's trust and understanding only when our inner thoughts are revealed clearly in our faces and words. When it has no lawful families or wise officials within and no enemy without, a nation will surely come to ruin. Then its people will understand that through calamity and grief we flourish, and through peace and joy we perish. (Hinton, 12.15)

This is not a call for perpetual conflict and tension. It is, rather, an exhortation to make the most of adversity. When a person finds himself in difficult circumstances, if he has done something terribly wrong and must now face the consequences, Mencius tells us that he first must look deep into his own conscience, examine his inner thought, and struggle through "worry and confusion." Then, self-improvement is possible: we all can make ourselves better through conscientious correction of our mistakes.

Parents and family members, who share in the responsibility of bringing a child to moral maturity, should be included in the processes of atonement and rehabilitation. Fathers and mothers can be drawn into the child-perpetrator's continuing education, learning lessons from bad behavior and identifying models of proper conduct. The child and family members together can also work to heal the social damage done by certain bad acts. This does not necessarily mean financial compensation for victims, though Confucian justice would be open to that. It might also entail meaningful service, performing some good to make up for the bad, for either the victim's family or society at large.

Ultimately, Confucians would look beyond the details of individual cases and ask into the broader social and economic causes of crime.

Why do children behave badly? What is it in their family situations that might engender improper or inhumane conduct? Personal and parental responsibility are important – children must take it upon themselves to "turn to learning" and their parents must encourage them in that direction. But governments also have an obligation to promote social policies that facilitate healthy child development and behavior. Mencius lists what a "true emperor," a good leader, should provide for the people:

> When every five-acre farm has mulberry trees around the farmhouse, people wear silk at fifty. And when the proper seasons of chickens and pigs and dogs are not neglected, people eat meat at seventy. When hundred-acre farms never violate their proper seasons, even large families don't go hungry. Pay close attention to the teaching in village schools, and extend it to the child's family responsibilities – then, when their silver hair glistens, people won't be out on the roads and paths hauling heavy loads. Our black-haired people free of hunger and cold, wearing silk and eating meat at seventy – there have never been such times without a true emperor. (Hinton, 1.3)

A key indicator of a well-ordered and just society, for Confucians, is the condition of elderly people. Older folks are safe and comfortable when economic inequality is limited by effective government policies, in this case ensuring that resources (mulberry trees) and opportunities (proper seasons) are provided to all. Education of children, however, is also an important duty of government in this regard. Good schools turn children toward moral understanding and, thus, the elderly are safe and content. When children are doing the right thing by their elders, they are acting properly, not committing crimes. Conversely, we can infer that if economic inequality is severe and if schools are substandard, social conditions will deteriorate and children will be more prone to behave badly. "True emperors" don't let that happen; they attend to both the broad social conditions that produce good children as well as the individual circumstances of those children who do bad.

Daoists, if asked, would initially hesitate to say how they would judge children who commit crimes. They would consider saying that such juveniles should not be treated as adults because children, in their youth and immaturity, are so fundamentally different than adults. After further thought, however, a Daoist would likely say "yes," children and adults can be treated in a similar manner, but only because the distinction between "child" and "adult" is meaningless and all things, since they move as "one and the same," can be treated equally in Way.

The apparent moral goodness of infants and very young children, their natural closeness to Way, would not afford children, in general, any special consideration or treatment by Daoists. In other words, children would not be presumed morally better than adults, even if they are potentially more in touch with Way. Teenagers, Daoists would assume, can exercise a certain amount of free will – indeed, younger children may also be willful – and that intentionality can produce un-Way-like behavior. Children can learn to transgress Way at a fairly early age. Thus, Daoists would not construct an overarching category of "children" and apply it to all individuals of a certain age or experience.

Conversely, "adult" would be a fairly useless generalization for Daoists as well. The variation – intellectual, physical, emotional, ethical – of all people above the age of eighteen or so defies simple classification. Although many adults are entrapped in humanly created distractions, "grappling and tangling with things," some may be able to relinquish their desires and follow Way. A few could be sage-like, consistently able to sense the best action for particular circumstances. But we cannot know, before we delve into individual histories, which mature person is more open to Way and which is hopelessly closed off from it. The mere title "adult" tells us virtually nothing about the integrity (*de*) of a specific man or woman.

Instead of pre-established classifications of "adult" or "child" a Daoist would suggest a process for determining whether a person had committed a bad act. A first set of questions might revolve around the nature of the act itself: Was it contrary to Way? If it was, how? Was it spontaneous or premeditated? A second set of questions could then be posed regarding the circumstances of the individuals involved and the context: Was the perpetrator incited or forced into acting? Did he or she understand the effects of the act? Was there something in the situation that might justify or explain what happened? Whatever particular questions are asked, they would be the same for persons of any age. For the very young, children under ten or so, immaturity might be a mitigating circumstance. Daoists could accept the idea that a young child may not understand the nature or ramifications of bad behavior. Such mitigation, however, would not be automatically assumed at the outset; it would have to be determined through consideration of the individual's integrity (*de*) and the broader social context.

We can go a bit further and posit some guidelines for how a Daoist might judge whether a particular action is good or bad. There is in Daoism an implicit "harm principle," the concept, made famous by John Stuart Mill, that people should be free to act as they want as long as they do

no harm to others.[5] This can be derived from various passages of the
Daodejing and *Zhuangzi.*[6]

To begin with, the *Daodejing* is generally against killing (passage 74) and
war (passages 31, 68), the most severe forms of harm. It is also critical of
selfish exploitation of others:

> The people are starving,
> and its only because you leaders feast on taxes
> that they're starving.
>
> The people are impossible to rule,
> and it's only because you leaders are masters of extenuation
> that they're impossible to rule.
>
> The people take death lightly,
> and it's only because you leaders crave life's lavish pleasures
> that they take death lightly,
> they who act without concern for life:
> it's a wisdom far beyond treasuring life.
>
> (Hinton, 75)

There is a clear sense of moral outrage here: the poverty and frustration
of average people is caused by rapacious and mendacious political leaders.
It's not right, not in keeping with what is possible in Way. The last two lines
of the passage swerve off in a different direction, suggesting that letting
go of our attachment to life can be liberating, but the main idea is the
unnecessary cruelty of those who hold power.

This suggests that people, adults as well as children, should not harm
other people, either physically or psychically. Selfishness, when taken to
extremes, can be harmful to others and should also be avoided. The primary
reason for Daoists to abandon selfish behavior is to get close to Way, which
actually brings a more authentic self-preservation, or preserves a more
authentic self. But there is a moral sensibility here, also. Pursuit of material
self-interest, craving "lavish pleasures," hurts others, by distorting their
sense of themselves in Way, and is wrong.

If we apply these ideas to questions of juvenile behavior, we end up
with a rather conventional ethical standpoint: harming others is wrong;
selfishness should be constrained. Although these ideas are the rudiments
of ethical reciprocity – do unto others as you would have them do unto
you – Daoism does not take that step. The relativism of not judging one
thing by the experience of another limits Daoist morality. But it is still

possible, by appealing to a more diffuse harm principle, for a Daoist to judge the actions of any person, even without adopting mutually exclusive categories of "child" and "adult."

Daoism resists the construction of strict and comprehensive legal codes and lawyerly thinking. Immediate conditions and individual circumstances are all that can be known of Way at any given moment. That is why Daoists would not rely on a universal process of moral education in the manner of Confucians. The simple Daoist harm principle is easily expressed and conveyed. What is difficult about ethical judgment is understanding what "harm" or "selfish" might mean in specific situations. Sensing the right thing to do is not so much a matter of applying general rules as it is an instinct cultivated through openness to Way. That, for a Daoist, is what children need to learn.

Neither Daoists nor Confucians, then, would agree with those in the contemporary United States who believe that children who commit terrible crimes should be treated legally as adults. Confucians would concur with those Americans who contend that children are fundamentally different than adults, especially in the realm of moral maturity, and that juvenile justice must have distinct standards and procedures. Daoists would agree, in the abstract, that children can be treated as adults. But the Daoist approach to judgment, which requires that each thing be understood on its own terms and which rejects predetermined categories of "adult" and "child," is impossible to reconcile with modern American legal practice.

Notes

1. Michael Boylan, "Duties to Children," in Michael Boylan, ed., *The Morality and Global Justice Reader* (Boulder, CO: Westview Press, 2011), pp. 383–404.
2. General discussions of moral development of children can be found in: Gareth B. Matthews, *The Philosophy of Childhood* (Cambridge, MA: Harvard University Press, 1994), Chapter 5, "Moral Development"; Alison Gopnik, *The Philosophical Baby* (New York: Farrar, Straus and Giroux, 2009), Chapter 8, "Love and Law: The Origins of Morality."
3. Anne Behnke Kinney, "Dyed Silk: Han Notions of the Moral Development of Children," in Anne Behnke Kinney, ed., *Chinese Views of Childhood* (Honolulu: University of Hawaii Press, 1995), pp. 17–56.
4. Michele Deitch *et al.*, *From Time Out to Hard Time: Young Children in the Adult Criminal Justice System*, (Austin, TX: The University of Texas at Austin, LBJ School of Public Affairs, 2009), p. 9.

Childhood

5. John Stuart Mill, *The Basic Writings of John Stuart Mill* (New York: Random House Modern Library, 2002), p. 14.

6. Kuang-ming Wu argues that Chapters 29 and 30 of *Zhuangzi* demonstrate the myopia of violence, thus suggesting that harming others should be avoided: Kuang-ming Wu, "Violence as Weakness: In China and Beyond," *Dao: A Journal of Comparative Philosophy*, 3 (1) (December 2003), pp. 7–28.

4

Work

When obligations to work conflict with obligations to family, Confucians would generally counsel us to fulfill our family duties first. Professional careers are less important than our social duties, and profit-seeking behavior, or materialist desires beyond a modest minimum, can undermine our humanity. Daoists, while also profit averse, see work as potentially more important than social relationships. It is a realm in which we can discover our place in Way.

I did not want to get a "real" job when my college years ended. Karl Marx was still ringing in my ears: alienated labor, and the alienated life that goes with it, was all that the working world seemed to offer. So I went to graduate school instead, a place, I thought, that would shield me, for a time at least, from the necessity of selling my time and the products of my labor to someone else.

It worked for a while. Graduate school existence did take me out of the work force, though it paid hardly subsistence. I toiled away in classes and libraries, learning Chinese and an assortment of social science theories, some of which would prove to be useless beyond graduate school drudgery. After a few years, however, the real world of work once again rose up before me. It was time to get a job, and the market for college teaching positions was terrible: too many PhDs, not enough permanent positions. Marx was right, there was really no escaping the cash nexus of modern life.

It turned out that I was lucky. I had only one interview in the first few months of my search, after having applied for dozens of positions, and I

Life, Liberty, and the Pursuit of Dao: Ancient Chinese Thought in Modern American Life, First Edition. Sam Crane.
© 2013 John Wiley & Sons, Inc. Published 2013 by John Wiley & Sons, Inc.

landed that job. One thing led to another and I am now safely tenured at a good college. But whatever my fine fortune, the larger reality remains: costs of living seem never to decline, demands on time constantly escalate, tensions between family and work and self-fulfillment remain unresolved. The ivory tower may appear secure, but it does not shield me from the exigencies of work.

$$* * *$$

We work, in the first instance, because we must. Food, shelter, clothing and other necessities must be secured. In modern market economies that means selling our talents and knowledge and time to someone or some company that will pay us. We enter into contracts or find informal arrangements to earn money to satisfy our needs and, if we have extra resources, our wants. It's all rather straightforward, perhaps even impersonal.

Some of us might find ways not to work. Wealth can allow leisure; misfortune can limit employment. Most of us, however, most of the time, have to work.

There is, nonetheless, more to work than sheer necessity, or, at least, we want there to be more. Some of us are fortunate enough to like our work, to find a certain fulfillment in it. Whatever we create through our labor, either physical or mental, becomes an extension of ourselves.[1] We are what we produce. And that can be a very important part of how we define ourselves and how we determine whether our lives are worthwhile. A person unhappy in work can easily carry that frustration into other aspects of his or her life.

Here, then, is created one of the great tensions of work experience: material necessity versus personal gratification. Each of these produces a distinct definition of what constitutes a "good job" and those disparate understandings can, at times, pull an individual in opposite directions.

On the material side, a good job is one that provides sufficient pay and benefits to obtain the necessities of life. While this seems simple enough, it is quickly complicated by changing interpretations of "needs." How much is necessary? How much is enough? It may be true that, in the most basic physical sense, we absolutely need relatively little. Many people the world over survive on meager resources: a certain number of calories, particular types of nutrients, shelter, clothing, basic medical care and the like. A modicum of human interaction and some intellectual stimulation or cultural expression might also fall under a minimum definition of what is necessary for human existence. If we live in a relatively affluent society, however, our understanding of "need" is likely to expand to reflect prevailing social standards. We may feel a need to have certain types of provisions or entertainment or education, even though, strictly speaking, we could live without them.

In short, as affluence grows, as we earn more from the work we do and as certain basic needs are fulfilled, what had been superfluous wants can transform into new needs. Some say they *need* an ice maker built into the refrigerator door, or they *need* cosmetic surgery, or they *need* tickets to the big game. Materially secure middle class Americans may come to feel deprived if they do not have those things that bring them a higher level of physical or emotional comfort. Or, they imagine they must have more of everything. It might be tempting to scoff at such bourgeois anxiety as false and feeble, but, whatever our judgment, it exists as a social fact. Some people become dissatisfied with their jobs because they are not making enough money to buy that set of fashionable commodities or services which currently defines the lifestyle they feel they deserve.[2] In such cases, "needs" have expanded well beyond the necessary and the value of work is defined by how much stuff it provides.

On the other hand, a job can be understood as good, even if it does not pay well and thus offers only limited access to material wealth, when it allows a person to do that which affirms a sense of self-worth. We have all encountered the dedicated teacher or librarian or car mechanic who is perfectly happy with his work, though it provides only a modest livelihood. The job fits his individual talents and expresses his self-understanding. She finds and creates herself in her work. This sort of gratification is measured more in the quality of the work itself as opposed to the quantity of compensation that it brings. A person happy in his job in this manner might avoid higher paying alternative careers and hang on to a relatively low paying job because the particular type of work lends meaning to life.

Good jobs in this sense create social roles that feed into our identities. I am a teacher, a college professor. With that comes certain social expectations about what I should do and what defines excellence in my field. When I live up to those expectations, my sense of self is enhanced. I internalize the public effects of my labor. Conversely, when I fail to meet the standards of my profession, my self-confidence deflates: I am something less than I ought to be. Although feelings of self-worth can be influenced by pay and benefits, they are also shaped by the pursuit of normative ideals of what we want to be and what we ought to do. If I am a good teacher, that is a good in itself, and it can make me feel good about myself, regardless of whether the pay is good or not.

There is a danger here, however. Identities are multifaceted; our work lives are only one source of our self-definition. We all have family roles that claim some portion of our total sense of self; we all have networks of friends and acquaintances and neighbors who fill parts of our lives. If we pursue our work to the detriment of our other social roles, if we allow the time and attention given to our jobs to draw us away from others, we could diminish ourselves. I do not want to be known as a good teacher at the cost of being a bad father or husband or friend.

Our jobs, then, create various tensions and choices. How much time should we spend at work and how much attention should we give to family and friends? Should we work in a way that produces the greatest material compensation or should we work at something that provides more self-expression and personal satisfaction? What if a certain level of income is required for self-expression? A "good job," in other words, is hard to find.

Confucians and work

Confucianism offers lucid and direct responses to the various questions raised by the work imperative. At the very outset, Confucius tells us not to get caught up in the pursuit of profit, the material benefits of our business or labor:

> The Master said: "If profit guides your actions, there will be no end of resentment." (Hinton, *Analects*, 4.12)

> The Master said: "The noble-minded are clear about duty. Little people are clear about profit." (Hinton, *Analects* 4.16)

> The Master said, "If wealth were an acceptable goal, even though I would have to serve as a groom holding a whip in the marketplace, I would gladly do it. But if it is not an acceptable goal, I will follow my own devices." (Ames and Rosemont, *Analects* 7.12)

Resentment, small-mindedness, dishonor: that is what the quest for profit brings. The reference to duty is the key here. For Confucius, our primary obligations are to our family and other close social relationships, it is there that we create and reproduce moral goodness, humanity. This is absolutely fundamental and if we allow ourselves to be distracted from familial and social responsibilities by the demands or rewards of our work, we would fall into the category of ethically deficient, petty "little people." Profit can be a diversion. If we are drawn away from our duties, then wealth is not an acceptable goal.

Material success in business or professional life, besides potentially undermining family roles, also breeds a broader public resentment: the wealth so obtained and amassed becomes a sign to others of what they do not have, and such disparity can infect interpersonal relationships. Instead of looking at each other and asking, "how can we work together to advance humanity," we think to ourselves, selfishly, "how can I work to get what I want from this person." Taking from others, or using others for selfish material interests, pushes us into a moral isolation that renders ethical reciprocity impossible. Goodness, from a Confucian perspective, is viable only when individuals work for the good of others.

Just as they reject the profit motive, Confucians also reject a fame motive. Proper action is generated by a genuine concern for fulfilling obligations to others; it is not intended to create celebrity and renown. *The Analects* speaks directly to this:

> The Master said: "The noble-minded worry about their lack of ability, not about people's failure to recognize their ability." (Hinton, 15.19)

> The Master said: "Don't grieve when people fail to recognize your ability. Grieve when you fail to recognize theirs." (Hinton, 1.16)

> The Master said: "Don't' grieve when people fail to recognize your ability. Grieve for your lack of ability instead." (Hinton, 14.30)

In the latter two references, the first phrase is literally repeated: don't grieve – or worry or be concerned – when people do not recognize your ability. What is important is that we are doing the right thing for the right reasons. Whether that is seen and acknowledged by others is of little import. There is a presumption that, eventually, the good will out, and public recognition of moral action will follow, but acclaim and prominence are not valid Confucian motivations.

It is not easy to live up to these Confucian ideals in a modern economy. Increasingly competitive and globalized job markets – with manufacturing employment shifting to China and service sector positions moving to

India – amplify the pressure of work on everyone, everywhere.[3] To keep up in the new world economy, to earn enough to pay for housing and education and health care, many of us put in more hours or seek ways to raise the productivity of the hours we log. Others struggle to augment the visibility of their work, to gain a modicum of fame that might be converted into money. A middle-class, middle-aged American man, down-sized from a previously gainful corporate career, now must work two or three jobs to maintain his family's accustomed lifestyle. He must promote himself incessantly. That, or depend more on the greater number of hours his spouse must work. Or, accept a lower standard of living. Confucians would tell us to accept the latter, if it provided more time with our families, but popular culture and the fear of falling out of the "middle class," or more dire anxieties of lost income and prospects, push many Americans toward more work.

Recognizing the stressful reality of contemporary working life, a Confucian political leader would advocate for government programs to relieve the pressure on families. From this point of view, the public good is well served when working individuals are able to take the time necessary from their jobs to fulfill their family obligations. Thus, generous family leave policies, maternity and paternity leaves, high quality child care and universal health insurance are all consonant with a modern Confucian public policy. Fathers and mothers, sons and daughters, sisters and brothers should not be confronted with agonizing conflicts between work and family. A company's pursuit of profit should not be allowed to destroy the moral integrity of a household.

A contemporary Confucian, however, would also expect family members to sacrifice material comfort for moral obligation. If faced with leaving a well-paying job or caring for a close family member, the latter would clearly be the right Confucian thing. Indeed, happiness can inhere in poverty:

> The Master said, "To eat coarse food, drink plain water, and pillow oneself on a bent arm – there is pleasure to be found in these things. But wealth and position gained through inappropriate means – these are to me like floating clouds." (Ames and Rosemont, *Analects*, 7.16)

Appropriateness, of course, is all about doing one's duty, and family is duty number one. If we are taking time to attend to the personal and human needs of our loved ones, then we should be happy, joyful even, to "pillow oneself on a bent arm." An objection could be raised here that allowing one's relatives to descend into destitution could very well be wrong. It might be harder to fulfill our obligations to those closest to us if we are consumed by a struggle for basic survival. A Confucian would reply that the worst inequalities are a matter of public interest. Humane political leaders – and, after all, only the humane should rule by these lights – should advance government policies to ensure subsistence for all well meaning families. Ultimately, however, Confucianism is optimistic. Doing the right thing will usually bring about sufficient material reward. We can never know our fate, but by fulfilling duty, the Confucian method of following "Way," we discover an intrinsic goodness:

> The Master said: "The noble-minded devote themselves to the Way, not to earning a living. A farmer may go hungry, and a scholar may stumble into a good salary. So it is that the noble-minded worry about the Way, not poverty and hunger." (Hinton, *Analects*, 15.32)

Way, here, is not an absolute goal, but a daily process of performing our social responsibilities. If we attend to those immediate and lasting commitments, good things, in the form of a healthy family and stable society, will probably follow. Uncertainty will still shroud specific personal outcomes – a good farmer might go hungry, a mediocre scholar may land a great job – but we cannot be distracted by the possibility of poverty. Better to be poor and benevolent than rich and irresponsible.

Mencius echoes the Confucian aversion to wealth and profit. The moral of the very first passage in the book that bears his name is: "Don't talk about profit" (Hinton, 1.1). To do so takes us away from our primary purposes of humanity and duty. He is especially concerned about materialistic calculations, even when introduced outside the family circle, contaminating domestic relationships. In this excerpt, Mencius is arguing against a man who is trying to stop a war by demonstrating to the adversaries that there is no profit in it:

> If you, sir, use profit to persuade the kings of Qin and Chu, and if the kings of Qin and Chu, being amenable to the idea of profit, stop their armies, the personnel of those armies will be delighted with the cessation of hostilities and amenable to profit. Ministers serving their rulers will be preoccupied with profit; sons serving their parents will be preoccupied with profit; and younger brothers serving older brothers will be preoccupied by profit. Finally, rulers, ministers, parents, children, and older and younger brothers will abandon humaneness and righteousness and encounter one another based on a preoccupation with profit. Whenever this has happened, loss has always ensued. (Bloom, 6B4)

The appeal to profit-making, even when used for good purposes like peace-making, can have a corrosive effect on the source of our humanity. Confucians expect that sons will serve fathers, and fathers sons, not out of material interest but for moral uplift. It may be that some personal benefit follows from the fulfillment of family duties – a son may have a more comfortable life if his father's income is substantial – but that should not be the motivation for realizing one's duty.

In eschewing the profit motive, Confucianism would not require us to drop out of work altogether. Obviously, we must do something to secure the necessities of life. Mencius explicitly recognizes the social utility of the "hundred crafts" (Hinton, 5.4), the work of artisans and traders, and he embraces a division of labor in a manner that roughly anticipates Adam Smith. In an encounter with a man who is attempting a rather extreme economic self-sufficiency, Mencius defends specialization and trade:

> "To exchange grain for these various implements and utensils is not to burden the potter or the founder, nor could the potter and the founder, in exchanging their implements and utensils for grain, be burdening the agriculturalists...
> In the case of any individual person, the things the craftsmen make are available to him; if each person had to make everything he needed for his own use, the world would be full of people chasing after one another on the roads." (Bloom, 3A4)

Running about on the roads is not a good thing. It is not simply inefficient and unnecessary, but chaotic and socially disruptive. Each person has particular capacities and talents, and a division of labor allows each to find a productive niche in society. Labor and trade are not, in themselves, bad things. The Confucian admonition is more specific: we should not allow ourselves to be driven or defined by our jobs. More important to the fullness of an individual's identity are his or her intimate social relationships, starting within the family and radiating out into the world at large. These ties must be nurtured and preserved, and protected from the demands of time and attention given over to employment.

Indeed, there is something fundamental in all of this, fundamental at least for a Confucian worldview. This can be seen in one of the most cryptic of lines in the *Analects*:

> The Master said: "A noble-minded man is not an implement." (Hinton, 2.12)[4]

What this means is that the person who seeks humanity, who is trying to do the right thing in the world, should not allow herself to be used solely for someone else's purposes. Although none of us is wholly autonomous, bound as we are by social relationships, we each must exercise a certain moral initiative to act for the good, for humanity. We should not allow ourselves to be manipulated to serve the malign or selfish interests of some other person.

Notably, a similar notion is to be found in contemporary American slang. It is derogatory to refer to someone as a "tool," an individual manipulated by another. This idea is also an element of Immanuel Kant's ethics, which go something like this: "Act in such a way that you treat humanity, whether in your own person or in the person of any other, always at the same time as an end and never merely as a means."[5]

It must be said that Confucianism is not Kantian; the latter's universalism sits uncomfortably with the particularism of Confucian ethics.[6] But there is this common point: a gentleman is not a tool; a person should not be used as a means to another's ends.

The implication for our work experience is this: we should not allow our jobs, which to some degree require that we be used for our employer's ends, rule our lives. We are always more than our work; the most important aspects of our lives lie outside of the jobs we do to earn subsistence. Work is crude and uncivilized, albeit necessary, a coarsening struggle for survival. Duty and humanity and ritual are what separate us from animals, lifting us up to higher moral accomplishments. Confucius gives an intriguing hint of this attitude here:

> A villager of Daxiang said, What a great man Confucius is! He has studied widely, but he doesn't make any particular name for himself.
>
> When the Master heard this, he said to his disciples, What should I specialize in? Should I specialize in charioteering? Should I specialize in archery? I think I'll specialize in charioteering. (Watson, *Analects*, 9.2)

Confucius is joking. He might accept the compliment that his wisdom is great but he mocks the idea that moral accomplishment can be expressed in the mere titles of "charioteer" or "archer." It is laughable, at the villager's expense, because the whole point of his ethics is not to reduce oneself to an oversimplified specialization. He is not merely an archer nor, for that matter, a government counselor, nor an appreciator of music, even though he has a certain expertise in all. "Teacher" might be expansive enough a category to do some justice to his life's project, extending as it does from the pragmatic to the moral to the technical. It is more likely, however, that he would want to be known as "noble-minded," or "exemplary," or as a "gentleman" or whatever term is used for a person who, in all that he does, strives to progress toward humanity.

In the world of work, then, we should not get caught up in our titles. It may seem important to be able to say "I am a lawyer" or "I am a doctor" or "I am a professor." We might even expend a great deal of energy and time and attention to be able to say "I am a partner" or "I am an associate" or "I am tenured." But none of these matters much to a Confucian. Best to say, "I am a father, a son, a husband" – that is, I am a person who follows ritual, lives up to duty, and seeks to create humaneness. None of which can be reduced to a mere job description.

Right action toward others, especially those closest to us, is something we must pursue, according to Confucians, in all aspects of our lives. Family and social obligations clearly take precedence over material and job-related concerns. When we attend to the former, we do not merely follow Way, as Confucius suggests, but we actively create and reproduce Way, humane and stable social order, through our considered actions, and that is something we must never lose sight of, even "in confusion and distress":

> The Master said, Wealth and eminence are what people desire, but if one can't get them by means that accord with the Way, one will not accept them. Poverty and low position are what people hate, but if one can't avoid them by means that accord with the Way, one will not reject them.
>
> If the gentleman rejects humaneness, how can he be worthy of the name gentleman? The gentleman never departs from humaneness ever for the space of a meal – in confusion and distress he holds fast to it; stumbling, faltering, he holds fast to it. (Watson, *Analects* 4.5)

Daoists and work

Daoists concur with the Confucian disdain for profit and wealth. Pursuing more and ever more material possessions simply takes us away from Way:

> The five colors blind eyes.
> The five tones deafen ears.
> The five tastes blur tongues.

Fast horses and breathtaking hunts make minds wild and crazy.
Things rare and expensive make people lose their way.
That's why a sage tends to the belly, not the eye,
always ignores that and chooses this.

(Hinton, *Daodejing* 12)

Tending to the belly is all about fulfilling basic needs, providing the most elemental sustenance. The belly is at the center of the human body, it is the core our existence. It is inside, a source of our integrity (*de*), our inherent nature, and that is what needs to be tended. The things that our eyes see are outside of us, external and impermanent, fleeting as a flash of lightening, plainly unnecessary. That is the distinction being drawn here, between essential and superfluous. We should not get caught up in apparent beauty – colors, tones, tastes – because they can cause us to "lose our way," to be enthralled by "things rare and expensive." By contrast, Way itself is described elsewhere in the *Daodejing* as "the thinnest of bland flavors" (Hinton, 35). It is simple and weak and cheap. We do not need much money to find it.

For Daoists, affluence creates its own misfortune, as this excerpt from passage 9 of the *Daodejing* suggests:

Once it's full of jade and gold
your house will never be safe.
Proud of wealth and renown
you bring on your own ruin.

(Hinton)

The things we acquire become emblems of affluence that others covet. Envious neighbors and relatives calculate their interactions with us with an eye to gaining some of what we have; and, so, our houses are "never safe." And the arrogance of affluence stokes selfishness and greed, creating the conditions for the rich man's demise. Elsewhere (passage 58), the *Daodejing* tells us that:

Disaster is that on which good fortune depends.
Good fortune is that in which disaster's concealed.
Who knows where it will end?
For there is no fixed "correct."
The "correct" turns into the "deviant."
And "good" turns into "evil."

> People's state of confusion
> Has certainly existed for a long time.
>
> (Henricks, 58)

This seems rather bleak. The rich, who have benefitted from good fortune, will eventually face disaster. Their "good" will be transformed into "evil." The allure of wealth will turn against even the most well intentioned. It is not as bad as it sounds, however. Even though people are confused, and have been confused for a long time, the *Daodejing* holds out the hope of enlightenment. The mere act of reading this text brings the problem to our attention and, thus, opens the possibility of turning us back to tending to belly instead of eye. We can't rely on some great man to save us from our own avarice, we must do it by ourselves and for ourselves, from the inside out.

Returning to the question of work, the Daoist sensibility clearly pushes against defining the value of labor in terms of the monetary rewards it brings. A modest standard of living is sufficient; all of those modern "needs," which are really desires and preferences made into ersatz necessities, can be done without.

Work, however, shorn of its materialist imperatives, does have a certain significance for Daoists. In brief, work can be an avenue for the expression of Way in particular lives. This is the message conveyed by the story of King Wen Hui of Wei and the cook found in chapter 3 of *Zhuangzi* (sometimes referred to as Cook Ding).[7] It requires quotation at length:

> A cook was cutting up an ox for Wen Hui, the King of Wei. Whenever his hand probed or his shoulder heaved, whenever his foot moved or his knee thrust, the flesh whirred and fell away. The blade flashed and hissed, its rhythm centered and ancient and never faltering like a rainmaker dancing "Mulberry Grove" or an orchestra playing "Origin Constant and Essential."
>
> "Unbelievable!" said King Wen Hui. "A skill so perfected – it's unbelievable!"
>
> The cook put down his knife and replied: "Dao is what I care about, and Dao goes beyond mere skill. When I first began cutting up oxen, I could see nothing but the ox. After three years, I could see more than the ox. And now, I meet the ox in spirit. I've stopped looking with my eyes. When perception and understanding cease, the spirit moves freely. Trusting the principles of heaven, I send the blade slicing through huge crevices, lead it through huge hollows. Keeping my skill constant and essential, I just slip the blade through, never touching ligament or tendon, let alone bone."

"An exceptional cook cuts, and so needs a new knife every year. An ordinary cook chops, and so needs a new knife every month. Now, I've had this knife for nineteen years: it's taken apart thousands of oxen but it's still sharp, still fresh from the grindstone. There's space in a joint, and the blade has no thickness. Having no thickness, it slips right through. There's plenty of room – more than enough for a blade to wander. That's why, after nineteen years, it's still fresh from the grindstone."

"Even so, I often come up against a knotty place where I stop and study the difficulties. Growing timid and cautious, I focus my vision, then work slowly, moving the blade with great delicacy – and suddenly Thomp! Thomp! Things come apart, like clumps of dirt falling back to earth. Holding the knife, I stand back and look all around me, utterly content and satisfied. Then I wipe my blade clean and put it away."

"How marvelous!" Said King Wen Hui. "I listen to the words of a butcher, and suddenly I've learned how to care for life itself!" (Hinton, 39–40)

The first thing to notice here is the inversion of status hierarchy: the mighty king learns from the lowly cook. This conveys the general Daoist admiration of the weak and the powerless, where Way is more likely to be found. In this case, the cook, slopping about in the blood and sweat of his work, has perfected a daily routine that allows him to connect with the natural unfolding of things. He not only cares about *Dao*, he performs it.

He does this by both intention and intuition. In the first instance, he has to work consciously at wielding the blade – three years of practice were required before he could see beyond the immediate details of the task. With rehearsal comes liberation: he frees himself from studied strokes and stops thinking about what he is doing. He just does it, meeting the ox in spirit, following his instincts and moving with the moment. That surrender to *Dao* carries him beyond mere skill. His work merges with Way.

The cook thus finds himself in his occupation. He is not concerned about the material results or benefits of his toil; he is not talking about how much he is getting paid or what he might deserve for the work. Rather, it is all about process. It doesn't really matter that he is a cook focusing on butchering oxen. The particular project could be just about anything – a carpenter, a seamstress, a writer, even. What matters is using the activity of work, the daily repetition of bodily and mental action, as an expression of Way. And through Way he finds a deeper satisfaction in his life.

By "trusting the principles of heaven," the cook gives himself over to fate and destiny, not trying to impose pre-conceived human expectations on the natural world. He does not force the knife to cut against the organic pattern of bone and muscle and ligament. Instead, he follows where the anatomy of the oxen leads, taking what nature, or *Dao*, allows, nothing more. As the *Daodejing* (7) suggests, he therefore finds himself by giving himself up:

> Therefore the Sage:
> Puts himself in the background yet finds himself in the foreground;
> Puts self-concern out of his mind, yet finds that his self-concern is preserved.
> Is it not because he has no self-interest,
> That he is therefore able to realize his self-interst?
>
> (Henricks, 7)

That is what work can do – preserve the spontaneous self – if we let go of worries about pay and benefits and perquisites, and just live in and through the activity of it.

There is something unrealistic about all of this, unrealistic, at least, from the perspective of survival in a modern world economy. We cannot relinquish all concern for our material subsistence, unless we are independently wealthy. And few of us have the opportunity to use our work consistently to discover Way – think of a harried office employee, harangued by bosses demanding higher productivity, worried that his job will be outsourced to India, never able to call his time his own. Under such circumstances, trusting the principles of heaven can be difficult, indeed. Yet if we cannot be full time on-the-job Daoists, we may still be able to bring some of what King Wen of Hui has learned into our lives: to find satisfaction in work requires complete immersion in the particulars of the task and the moment.

Another important lesson of the Cook Ding passage is that Way can be learned. It is not a matter of sitting with books and studying, though reading the foundational texts of Daoism might help a bit. Apprehending Way is not really "knowledge" in the intellectual sense, since "the knowing are never learned, and the learned never knowing." (Hinton, *Daodejing*, 81) Rather, appreciation and understanding of Way emerge from the events of everyday life, from the repetitive exertions of menial work. When you can carry out your daily routine without thinking about it, when you can do it by feel more than by calculation, when you are, as athletes sometimes say, "in the zone," then you are on the cusp of Way. You come to know it by doing it, relying on physical memory and intuitive sensitivity instead of conscious purpose.

Knowing Way through work does not, for Daoists, involve domestic or social relationships. They do not share the Confucian worry that employment might impinge upon family life. The cook in Zhuangzi's story makes no mention of his parents or spouse or children. He is finding himself by himself through his solitary engagement with his work. Although it may be true for some people that they can best discover Way in association with their closest loved ones, this is not, from a Daoist perspective, necessarily true for all. It is equally possible that a person can best find Way alone. The stance is not actively anti-family – Zhuangzi himself was married – but neither does it make familial duty a supreme ethical principle. Daoist support, therefore, for family leave policies and child care policies and the like would be decidedly weaker than Confucian advocacy. Such things might be nice, they might remove the pressure of the profit motive, but they are not required for the discovery of Way through work.

Daoists find more promise in work in and of itself, not for what it might provide for our families or social relationships, but what it might offer each individual. Giving more time to work than to family might actually be good for some.

Yet even with this obvious difference versus Confucian notions of duty, the Daoist aversion to profiteering brings it closer to Confucian attitudes about work than to modern American sensibilities. Many of us today are unable to detach ourselves from the material compulsion of labor and employment. We focus on pay and benefits because we fear poverty and deprivation. Daoists and Confucians would counsel us to find other sources of self-worth and happiness, either in the immediate tasks of work itself or in the social obligations that transcend work. Then, we might find joy in either a "crooked arm for a pillow" or "the thinnest of bland flavors."

Notes

1. Al Gini, *My Job My Self: Work and the Creation of the Modern Individual* (New York: Routledge, 2001).
2. Karl Marx, *Capital*, vol. 1 (New York: Random House, Vintage, 1976), "The Fetishism of the Commodity and Its Secret," pp. 163–177.
3. Richard Sennett, *The Corrosion of Character: The Personal Consequences of Work in the New Capitalism* (New York: W.W. Norton, 1998).
4. I've always liked Simon Leys' translation of this aphorism: "The Master said: 'A gentleman is not a pot.'" Simon Leys, *The Analects of Confucius* (New York: W.W. Norton, 1997), p. 7.
5. Immanuel Kant, *Grounding for the Metaphysics of Morals* (Indianapolis: Hackett Publishing Co., 1993), p. 36.

6. The comparison of Confucius and Kant is an immense topic, the subject of two recent special editions of *The Journal of Chinese Philosophy*, 38 (4) (December 2011) and 33 (1) (March 2006).
7. James Behuniak argues that the Cook Ding passage illustrates how "ordinary practice," what we might call "work," is a means to a moral life: James Behuniak, "John Dewey and the Virtue of Cook Ding's Dao," *Dao*, 9 (2) (June 2010), pp. 161–174.

5

Marriage and Family

Confucians are famous for the importance they attach to family, the source of our closest human relationships and, therefore, our humanity. Ritualized performance of family duties through marriage is the best, though not only, avenue to moral goodness. By its own logic Confucianism, since it emphasizes daily commitment to duty and ritual in family life, should be supportive of same-sex marriage. Daoism is much less concerned with marriage and family. Such arrangements may be part of the natural unfolding of things for some people, but they are not necessary for all to find their places in Way. Family ties are as fleeting and ephemeral as any other aspect of Way.

I didn't think much about getting married. It just seemed like something that would happen. I wasn't averse to it, but neither was I consumed by it. Some time in my last year of college, after my wife-to-be and I had been together as something more than friends for close to two years, I gave her a ring. An opal. Money was a problem for me and diamonds were not in the picture. The word "engagement" did not pass my lips, but my intention was conveyed and understood. I wanted her to come with me when I would leave for graduate school in Wisconsin later that summer.

My reticence about marriage came from my parents. Theirs was not a happy union. My childhood was pervaded by a sense that holy matrimony (we were Catholics, of a sort) was both inevitable and doomed. They fought and raged but stayed together, because that was what was done. Their

Life, Liberty, and the Pursuit of Dao: Ancient Chinese Thought in Modern American Life,
First Edition. Sam Crane.
© 2013 John Wiley & Sons, Inc. Published 2013 by John Wiley & Sons, Inc.

defiant unhappiness stood for me as a negative example, everything that my life would not become.

Somehow that sense of inevitability carried forward in me. Of course I would get married, some day. And, of course, there would be children, because that was a part of life I wanted to experience. And if I did it right, I would do it better than my parents.

We moved to Wisconsin in August, a fateful trip that would open unknowable new chapters of our lives. Our cohabitation, far away from parental supervision, was a problem, however, for her father. He stopped talking to her. She withstood it for a while but it wore her down. She started to think about making us legal. One day, later that autumn, she came into our threadbare study and said: "The price of gold is exploding; we should probably go get wedding rings before it gets too expensive."

"Okay," I replied. Such was the proposal.

The decision to have children was more thoroughly considered. We did not want to have a child until we were more settled in jobs, more secure in our livelihoods. That took eleven years. We tried to manage the circumstances of Aidan's birth but, in the end, we really could not. The thing we tried to control, the birth of our first child, defied our plans; and the thing we just let happen, our marriage, has endured for more than thirty years.

* * *

Marriage in the contemporary United States is not what it used to be. One hundred and fifty years ago, American marriage was more of an institution, a fundamental building block of society held together by prevailing patriarchal cultural norms, resolutely defined social roles, and inescapable economic necessity. As modernization progressed through the twentieth century, with attendant processes of industrialization, urbanization, and cultural liberalization, marriage changed as well. By the post-WWII era, what social scientists call "companionate marriage," based on more personal ties of love and friendship among husband and wife, became the standard. And when society and culture transformed further in the 1960s, bringing to the fore personal liberation and freedom, views on marriage shifted once more. Today, spouses have a much stronger expectation of realizing individualistic fulfillment within the union of wedlock, and if those discrete goals are not attained, divorce can readily follow.[1]

Instability is more common now. Americans are mobile not only geographically but also interpersonally. We marry more and divorce more than

Europeans.[2] Paradoxically, people in the United States seem to value marriage but are quite willing to walk away from it if it is not working to fulfill individualistic interests. The promise of a greater good through partnership pales in comparison to the prospect of maximal personal advantage.

All of which raises a rather simple question: why bother?

In the past, conceiving and raising children was a primary purpose of matrimony. But now, more than half of the births to mothers under thirty years of age happen outside of marriage.[3] It seems that more and more women are eschewing traditional family practices and redefining maternity. Men, too, are increasingly acting as unwed fathers. Unfortunately, while single parenthood might fulfill the personal interests of the mothers and fathers involved, children are not well served by these new arrangements. Children in households with single mothers are much more likely to be living in poverty than those in two-parent households.[4]

The plight of children in poverty, however, does not seem to be sufficient to bolster the case for marriage. Economic and cultural forces continue to work against it: numerous people feel they do not have the financial security to enter into a putatively lifelong commitment and many no longer believe that pregnancy requires marriage. Indeed, marriage is commonly viewed not as something that should happen at the beginning of adulthood, but as a culmination of sorts, something that symbolizes a certain level of economic achievement and relationship maturity.[5] It is more of a luxury good than a basic human experience.

Surprisingly, at least for someone my age, just as it seemed that marriage was losing its *raison d'être*, a new issue has emerged to breathe life into the debate: same-sex marriage. In the 1970s, homosexuality carried more of a transgressive cultural valence. Gays and lesbians were excluded from the mainstream of American society, and many seemed to revel in that nonconformist status. But, of course, human diversity is always more complex than social stereotypes suggest, and, by the 1980s and 1990s, more homosexuals were pressing the case for same-sex marriage. It seemed a stunning turnabout, from determined anti-traditionalism to an embrace of social conformity.[6]

The debate that has raged in the United States over the issue has been salutary in a number of ways. It has revealed, especially along generational lines, a greater acceptance of homosexuality; not universal, to be sure, but certainly greater than, say, the 1970s. In those places that have adopted same-sex marriage legally, it has opened new possibilities for the strengthening of gay and lesbian relationships. And, for the purposes of this book, it has reinvigorated arguments about marriage more generally. Before the same-sex issue, we all knew how marriage was declining. Now, all of us, gay and straight alike, are reminded of the power of that very deep human aspiration to connect our individual fate to another and lovingly cultivate meaningful lives together.

Confucians on marriage and family

Marriage and family are obviously central to Confucian ethics. Perhaps the most oft-repeated exhortation in the *Analects* is the duty of children to care for parents. Those parents, we can safely assume from historical context, are a man and a woman who have entered into a lifelong matrimonial union recognized by established ritual and custom.[7] Marriage and child-bearing and child-rearing are inextricably linked in the Confucian mindset. One marries in order to have children to carry on the enactment of humanity in the world; and children should get married likewise to extend the moral life to yet another generation, thus also honoring their parents in the process.

Creating and raising a family, though perhaps the best Confucian justification of marriage, is not the only such justification. Even without children, a marriage is a solemn commitment, witnessed by relatives and society, to care for another person for ever. The fulfillment of that vow, the cultivation of our closest loving relationships, is the truest expression of our humanity and thus the best thing we can do. It is better, for a Confucian, to enter into married life without children than to maintain a solitary existence. Or, short of marriage, it is better to affirm and perform duties to others than to escape into an amoral isolation. Of all of these situations, however, marriage with children provides the greatest potential for Confucian moral goodness.

Something needs to be said, however, about the notion of carrying on the father's family line as a reason for marriage. Historically, having a male heir to carry forward, generation to generation, a father's surname was a major concern for Confucians in their decisions about marriage and family. And that caused a great deal of pain and misery for Chinese women, who suffered all sorts of injustices and slights in their subordination to the patrilineal name. There is nothing, however, morally necessary for Confucianism in the practice of patrilineality. In other words, in a modern context we can detach the Confucian argument in favor of marriage from the practices of patriarchy and still be true to the ethical core of Confucianism.[8]

In Confucianism's most basic moral formulation, what matters is not so much the name of the family as the practice of humanity. We can see this in the story of mythic sage-emperor Shun, as recounted by Mencius.

Shun was extraordinarily virtuous. He was a commoner, a farmer, who maintained his love for his family even though his father and his brother attempted to kill him. His patience and rectitude and wisdom are the standards against which all other Confucian exemplars are measured.

Shun, however, poses a dilemma for Confucian ethics. It seems that his depraved father did not want him to get married. But, if Shun did not get married and have a child, there would be no heir to sustain the humanity-generating practices of the family into the future. That failure would undermine the larger process and purpose of humaneness and, thus, be disrespectful to Shun's father, since any father is shamed when his children do not follow the path of humanity, duty, and ritual. To be filial, then – to be respectful and loyal to his father – Shun would have to disobey him and get married so as to start a family of his own. As it turns out, that is what Shun does: in pursuit of the greater filiality of maintaining the family, he violates the more immediate filiality of obeying his malevolent father. The most obedient thing to do is to disobey his father.

This story might be interpreted as a confirmation of the importance of preserving the father's family name. But further consideration pushes against such a narrow meaning. Returning to *Mencius*:

> Mencius said: "There are three ways you can fail to honor your parents, and the worst is to have no heir. Shun married without telling his parents because he was afraid he might have no heir. For the noble-minded, this is no different than telling them." (Hinton, 7.26)

The disobedience – marrying without telling his parents – is justified by the larger purpose of having an heir. We must ask, however, why have an heir? What is so important, to Shun and to Mencius, about creating a new generation of the family? Notice that nothing is said here, nor elsewhere in Mencius' rendition of the Shun legend, explicitly about the family name. Although it is historically true that patrilineality was vitally important in ancient China, it is not clear that it is a necessary element of Shun's morality.

Confucius himself directly invokes family name once in the *Analects*:

> The Master said: "Leaving a name that carries no honor through the ages following their death – that is what the noble-minded dread." (Hinton, 15.20)

It is not certain that the dread mentioned here creates an absolute moral imperative to have a son. Of course, the noble-minded want to preserve the reputation of the family. But this passage could mean that the actions of a noble-minded individual in his or her own life are what really matter: how we act determines our reputations, our names. Our own actions are what bring honor to our families, not our gender or the gender of our offspring. At the very least, we have reason to question whether carrying on the family name should be taken as the primary reason for marriage because Mencius suggests other factors that need to be considered as well. When answering an inquiry about how it could have been right for Shun to marry without telling his parents, he says:

> If he had informed them, they would not have allowed him to marry. For a man and a woman to live together is the greatest of human relationships. To have informed his parents, and then to have had to forgo this greatest of human relationships, would have resulted in antagonism between him and his parents. This is why he did not inform them. (Bloom, 5A2)

Marriage creates "the greatest of human relationships." It establishes a new family union within which duty and ritual can be performed that, in turn, extends humaneness in the world. That is why we should marry. Of course, if we do our best and sincerely live up to the new family obligations created by marriage, we also honor our parents. There can be no greater honor than to be associated with the reproduction of humanity. Indeed, "the greatest of human relationships" forged by marriage is so important morally that its formation justifies Shun's deception of his parents.

Thought of in this light, an heir is significant not so much for the continuance of the father's surname, which is subsidiary in any event to the performance of moral duty, as it is necessary for the propagation of humaneness. A family's name would hardly matter, for Confucius or Mencius, if it signified dissolution and depravity. Shun himself saved his family's name by his moral acts, not by his mere existence and surname. Had he allowed himself to be provoked by his father into committing patricide, we would not be discussing him today; he would not have been preserved in the Confucian canon as a moral exemplar and his family's name would be lost to history. Or, worse, his family's name would forever be linked to inhumanity and iniquity, a dreadful outcome in Confucian terms. Heirs matter, in short, only to the extent that they can potentially do the right thing.

We can push this line of thought a bit further to argue that the gender of an heir should not matter to Confucian ethics. While social convention might have defined families in terms of the father's surname, the performance of humanity can be accomplished by female heirs as well as male heirs. Daughters can care for parents, a principle Confucian duty, and fulfill other social obligations as effectively as sons, perhaps more so. If actual moral achievement is what matters most – and I believe that is the spirit of Confucianism – then gender is hardly important.

In sum, marriage and family are, for Confucians, the best way to do good in the world – not the only way, but generally the best way. The commitment to care that lies at the heart of marriage creates, when it is enacted, a "great bond of humankind." It is the very stuff of moral accomplishment. Children, too, sons and daughters both, call forth from us, and return to us, a visceral love and attachment, the most elemental of human experience. On this powerful emotional foundation, Confucius builds his ethical edifice: we care for our family, and we should care for our family, because we love them so deeply and, in doing so, we improve not only ourselves but the wider world.

Daoists on marriage and family

There is little in the *Daodejing* or *Zhuangzi* on marriage and family. That relative silence suggests that Daoism does not place much importance on the formal institutionalization of interpersonal commitments. To someone who refers to "marriage as an institution" or "the institution of the family," Daoists might reply, "why tie yourself to rules and expectations when we know that circumstances change and human relationships evolve?" Formalized family arrangements are not explicitly rejected by Daoism, but they make sense only to the extent that they reflect the natural unfolding of Way and do not become obstacles to individuals finding themselves in Way. Family life may be natural for some, perhaps for many, but it should not be assumed as a model for all.

Those passages in the *Daodejing* that do make reference to family life present it as a habitual element of human experience. It is what many people do and, thus, is taken for granted. But it is not idealized or universalized as the best means to a moral life. Passage 54, for example, reflects upon how Way can be brought into one's life, without ever using the word "Way."

Something planted so deep it's never rooted up,
something held so tight it's never stolen away:
children and grandchildren will pay it homage always.
Cultivated in yourself
it makes integrity real.
Cultivated in your family
it makes integrity plentiful.
Cultivated in your village
it makes integrity enduring.
Cultivated in your nation
it makes integrity abundant.
Cultivated in all beneath heaven
it makes integrity all-encompassing.
So look through self into self,
through family into family,
through village into village,
through nation into nation,
through all beneath heaven into all beneath heaven.
How can I know all beneath heaven as it is?
Through this.

(Hinton)

In this passage, "something" and "this" refer to Way. Family here is just one of a variety of human groupings, from individual isolation to all beneath heaven, which are manifest in Way and in which Way is manifest. There is nothing to suggest that family is any more important than village or nation; it is simply a matter of scale. No moral assessment is proffered. Nothing is said about the goodness or badness of any particular form of human association. It's just what people do.

The *Daodejing* tells us that by cultivating Way in our various social surroundings, yielding to its natural movement and transformation, we will discover our integrity (*de*), the innate possibilities and tendencies within us. Embracing Way opens us to who we really are. Similarly, by cultivating Way in our families, we allow for the fullest expression of the integrity of each family member. Family is important only to the extent that it serves as a locale or avenue for Way.

What does it mean, however, to cultivate Way in the family? It could suggest just letting relationships develop on their own, without imposing any preconceived notions of parental or juvenile roles. Just let daily practices emerge as they will. If a man likes to cook, let him cook. If a woman likes to mow the lawn, let her mow. If no one is especially interested in vacuuming, don't worry about it. Certain things will happen one way or another; food will be secured and prepared; shelter maintained; clothing arranged. There may be unspoken Daoist assumptions that parents will naturally care for their children, and children will naturally follow, for a time at least, their parents, assumptions rooted in enduring patterns of human emotion and attachment. Such is suggested in this excerpt from *Daodejing* passage 80, which looks toward a simplified and harmonious utopia:

> Let people knot ropes for notation again
> and never need anything more,
> let them find pleasure in their food
> and beauty in their clothes,
> peace in their homes
> and joy in their ancestral ways.
>
>   (Hinton)

No computers for calculation and word processing in this idealized village. Only simple pleasures: modest food, adequate clothing, and peaceful family life. The text implies that, when left to their own devices, people will find solace in supporting one another in small-scale family contexts. These sorts of loose expectations, however, should not, from a Daoist perspective, crystallize into hard and fast social codes. If family members truly love one another and stay together, that's fine; and if a family grows apart and disintegrates, that would not be seen as a tragedy by Daoists, just the natural divergence of individual integrities in Way. Should family relationships become insincere or forced or abusive, it might be in keeping with Way to let them go.

It is in this manner that *Daodejing* passage 54 tells us to look "through family into family," just as we should look "though self into self." The first use of "family," in this case, connotes rigid social conventions, the humanly created principles and beliefs that attach to ritualized matrimony. This is what must be seen through because such customs can take us away from the spontaneous dynamism of Way. It is only when we give up on tradition and ritual and dogma that we might be able to begin to create genuine family relationships, connections founded on intuitive love and attachment. Like so much else in Daoism, "family," when we make too much of it, distracts us from what family can really be.

Those families that do come together and stay together naturally will most often, consistent with *yin–yang* dynamics, be centered on the mutual attraction of opposite sexes. Heterosexuality, like marriage and any other human practice, is not, for Daoists, a moral category; it is simply a common experience. Homosexual relationships would not be degraded and disparaged in a Daoist world; rather, male and female pairings would be understood as expressions of deep and pervasive forces of difference and balance in Way. Passage 28 from the *Daodejing* provides this sort of image:

> Knowing the masculine
> and nurturing the feminine
> you become the river of all beneath heaven.
> River of all beneath heaven
> you abide in perennial integrity
> and so return to infancy.
>
> (Hinton)

Male and female instinctually complement one another, and their pairing opens the way to reproduction, a major theme of the *Daodejing*. Many of its references to fertility and birth highlight the female side of the story: "the mother of all beneath heaven" (Hinton, 25, 52), "dark female enigma" (Hinton, 6), but the male aspect is not ignored. Indeed, the book, in its own time, was written by men for men to read (in ancient China few women were given the chance to become literate). In a sense, then, its emphasis on female, *yin* forces in nature – valleys and water – is a challenge to men to balance their innate masculinity with openness to feminine energy and possibilities. And a common way of doing so is entering into a long-term relationship with a woman.

Again, this would not necessarily negate homosexuality. Daoism is not so rigid as to assume that expressions of *yin–yang* balance can only be manifest in male–female pairings. If each individual is a unique amalgamation of both tendencies, which is what Daoism suggests, then it is easy to foresee a wide variety of balanced relationships, irrespective of biological sex. A particular man may have more female *yin* qualities than other men; and a particular woman may have more male *yang* qualities than other women. Thus, a homosexual relationship could express a balanced *yin–yang* interaction.

The Daodejing, however, certainly suggests that heterosexual unions are commonplace and potent. A rather famous Daoist opposite-sex marriage was that of Zhuangzi. His wife is only mentioned once in the book that bears his name, and that recounts his response to her death. The brief scene opens with a friend going to console Zhuangzi and finding him inappropriately pounding on a tub and singing. The friend rebukes him for his cavalier attitude. But Zhuangzi tells him, and us, that when she first died he did "grieve like anyone else" (Watson, 191). His tie to her was emotionally genuine. It was only after some reflection on the meaning of death more generally that he was able to step beyond his heartache and find some solace, even if he expressed it in an unusual manner. But it is that initial sense of loss I want to highlight here. It shows that even though Zhuangzi often tells us to let go of both our sorrows and our joys, he himself was compassionately attached to his wife. His apparent detachment was not absolute; his integrity included the love of his wife.

We can relate the story of his wife's death to another of Zhuangzi's images to get at the Daoist understanding of marriage. It is a vignette about pigs:

> Confucius said, "I once went on a mission to Chu, and as I was going along, I saw some little pigs nursing at the body of their dead mother. After a while, they gave a start and all ran away and left her, because they could no longer see their likeness in her; she was not the same as she had been before. In loving their mother, they loved not her body but the thing that moved her body." (Watson, 73)

Don't be confused by the invocation of Confucius; it is a trick Zhuangzi uses – putting his own words in the mouth of Confucius. What is important here is the understanding of love. The baby pigs – or for that matter any living creature, humans included – love others based not on physical or social form but on something else, the spirit or energy or integrity that animates form, the thing that moves a body. When we encounter a person who has that indescribable life force, not only are we attracted but we also see ourselves in him or her. For Daoists, it is not too far a step to say this same feeling is what also animates marriage: it is the love that brings individuals together and, if circumstances allow, holds them together for life. It is not a social institution or a moral obligation but a natural, and possibly fleeting, human impulse.

Much the same can be said about the Daoist perspective on child-bearing. There is no commanding moral reason to have children. It is neither good nor bad. Birth and child-rearing are not especially well suited for the creation and propagation of humanity, because Daoists reject the very idea of a self-conscious project of cultivating "humanity." Of course, many people do come together into family units and have children. Such is the Way of human beings. And it will happen whether it is recognized as morally excellent or not. It is a mere inevitability.

There may be a certain beauty in family life, the hearth and home of mother and father and children. But for Daoists that beauty cannot be planned or managed or controlled. It has to be a natural expression of intrinsic love and care, otherwise it may become a contrived and distorting falsity. Our greatest joys may arise from our children, but so may our greatest sorrows. Children, as family, are as complex and uncertain as any other aspect of Way.

To a young couple contemplating marriage and children, then, a Daoist might say: "go ahead, if your intuition impels you, but don't make it into something it cannot be. Just do it and follow along where it leads you."

Same-sex marriage?

The very notion of homosexual marriage would seem to be alien to the experience of Confucianism and Daoism. It is only in recent decades that the possibility of gay and lesbian persons marrying one another has been seriously debated or realized, as in my home state of Massachusetts. But historical novelty does not imply philosophical irrelevance. Both Confucianism and Daoism have something to say about gay marriage.

A modern Confucian perspective could be affirmative. If we take the most basic Confucian principles – humanity, ritual, and duty – shorn of any gender implications, it is by no means necessary that they would deny same-sex marriage. Although, as mentioned above, there is likely to be an initial Confucian assumption that most marriages will be between a man and a woman, and that a certain morality inheres in heterosexual unions, it does not follow that all marriages must be heterosexual or that only heterosexual marriages can be good. For Confucians what matters most in all human relationships is the enactment of duty according to ritual as a means of building humanity in the world. If gay marriages can realize those ideals they should be acceptable to Confucianism.

But first, let's talk about sex. Confucius, for the most part, disdains sex. It is obviously necessary for familial reproduction but he tends to see it as a distraction. A person overly concerned with sex may fail in his social duties. *Analects* 16.7 gives a warning of sorts:

> Confucius said: "The noble-minded guard against three things: in youth, when *qi* and blood are unsettled, they guard against beautiful women; in their prime, when *qi* and blood are unbending, they guard against belligerence; and in old age, when *qi* and blood are withering, they guard against avarice."
> (Hinton)

Qi is a kind of energy or life force that courses around us and through us. It shapes our destiny. It can be controlled, in part, but is always larger and more powerful than human efforts to contain it. Sometimes you can manage your *qi* and sometimes your *qi* manages you. Confucius obviously believes that good will and proper behavior enable people to channel their *qi* in positive ways. The idea in 16.7 is that at different stages of life, different challenges are posed by our natural *qi* proclivities. In youth, the challenge is sex, symbolized here by "beautiful women." If you allow yourself to be driven by sexual desire, you can be diverted away from the work of noble-mindedness; you can be distracted from the fulfillment of your social duties. Presumably, Confucius sees this as somewhat less of a problem as life goes on and *qi* flows in other directions.

The idea of sex as distraction is echoed elsewhere in the *Analects*, in various passages (e.g. 15.13) that repeat the refrain most concisely captured in 9.18:

> The Master said: "I've never seen anyone for whom loving integrity is like loving a beautiful woman." (Hinton)

This is a lament of sorts. He bemoans the fact that men (his students were men, after all) tend to be more interested in pursuing the delights of the opposite sex than in attending to the obligations that are part and parcel of their integrity. Sex, too much sex or too much attention to sex, is a problem. This is not to say that all sex is necessarily bad; rather, the illusory pleasure of cheap attraction is bad. This would be true for homosexuality as well as heterosexuality.

There are no explicit references to homosexuality in the *Analects* or *Mencius*. It no doubt existed in Confucius's time. Indeed, by the third century BCE, homosexuality was common enough to be mentioned by Han Fei Tzu as a standard means of political entrapment:

> There are eight strategies which ministers customarily employ to work their villainy. The first is called "Making use of bedfellows." What do I mean by this? The ruler is easily beguiled by lovely women and charming boys, by all those who can fawn and play at love.[9]

Sex, in this case, is a political danger, and the casual mention of gay sex ("charming boys"), and its political equivalence with straight sex ("lovely women"), suggest that homosexuality was practiced and known in the ancient halls of power. Yet while they may have been aware of it, we cannot know what Confucius or Mencius thought of homosexuality per se. It could be assumed that they would reject it, generally, since it could be interpreted as mere hedonistic sensory satisfaction, detached from the socializing goodness of human reproduction. But straight sex can also lose its moral bearings, something that Confucius worried about.

A Confucian view, then, might focus more on the social context and purpose of sexuality and care less about any particular sexual orientation. Sex, of whatever flavor, should not be exaggerated or made the center of our identities. It is not nearly as important as the social roles we should fulfill, the duties we must enact. Thus, an overwrought gay personality might be frowned upon by Confucians, who would believe that we must control our physical desires, of whatever sort, gay or straight, and direct them toward the greater goal of humaneness. If heterosexual relationships can be either good or bad, depending upon how they fit into a set of duties and roles, then it might be possible for homosexual relationships, under the right social circumstances, to be morally constructive.

Gay marriage provides just those beneficial circumstances. Homosexuals who seek to marry are as likely as heterosexuals to be conscientiously working to build lasting relationships that are productive of family duties. The love and care shared by committed couples is, in and of itself, a generator of humanity. Each person, upon marrying, becomes a spouse and takes on new obligations. If both of them perform those duties, if they care for one another and each other's family, and if they nurture children and build humaneness into the future, then why shouldn't that be considered a good thing from a Confucian perspective?

Biological reproduction, of course, raises an issue, but one that is easily accommodated. Adoption by homosexual couples need not violate any Confucian principle. Indeed, if it led to nurturing and devoted child-rearing, it would be all for the good from a Confucian point of view. Adoption was common in ancient China, especially to secure a male heir. A male head of household was then understood as the best means for establishing a secure family setting in which duties could be defined and performed and humanity thereby constructed. As was argued previously, the production of a male heir is not (and never has been) necessary for the realization of Confucian virtue. And there are other good Confucian reasons for adoption: to enrich families that might otherwise not be afforded the humanity-creating experience of raising children. Adoption, when parents fulfill their child-rearing obligations, is a noble practice.

And if adoption is generally justifiable, it should also be acceptable, and even encouraged, in the context of a homosexual marriage since it would be fulfilling the same moral function. What matters for parents is not their sexual orientation but their actual performance of parental duties.

A modern Confucian view could thus accept the public expression and performance of mutual obligation of care and support that gay marriage represents. If sexual activity is constrained by social duty, as Confucians would hope in cases of heterosexual relationships as well, and if gay partners and parents conscientiously carry out their responsibilities to one another, then gay marriage would function very similarly to the moral ideal of straight marriage and would therefore be welcomed. Conversely, if gay partners stray from their family duties, if they allowed themselves to be distracted by the *qi* of sexual desire and infatuation, then their union would be subject to the same critique as a failed straight marriage. What matters is the enactment of duty, not the sexual identity of the enactors.

There are, however, at least two objections that might be raised from within Confucianism regarding gay marriage: tradition and filiality.

Confucius understood himself as a defender of tradition, not an innovator. In *Analects* 7.1 (Hinton) he describes himself as: "transmitting insight, but never creating insight, standing by my words and devoted to the ancients..." If he is strongly beholden to tradition, and if marriage is traditionally viewed as a heterosexual practice, then it might be reasonable to assume that a modern Confucian would reject gay marriage on the grounds that it violates tradition.

The issue is not quite that cut and dried, however. Although Confucius presents himself as a traditionalist, his arguments, in fact, were quite innovative in his own time. Perhaps most notably, he held that hereditary status, in and of itself, was not a sufficient claim for legitimate political rule (as will be discussed in the next chapter). He supported the idea of a moral meritocracy, that the virtuous should rule, and this notion disrupted what had been, to that point, the traditional practice of simple lineal succession. Mencius makes this point even more explicit and potent. All throughout the book that bears his name, Mencius stands up to hereditary leaders, calling them out for their transgressions, pressing against the political status quo. This is hardly the behavior of a hidebound traditionalist.

Confucius and Mencius also innovate in the realm of ritual. Recall, from the earlier discussion in Chapter 1, how Confucius takes traditionally defined ceremonial proceedings and creatively adapts them to his own purposes. The flexibility in interpreting tradition found in *Analects* 9.3, where Confucius decides to depart from customary practice in wearing a particular cap, suggests that he is open to change. Most imperative in this regard are the intentions and purposes of our actions. If we are able to perform our obligations to respect elders, cherish the young, and welcome friends through new forms of social interactions and relationships, then those new forms should be embraced and enacted. Of course, Confucianism would not carelessly or hastily abandon tradition. Long-standing social practices are due a certain respect. But tradition by itself, without reference to the broader process of contextually understanding and accomplishing our duties toward others, should not obstruct morally progressive social change. The key question is not, "what is tradition?" but, rather, "what will create and expand humanity?" Thus, if gay marriage can be shown to be consistent with the aims of humaneness, as I believe has been done above, then the fact that it violates tradition should not cause a Confucian to reject it.

If appeals to tradition are, by themselves, not enough to refute a Confucian acceptance of gay marriage, what about filiality? If parents are opposed to gay marriage, wouldn't a modern Confucian, in a good faith effort to respect mothers and fathers and elders, then have to accept that judgment and reject gay marriage also?

Not necessarily. The example of Shun, mentioned above in reference to the ethical insignificance of male heirs, can also be invoked here. Shun disobeyed his parents – he married without their knowledge and consent – because he had to live up to a higher standard of filiality, remaining true to the broader practice of humanity and extending it into new family relationships. Though we can presume that when Mencius thought about marriage he envisioned heterosexual couples, even so, gender is never explicitly invoked as a normative necessity in his account of Shun. It is all about humaneness, with no reference to sexual orientation or gender. If a marriage is justified on the grounds of creating "a great bond of humankind," and if we judge the moral goodness of a marriage in how well each spouse lives up to his or her duties to the other, and to other family members, then why should sexual orientation matter?

Parents of gay children may not appreciate this. They may resist a homosexual marriage of their son or daughter because it seems so perverse to them. But, if sons or daughters are entering into the marriage in good faith, if they seek to create and perform duties to one another, and do so conscientiously, then their marriage could, like Shun's, be a matter of a higher filiality.

In sum, the objections based on claims of tradition and filiality are not decisive; they do not produce an irrefutable Confucian rejection of gay marriage. They do raise questions that a modern Confucian might ask when considering the issue. At most, they could lead to a contention that, especially in light of tradition, same-sex marriage is something new and, in that sense at least, different from heterosexual marriage. To the extent that the term "marriage" has historically had a heterosexual connotation, there might be a claim that it should retain that meaning. The notion of "rectification of names" might be invoked here, following *Analects* 13.3:

> If names are not rectified, then speech will not function properly, and if speech does not function properly, then undertakings will not succeed. If undertakings do not succeed, then rites and music will not flourish. (Watson)

But the rectification of names is a behavioral concern.[10] It suggests that our actions must live up to the standards of any given moral concept. We should name a thing "marriage" only if the reality of it fulfills the moral criteria of marriage, which at base is the mutual fulfillment of duties. If we do not realize correct behavior, then we should not call the relationship a "marriage" – it is something less than that. Although some modern Confucians might want to assert that "marriage," and the behavioral imperatives associated with it, presume a heterosexual relationship, the performative logic of rectification of names could accommodate same-sex unions.

Daoists would likely take a much more relaxed position on gay marriage. Since marriage and child-rearing generally have less moral significance for Daoists – these things occur but they are not afforded any particular ethical importance – then the question of sexual orientation in relation to these social practices would seem to be fairly trivial. The recent rise in the demand for, and recognition of, gay marriage in the United States would be noted, by Daoists, as an empirical datum. *Dao* has shifted and moved in such a manner that now persons who formerly had to hide and repress their sexual orientation can now practice and celebrate it in new social forms. This change would have no particular ethical valence for Daoists: it is neither right nor wrong, good nor bad. It just is. And so be it.

A philosophical Daoist might share the Confucian worry that sex can, if taken to excess, distract us from our integrity. It must be said, however, right at the outset, that this concern of philosophical Daoists is not shared by religious Daoists, who are famous for their focus on sexual practice as a means of extending life. Indeed, this may be one of the greatest differences between philosophical and religious Daoism: the former view sexuality as an organic element of human life that requires no special attention, while the latter understands sexual activity as vital to the pursuit of immortality, a goal not shared by philosophical Daoists. Since our subject here and throughout is philosophical Daoism, the analysis below concentrates on that stream of thought.

Sex is alluded to in the *Daodejing*. It is a part of the natural experience of humans in Way. Fertility is often referenced, especially through images of female potency. But the text also warns against over-indulgence generally, and this would apply to sex as to anything else. If we allow our natural sexual instincts to become conscious desires or purposes, if we orient our lives to the pursuit of sexual pleasure, to the exclusion of other facets of our experience in *Dao*, then we are making it into something it is not and, in that way, obstructing our openness to *Dao*. This is not the same as the Confucian moral opprobrium that attaches to sex as a potential distraction from our social duties. Daoists would not invoke duty and ritual; rather, they would rue the human propensity to desire more than is necessary, as in this excerpt from passage 9 of the *Daodejing*:

> Forcing it fuller and fuller
> can't compare to just enough,
> and honed sharper and sharper
> means it won't keep for long.
> (Hinton)

The prospect of "just enough" would include sex as well as wealth and renown. If we strive for more and more, for too much, if we yearn and grasp and horde, we will, ultimately, bring on our own demise. And that pertains to sexual immoderation of any sort, gay or straight.

Zhuangzi also comments on the human tendency to overdo:

> When men get together to pit their strength in games of skill, they start off in a light and friendly mood, but usually end up in a dark and angry one, and if they go on too long they start resorting to various underhanded tricks. When men meet at some ceremony to drink, they start off in an orderly matter, but usually end up in disorder, and if they go on too long they start indulging in various irregular amusements. It is the same with all things. What starts out simple in the beginning acquires monstrous proportions in the end. (Watson, 60–61)

Sexual activity would fit within the broad understanding of "all things". Sex, like games and drinking, can lead us into thickets of complex debauchery.

Daoists, it should be said, are not prudish. They would not reject or regulate sexual intercourse. Rather, they would simply counsel us not to obsess over sex. This would, again, be relevant for heterosexual and homosexuals alike. Too much emphasis on sexuality in our identities could distract us from the fullness of our place in Way.

In short, a Daoist would not reject gay sex outright, but would warn of over-indulgence in sex more generally.

The issue, then, of gay marriage for Daoists is not the morality of homosexuality but the nature of marriage. As mentioned earlier, what would matter is the genuine integrity (*de*), in Daoist terms, of the individuals entering into such a union. If a person felt that his or her inherent and unique combination of *yin* and *yang* tendencies made it most natural to enter into some sort of prolonged relationship with a person of the same sex, then there would be no Daoist reason to keep that relationship from developing. It would really be no different than heterosexual marriage. It might be obvious and easy for some but it should not be made into a standard for all. In other words, not all homosexual relationships would need to be justified by marriage. No justification of any sort, beyond the spontaneous proclivities of those involved, would be required.

Whether such a relationship should be inviolable is a question that brings us to the more general issue of divorce.

Confucian and Daoist understandings of divorce

Contemporary Confucians would have an initial presumption against divorce. Marriage, of any sort, is a solemnly declared commitment and, as such, it should be respected and preserved. All facets of duty are like this. We cannot simply stop caring for elders or cherishing the young or welcoming friends because it is inconvenient or even personally difficult. Indeed, given its central assumption that individuals do not exist autonomously in the world but are always embedded in, and defined by, social relationships, Confucianism would have a hard time conceiving of an appeal to something like personal liberation as a justification for divorce. Moreover, the notion of a "no fault" divorce would, on the face of it, be nonsensical. The logic of Confucianism suggests that the only legitimate grounds for ending a formalized obligation like marriage would be failure to perform one's familial or social duties, which suggests some sort of neglected responsibility or fault.

It must be noted here that Confucius himself was not a paragon of husbandly virtue, at least by modern standards. He left his wife.[11] It is not clear if he formally divorced her, or simply just dumped her when he embarked, in 497 BCE, on his journey from state to state dispensing nuggets of wisdom. Perhaps he was behaving in a manner perfectly consistent with the moral expectations of his time, a time when a husband's prerogatives were more powerful than is now the case in the contemporary United States. Wives, in ancient China, had less status, and certainly weaker legal standing, than they do in most modern societies. To the extent that spousal obligations have grown in moral significance over the centuries, in both the West and in China, we must then conclude that in his personal relationship with his wife, Confucius did not live up to the ethical standards of a modernized Confucianism. He appears to have failed to enact conscientiously his duty toward his wife.

But even if we make that judgment, Confucius's personal behavior could suggest how Confucianism might now weigh the question of divorce.

We cannot know precisely why Confucius left his wife. Her side of the story is not recorded. What we can know is what he did after he departed. He traveled in order to develop his moral theory further and to find ways to influence state policy to have a broader effect on the world. Yes, there is an inconsistency here: the moral theory that he articulated placed family duties at the center of our existence, but he walked away from his own family duties (his son and daughter were also without their father during his travels) as he expounded that theory. But let's put aside that inconsistency for a moment to ask a question: How might the actions of Confucius be justified, or not, in terms of the principles of his own moral theory?

If a spousal relationship is not working, if a husband and wife are not cooperating together to fulfill their responsibilities to one another and to other family members, then there could be a Confucian reason to end the marriage. This kind of failure cannot, however, be justified in terms of mere selfishness. Marriage requires the submergence of the ego; personal interests have to be compromised in concert with other family members. That can be hard sometimes. It can create resentments and jealousies. But the whole point of the exercise is to force us to turn back on ourselves, examine why it is we have those selfish reactions, and find the ways of changing ourselves for the better in relation to others. I think that's what Mencius means when he says:

> All the ten thousand things are complete in me. To turn within and examine oneself and find that one is sincere – there is no greater joy than this. To dedicate oneself in all earnestness to reciprocity – there can be no closer approach to humaneness. (Bloom, 7A4)

Since walking away from family ties is such a difficult, and morally fraught, move, the question that a Confucian divorce therapist would raise is: why? Why are you doing this? Some percentage of divorces in the United States today are driven not so much by one partner's failure to perform his or her obligations but, rather, by self-centeredness. The most prominent of divorces – the celebrity breakups that splash across tabloid covers – are very often exercises in selfishness: outsized personalities unwilling to accommodate one another. These egotistical spectacles may play an inordinate role in shaping choices made by others. A Confucian would say that selfishness is not, ultimately, its own solution. If all you can think of are your own interests, and not the connections and bonds you have with others, then you are failing to truly understand yourself in the world and, thus, will not be able to achieve what is genuinely best for you, individually. Better to try again to improve one's relationship with a spouse than to strike out into a morally isolated, and therefore deficient, existence.

If it were found that selfishness was not the motivator, if one of the partner's was truly failing in his or her responsibilities or, worse, acting in an abusive manner toward the other, then that might be sufficient for a grant of divorce. More specifically, if one partner was obstructing the other's ability to perform his or her duties to other family members – children or elders – that could be a serious breach of marriage vows and justify formal separation. But all of this would have to be demonstrated. Confucians would want to try to keep marriages together – they would support counseling and therapy – but, in the end, if it were shown that obligations were being ignored or thwarted, they would accept, sadly, divorce.

To turn this back to the question of Confucius's own behavior, we could ask: was he merely acting selfishly or was his duty to teach and expand the reach of his moral theory sufficient to justify his separation from his wife? Personally, it seems to me that he could have accomplished much of his public purpose without leaving his wife, but it is hard to come to a settled judgment with so little information about his and his wife's circumstances.

Daoists would have little care for the question of divorce. Marriage, like any other human activity in Way, is fluid; it can change along with the shifting feelings and experiences of the persons involved. If two people grow apart, if their interests diverge or their passions run elsewhere, there is scant reason to maintain a formal relationship that no longer truly reflects emotional and behavioral reality. Such changes are not a matter of failing or fault; they simply happen. The ebbs and flows of human life are unfathomable. All we can do is follow along where Way leads us.

Many marriages may remain intact by force of habit. Two lives may naturally intertwine and produce an instinctive collaboration. A certain comfort and ease can be achieved. People might find " . . . peace in their homes and joy in their ancestral ways," as passage 80 of the *Daodejing* suggests. And that is fine. But if that shared life is tense and painful and forced, staying together might be a conscious resistance to the natural unfolding of things. Divorce could be the most unconstrained and spontaneous choice.

A certain irony can be noted here. Zhuangzi seems to have been with his wife when she died (Watson, 192). We do not have much of a historical record to draw upon, but it would appear that he had stayed with her, or maintained his marriage, right up to the end of her life. On the face of it, Zhuangzi appears to have been a better husband than Confucius; the Daoist seems to have upheld his family duties more faithfully than the Confucian. This could be taken as a verification of passage 38 of the *Daodejing*, which begins:

> High integrity never has integrity
> and so is indeed integrity.
> Low integrity never loses integrity
> and so is not at all integrity.
>   (Hinton)

"High integrity" would describe Zhuangzi's approach to his marriage: he never consciously makes it into a formalized and inviolable institution, he doesn't define it explicitly in terms of "integrity," and in so doing he actually achieves a more genuine integrity in his relationship. By contrast, Confucius goes on and on about the importance of fulfilling family duties, which in a modern context certainly include spousal obligations, but in trying to never lose "integrity," he ultimately fails to accomplish it.

That may seem a harsh assessment of Confucius. Yet it might be one that his erstwhile wife would accept.

Notes

1. Paul Amato *et al.*, *Alone Together: How Marriage in America is Changing* (Cambridge, MA: Harvard University Press, 2007), Chapter 1, "The Continuing Transformation of Marriage in America," pp. 1–35.

2. Andrew J. Cherlin, *The Marriage Go-Round: The State of Marriage and the Family in America Today* (New York: Random House Vintage Books, 2009), pp. 16–19.

3. Jason DeParle and Sabrina Tavernise, "For Women under 30, Most Births Occur Outside Marriage," *New York Times*, February 17, 2012, p. A1.

4. Kristin Anderson Moore *et al.*, "Children in Poverty: Trends, Consequences, and Policy Options," *Child Trend Research Briefs*, publication #2009-11 (April, 2009), p. 2. Available at: http://www.childtrends.org/Files//Child_Trends-2009_04_07_RB_ChildreninPoverty.pdf, accessed March 4, 2013.

5. Cherlin, *The Marriage Go-Round*, pp. 139–143.

6. For me, a book that opened up these new arguments is Andrew Sullivan's *Virtually Normal: An Argument about Homosexuality* (New York: Knopf, 1995).

7. Melvin P. Thatcher, "Marriages of the Ruling Elite in the Spring and Autumn Period," in Rubie S. Watson and Patricia Buckley Ebrey, eds, *Marriage and Inequality in Chinese Society* (Berkeley, CA: University of California Press, 1991), pp. 25–57; Bret Hinsch, *Women in Early Imperial China* (New York: Rowman & Littlefield, 2011), Chapter 2, "Kinship," pp. 35–60.

8. As Goldin writes, when considering the question of whether Confucianism is sexist: "If it is, it does not have to be." Paul R. Goldin, *Confucianism* (Berkeley, CA: University of California Press, 2011), p. 120.

9. Burton Watson, trans., *Han Fei Tzu: Basic Writings* (New York: Columbia University Press, 1964), p. 43.

10. For a fuller discussion of this concept, from both Confucian and Daoist perspectives, see Zhang Dainian and Edmund Ryden, *Key Concepts in Chinese Philosophy* (New Haven, CT: Yale University Press, 2002), "Rectification of Names," pp. 461–474.

11. Annping Chin, *The Authentic Confucius: A Life of Thought and Politics* (New York: Scribner, 2007), p. 40.

6

Public and Political Life

For Confucians, public life – holding political office or assuming some sort of community leadership role – is a natural expression of moral accomplishment. Quite simply, the virtuous should lead and rule. Conversely, if a political leader is not fulfilling family and social duties, he or she should be willing to relinquish office in order to focus on these more pressing obligations. Daoists, on the other hand, care little about politics. While they recognize that some sort of political and social leadership is inevitable, they eschew competition for such positions. The hierarchy and power that undergird public life are likely to obstruct a person's openness to the natural unfolding of Way.

My time in public office was short and modest. When Aidan entered the school system, Maureen and I were invariably drawn into meetings and conferences and committees. Eventually a position on the school board opened up and I found myself appointed and responsible for setting policy and budgets. The next year I ran, unopposed, for election, and settled into what became a five year commitment.

It was a different slice of life for me. Academia, my profession, can often be a solitary world. For the most part, I prepare my classes by myself and I do my research and writing by myself. There are meetings, of course, and collegial exchanges, but those do not usually require the kind of deliberative give and take, the compromise and deal-making, required in local politics. I had to learn to listen more effectively and find, with others, workable solutions to specific problems.

Life, Liberty, and the Pursuit of Dao: Ancient Chinese Thought in Modern American Life,
First Edition. Sam Crane.
© 2013 John Wiley & Sons, Inc. Published 2013 by John Wiley & Sons, Inc.

For two years I served as Chair of the School Committee. Things were rather complicated. We were starting to build a new school while simultaneously restructuring administrative duties and hiring a new Superintendent. There were only five of us on the Committee. I appointed the others to immerse themselves in the details of our various projects and held myself in reserve. My expectation was that I, as Chair, would insert myself in any one of the unfolding issues, depending upon whether more attention or pressure was required. In a sense, I was leading by following, or leading by stepping back from the daily fray.

Somehow everything got done: the new school was built; a new administrative structure was defined; a new Superintendent hired. One of my colleagues, familiar with Daoism, noticed the similarity between my detached leadership and the *wuwei* – "do nothing" or "do little" – principle. She gave me a copy of the *Daodejing* when I stepped down from the Committee, and noted this line from passage 37: "Way is perennially doing nothing so there's nothing it doesn't do" (Hinton).

* * *

It is commonplace these days to hear complaints about political leadership in the United States. The President and Congress are at loggerheads. Serious public problems – crumbling infrastructure; growing economic inequality; substandard public education – worsen with little or no effective government policy. Moneyed interests dominate election campaigns, which produce non-stop negative advertising, an unending stream of distortions and attacks. Ideology and cash have overwhelmed character and compromise. The optimism of 2008, when the election of an African-American president seemed to shatter historical barriers and open the way for a new era of good feeling, quickly disappeared into a miasma of heightened partisan division, doctrinal rigidity, and policy gridlock.

In a broader historical perspective, there is not much new here. American politics, from the earliest days of the Republic, have always been marked by cut-throat competition. The long and contentious rivalry between Alexander Hamilton and Aaron Burr ended in a duel and a death. The Gilded Age was rife with plutocracy and corruption. More recently, Richard Nixon set a modern standard for the abuse of public office in the service of personal political power. In each period, disillusionment with political leadership inspired debate on the questions of who should rule and how they should rule.

The last couple of decades provide ample examples of this dynamic: political malfeasance sparking discussion on the ethics of leadership.

Whatever public policy accomplishments he might have to his name, Bill Clinton will be forever tied to scandals that led to his impeachment. His unfaithfulness to his wife, details of which were embarrassingly displayed in public, centered attention on questions of character: should an individual's personal life be taken into account when judging his or her leadership capacities? Ultimately, the American political system answered with a qualified "no" to that question. The fact of his marital infidelity was, in and of itself, insufficient to remove him from office. His popularity in opinion polls remained relatively high throughout the impeachment ordeal. The legal issues, questions of perjury and obstruction of justice, were decisive, and there it was found that the particulars of his case, however lurid, did not justify expelling him from the presidency.

Moreover, Clinton himself did not believe that his personal behavior should determine his political fate. He did not resign. His political enemies certainly made the most of his faults, and Clinton no doubt felt that if he resigned he would simply be caving in to political pressure. In this he was not alone. American politicians seldom resign. They tend to hold on to office, at least until legal or political processes force them out. The separation of private and public life becomes a barrier or sorts, insulating a leader's personal shortcomings from his or her civic experience.

There was, however, a certain queasiness in the acceptance of Clinton's leadership. Many people felt that his transgressions did not justify his political downfall, but they were uncomfortable with his philandering. From this emerges an odd contradiction in American politics. It seems that "character" matters to voters and citizens. Or, at least, they say it does when asked at election time.[1] But, then, they are willing to suspend judgment and tolerate scoundrels who argue that their personal moral failings – whether those are sexual or financial or other – should not be used against them politically. Clinton's impeachment brought this tension to the fore. He was mercilessly attacked for his intemperance but praised for his competence.

That same tension is at the heart of political advertising. Consultants and image-makers strive to present their candidates as being both morally upright and politically effective: a good person who can get the job done. And they work hard to define their opponents as neither. The most cutting attack ads, however, are those that focus on integrity and honor. Obliquely, negative advertising demonstrates the political value of "character," by making it the primary target of vilifying critique. If a candidate is shown to be a liar or a "flip-flopper," unconcerned with the truth while seeking only political expediency, then the public will lose trust and seek out other leaders who are more genuine. Americans, it is presumed, esteem sincerity and authenticity in their politicians. They want their presidents and governors and representatives to say what they mean and be who they are. Negative advertising is designed to rob opponents of those very characteristics.

The political competition that has spawned pointed personal attacks has also created a more rigid ideological polarization. Compromise, which had once been a signal virtue in American government, has become something of an epithet. In the aftermath of President Obama's signature legislative accomplishment, the Affordable Care Act, Congress has fallen into partisan deadlock. Republicans, in an effort to deny Obama any further achievements, have used any means necessary to stymie legislative action.[2] Any conservative who dares to cross ideological lines in search of pragmatic public policy solutions, such as Chief Justice John Roberts in his opinion to uphold the constitutionality of the health insurance law, faces charges of betrayal, duplicity, and treason.[3]

The Roberts decision is instructive. His careful compromise could be taken as an act of statesmanship, carefully attempting a synthesis of various points drawn from both the liberal and conservative wings of the Court. If we assume he acted in good faith, we might then view his efforts as exemplary, a combination of personal character and policy innovation that American citizens seem to desire. It remains to be seen, however, if that more positive image will transcend the continuing partisan warfare that defines him in more dire terms.

Confucian leadership

Confucians would disdain Bill Clinton. They might appreciate his political competence, at least to the extent that his policies may have enabled people to carry out their familial and social duties with the dignity they deserve. But, ultimately, his moral failings and the poor example he set would have turned Confucians against him. John Roberts, on the other hand, comes closer to the Confucian ideals of personal integrity and situational awareness in decision making.

What matters for Confucians, in determining who should serve in public office, is moral accomplishment. Economic and social status are, by themselves, insufficient criteria for choosing leaders. Confucius and

Mencius put forth arguments that undermine hereditary prerogatives. Ethical qualifications are front and center. If a person from a rich and influential family is seeking public office, but he or she is known to shirk family obligations and behave in a generally dissolute manner, then that individual should be discouraged, or perhaps even barred, from serving. Conversely, if a person of modest means has parents of questionable character, but he or she is sensitive and alert in performing family and social responsibilities, then that individual should be elevated to a leadership position. The good, not the well born, should lead.

Clinton was certainly not born to an elite family. His experience, however, is a reminder that even for those who have worked their way up from modest means, and presumably acted ethically along the way, Confucian leadership requires continuing moral fitness. Goodness is performative, not existential.

In their own time, in a society where only a very small elite was literate and educated, Confucius and Mencius generally assumed that there would be a strong correlation between the well born and the good. Those who had access to the means of proper education would more likely make progress toward moral improvement than those who were unable to read or write. And the rich and powerful clearly had more access to education. But Confucian thinkers knew that the correlation was not perfect. There were many among the elite whose selfishness and arrogance undermined their ethics. Mencius is famous for confronting kings and dukes, all no doubt from wealthy and influential families, and excoriating them for their misrule. He accepts the removal, or even the violent overthrow, of rulers who have done wrong.[4] The message is clear: family status alone does not legitimate a ruler or office holder. What matters for Mencius is enacting humanity:

> Therefore only the humane should be in high positions. When one lacking
> in humaneness occupies a high position, his wickedness spreads to everyone.
> (Bloom, 4A1)

Even if a person comes from the ruling house and can make a hereditary claim to office, he or she still has to enact duty, in all of its social and familial aspects, according to ritual to progress toward humanity in order to maintain a legitimate basis of political power. Conversely, if a disadvantaged person, even a commoner, demonstrates a certain instinct for proper behavior, and if that quality is further developed through careful moral education, then that individual could make a better leader than his or her more privileged peer. This point is best gleaned from the story of mythical sage-emperor Shun, as recounted by Mencius.

We encountered Shun earlier, in discussing filial piety, because no one in the Confucian cannon exceeds his moral standing in that regard. Legend has it that Shun was a commoner, the son of a farmer, who toiled in the fields. Thus, he was probably not educated as a youth; perhaps he was illiterate. But when the reigning sage-king, Yao, started to think about a successor he did not turn to his own sons, whom he found to be lacking in character. Rather, he asked his ministers and counselors who should succeed him, and they recommended Shun. Neither Mencius nor Confucius explain precisely how Yao and his court could have known that Shun was a morally excellent person, but the Grand Historian, Sima Qian, writing in the Han Dynasty, gives us a more detailed view. Qian tells us that Shun was, at an early age, already known far and wide for his extraordinary filiality, even in the face of very difficult family circumstances:

> Shun's father, the Venerable Blind One, was obstinate, his mother mean, and his younger brother, [Xiang], presumptuous. They all had a desire to kill Shun. Shun was obedient and compliant and never strayed from the way of being a son, and was fraternal to his young brother and filial to his parents. When they wanted to kill him, they were not able to find him. But when they needed him, he was always around.[5]

Shun's reputation impressed Yao, who was looking for someone whose judgment was refined through conscientious attention to familial and social obligations. Yao sent his two daughters to marry Shun, and then watched to see how Shun responded. The modest farmer performed magnificently: he cultivated filiality in his new wives; he cooperated with others around him to improve economic and political life; and he remained respectful of his immediate family members. But the jealousy and hatred of his parents and brother only grew and they twice acted upon their desire to kill him. Yet even in the face of such cruelty, Shun kept his filial composure. He did not strike back against them, but simply continued to treat them in a manner proper to their familial roles. After some years, Yao realized that Shun truly was an exceptional person, and he invested him with public duties, the beginning of a twenty-eight year apprenticeship that ultimately resulted in Shun's succession to emperor upon Yao's death, an outcome, according to both Sima Chen and Mencius, universally seen as legitimate by elites and commoners alike.

By foregrounding the story of Shun, Mencius makes the point that good political leadership is rooted in consistent ethical behavior, first at home and then in the community at large. Leadership is a culmination of sorts, to be conferred only after a track record of proper behavior has been established. But it is also an avenue for the continued development and expansion of moral action. In each phase of his life – as a son and brother; as a husband; as a member of the community; as a leader-in-training; and, finally, as emperor – Shun rose to the occasion and did the right thing on a successively wider scale.

But what made exemplary leadership possible, in Shun's case, was the character forged in his early family life. He learned how to be a good emperor by first being a good son and brother and husband. For Confucians, lovingly and carefully attending to those family duties are the basis, ultimately, for political judgment. *Analects* 2.21 suggests as much:

> Someone asked Confucius: "Why aren't you in government?"
>
> The Master replied: "The Book of History says: Honor your parents, simply honor your parents and make your brothers friends – this too is good government. That's really being in government, so why govern by serving in government?" (Hinton)

The figure of Shun further suggests that some people are morally excellent by nature. They have an innate instinct for understanding how to do the right thing in the most difficult of circumstances. Of course, Mencius is famous for believing that everyone has a certain capacity for goodness. But in many cases that capacity has to be developed by close parental guidance and careful moral education. Shun stands as an example of the person whose ethical sensitivity is prior to education as well as independent of family lineage. He was good even when his parents and brother were bad. He was good without an early education. He was just good in his bones. And that is the sort of person who makes the best leader, as Confucius suggests in *Analects* 16.9:

> Confucius said, Those born with understanding rank highest. Those who study and gain understanding come next. Those who face difficulties and yet study – they are next. Those who face difficulties but never study – they are the lowest type of people. (Watson)

Not everyone is a Shun. There may be few who have his inherent moral sensitivities but Confucius and Mencius both believe that we can study and become enlightened; we can all become Shun-like, if we just concentrate on behaving as he did. And those who commit themselves to that ethical course will be the best leaders and rulers.

The development of Confucian leadership skills thus starts at home. In the *Analects*, Confucius is quoted as saying that a person should not worry about attaining a political position (Hinton, 8.14, 14.26), but should concentrate on fulfilling the duties he or she bears at the moment. And in a widely quoted, yet somewhat cryptic, passage he suggests that when everyone is attending to their family duties, social and political order will emerge:

> Duke Jing of Qi asked Confucius about governing effectively. Confucius replied, "The ruler must rule, the minister minister, the father father, and the son son."
> "Excellent!" exclaimed the Duke. "Indeed, if the ruler does not rule, the minister not minister, the father not father, and the son not son, even if there were grain, would I get to eat of it?" (Ames and Rosemont, *Analects*, 12.11)

Leadership at the top of the political hierarchy, that of the ruler, is founded upon the enactment of social roles at the bottom, that of the son and, we can now add, daughter. And this organic network of obligations, which connects the filial efficacy of children with the political efficacy of rulers, creates a universal paradigm for supervision and management of all sorts: if you want to be a good ruler, be a good son or daughter. The practice of being a good child cultivates within the individual son and daughter the sensibilities and habits required for leadership in other contexts, and creates a good example for others to follow. Confucius is quite explicit on this account:

> Master You said, A man filial to his parents, a good brother, yet apt to go against his superiors – few are like that! The man who doesn't like to go against his superiors but likes to plot rebellion – no such kind exists! The gentleman operates at the root. When the root is firm, then the Way may proceed. Filial and brotherly conduct – these are the root of humaneness, are they not? (Watson, *Analects*, 1.2)

Filiality, children fulfilling their obligations to parents, creates political stability. It should be said that filiality is, first and foremost, inherently moral. Confucius is not arguing that filial behavior is valuable merely for its political effect. Rather, respecting and caring for parents is the fundamental means of realizing our humanity, in all of its aspects. Political order is a secondary effect of what we should be doing anyway.

But how do we get from children doing right by their parents in myriad localized contexts to macro-scale political legitimacy and organization? What is the mechanism that translates private morality into public good? For Confucians the answer is at once tangible and idealistic: exemplary leadership.

Confucius strongly believes that persons of high moral character, committed to doing the right thing, will provide powerful examples of proper behavior that others will naturally follow. One of the most famous passages from the *Analects* that articulates this notion of leading by example is 12.19:

> Asking Confucius about governing, Ji Kangzi asked: "What if I secure those who abide in Way by killing those who ignore Way – will that work?"
>
> "How can you govern by killing?" replied Confucius. "Just set your heart on what is virtuous and benevolent. The noble-minded have the integrity of wind, and little people the integrity of grass. When the wind sweeps over the grass, it bends." (Hinton)

There are several points made in this stanza, but to get at exemplary leadership we might begin by considering the latter lines. In resisting the lord's initial impulse toward violence, Confucius counsels him to simply focus on finding the most humane course of action, which for a Confucian is always a matter of carefully considering and cultivating our closest loving relationships and extending that consideration to all of our social interactions. This is a matter of integrity – *de*.

In the Confucian lexicon, the meaning of "integrity" overlaps partially with the Daoist usage. Both suggest that each person has certain natural characteristics and proclivities. But where Daoists make no moral judgments about those natural characteristics, Confucians, at least those who follow the Mencian line of thinking, believe that everybody has an innate capability for goodness. Some people, however, are more naturally able to understand and follow through on doing what is right, whatever the circumstances may be. There is a kind of Confucian hierarchy of ethical proficiency. Everyone possesses the capacity for moral action, but some are better at modeling and demonstrating it. Thus, the integrity, or innate character, of some people is to take the lead in showing others how to behave properly. These are the noble-minded: a nobility not of vaunted lineage but of realized virtue. Others, the "little people," have an intrinsic ability to learn what is right but they must be taught. That is their integrity: to follow the example of the noble-minded.

There is a certain idealism here. Confucius seems to believe that most people, most of the time, want to follow their innately good human nature and will do so. That is why, as in the first lines of passage 12.19 above, he wards us away from coercion. "How can you govern by killing?" Even if, as Ji Kangzi is suggesting, we focus coercive power against only those who are purposefully doing wrong – not following the Confucian Way – the results, in terms of social stability and political order, are not as effective as exemplary leadership of the noble-minded. If the good rule, force is unnecessary. And if force is systematically invoked, most likely it is because the good are not ruling.

The metaphor of the wind and the grass suggests that exemplary rulership flows from a kind of natural force. People will instinctually follow the morally upright leader. Confucius elsewhere implies that something like celestial gravitation (which he obviously did not conceptualize in a Newtonian sense) is at work:

> The Master said: "In government, the secret is integrity. Use it, and you'll be like the polestar: always dwelling in its proper place, the other stars turning reverently about it." (Hinton, *Analects*, 2.1)

This could imply something like charisma. The good ruler, through the demonstrable rightness of his or her judgment and actions, will inspire the allegiance of other "little" people who themselves naturally long for moral improvement. The connection is not necessarily rational. People may not stop and think and calculate the precise personal and social benefits that might come from doing what the morally charismatic leader does. Rather, the inspiration is affective and emotional, perhaps even spiritual. "Little" people are simply swept along, like grass in the wind or smaller stars turning around the North Star, by something beyond their conscious control.

The attraction is generated, however, not by the person or family ties of the morally charismatic ruler but from his or her actions. If the good ruler does bad, the basis of leadership is undermined. And if the good ruler continues to do bad, then the description "good" no longer applies and removal from office is a possibility. The moral charisma of a ruler must be earned, day in and day out; it is contingent.

It is also essential. Confucius and Mencius both assume a social–political context in which laws are promulgated and implemented by a centralized authority. They are not anarchists; but neither are they Legalists.[6] The pessimistic assumption that people are by nature selfish and bad, and must therefore be restrained, even repressed, by strict laws and harsh punishments, is alien to the Mencian stream of Confucian thought. (The Confucian Xunzi, however, famous teacher of the Legalist Han Feizi, embraced gloomier assumptions about human nature.[7]) Laws and punishments, for Mencius, might be necessary for social and political order, but they are insufficient (Bloom, 2A3). Without exemplary moral leadership they would actually produce the inconsiderate and socially harmful behavior they were designed to prevent. Confucius, as usual, is the inspiration here:

> The Master said: Guide them with government orders, regulate them with penalties, and the people will seek to evade the law and be without shame. Guide them with virtue, regulate them with ritual, and they will have a sense of shame and become upright. (Watson, *Analects*, 2.3)

Without the exemplary ruler to show the way, people will simply not know how to behave properly, even when they are operating within a fairly clear and consistent legal system. People need moral instruction and inspiration, and that is what good leaders provide.

What happens, however, if an inhumane person seizes a leadership position? This is a dire situation for Confucians, and Mencius, in particular, considers how it might be handled. In the first of two rather famous passages, he seems to justify regicide:

> King Xuan of Qi asked, "Is it true that Tang banished Jie and King Wu assaulted Zhou?"
> Mencius replied, "It is so stated in the records."
> "Then can a minister be allowed to slay his ruler?"
> "One who offends against humaneness is called a brigand; one who offends against rightness is called an outlaw. Someone who is a brigand and an outlaw is called a mere fellow. I have heard of punishment of the mere fellow Zhou but never the slaying of a ruler." (Bloom, 1B8)

Jie and Zhou are infamous villains in Chinese history: the former is the depraved final ruler of the Xia dynasty, the latter the wicked last king of the Shang dynasty. The heroes here – Tang and King Wu – are the virtuous founders of successor dynasties. In the morality tale that is classical Chinese historiography, founders are always virtuous and dynastic finales are always tyrannical. In any event, what we should notice in this passage is the standard for determining good leadership. If a king is acting against humanity, he is not living up to the primary responsibility of political rule, and, thus, should not be given the name "king," in keeping with the rectification of names (*Analects*, 13.3) nor enjoy the prerogatives and protections that appertain to kingliness. Zhou (final ruler of the Shang, not to be confused with the Zhou dynasty – a different "Zhou" – that replaced him) was so bad, a brigand and an outlaw, that he should be punished as any commoner would. That he died as a result of King Wu's attack on his army and palace is thus justified, an appropriate punishment given his enormous violations of humanity.

To some degree, this is a *post hoc* justification for the institution of a new political regime. It should not, however, be taken as a license to kill the king at any slight provocation. Zhou is generally understood to be a truly horrible fellow, much worse than the unfaithful Clinton. The bar for regicide is thus set rather high. Be that as it may, what matters most here is the criterion of humanity. If a ruler is not creating the conditions for the population to carry out familial and social duties, if economic inequities are too onerous and legal injustices too severe (more on this below), then he or she has no claim on political office. The same message, absent the suggestion of violence, is echoed by Mencius here:

> King Xuan of Qi asked about high ministers.
> Mencius said, "Which high ministers is the king asking about?"
> The king said, "Are the ministers not the same?"
> "They are not the same. There are ministers who are from the royal line and ministers who are of other surnames."
> The king said, "May I inquire about those who are of the royal line?"
> "If the ruler has great faults, they should remonstrate with him. If, after they have done so repeatedly, he does not listen, they should depose him."
> The king suddenly changed countenance.
> "You should not misunderstand. You inquired of me, your minister, and I dare not respond except truthfully."
> The king's countenance became composed once again, and he then inquired about high ministers of a different surname.
> "If the ruler has faults, they should not remonstrate with him. If they do so repeatedly, and he does not listen, they should leave." (Bloom, 5B9)

Mencius here makes the point that if a leader is not doing the right thing, if he or she has "great faults," they can and should be removed from office. Ministers, from both aristocratic and commoner backgrounds, have a duty to point out a leader's shortcomings, to remonstrate, and set him or her in the right direction. The capacity to actually remove the ruler, however, rests only with the royal ministers. Other high ranking officials, whatever their status and accomplishments, can simply remonstrate and, if that yields no change in the direction of more humane rule, resign. This suggests that deposing a ruler is a potentially fraught undertaking. Mencius might well be concerned with the legitimacy of a new regime. To best ensure a smooth transition, the ultimate decision for change should rest with those closest to the bad ruler, his or her family line. They may best understand the failings of a wayward king, the reasons why he is not living up to the standard of humanity.

If presented with the example of President Clinton's indiscretions, Mencius would likely expect those closest to him to urge him to do the right thing and resign. And he would expect Clinton, if he was truly a man committed to humanity and duty, to ultimately make that move himself. Shun was said to be willing to give up his kingship as easy as "casting aside an old sandal" (Bloom, *Mencius*, 7A35), if fulfilling his family duties contradicted his official responsibilities. For Clinton, the public embarrassment, the evasion and dissembling, not only raised questions about his personal integrity but set a very bad example for society at large from a Confucian point of view. Under such circumstances, a noble-minded person should put ethics over politics and step down.

It should be noted that the excerpts cited above do not authorize a general "right to rebel." Over the centuries, various commentators have found this idea in *Mencius*, and these two passages are often cited in this regard.[8] However, it seems plain that Mencius is putting forth a more limited idea here: not that the people have a right to rebel, but that the elite has a responsibility to act when a leader is ignoring his responsibility and abusing his power.

To summarize: Confucius and Mencius believe the morally good should lead. Morally charismatic leadership is indispensable to social and political harmony; it provides a basis of legitimate rule that does not rely upon force and violence. Moral goodness is a function of fulfilling familial and social duties; thus, leadership is cultivated in, and must be based on, the continuing nurturing of one's closest loving relationships. If a leader fails in his personal or social obligations, he should yield the leadership position; and if he does not yield, he should be removed.

Beyond telling us who should lead and why, Confucius and Mencius give us some suggestions for how a good leader should lead. Of the various points they make, two might be most relevant for contemporary application: don't be dogmatic; and work to lessen socio-economic inequalities while recognizing that perfect egalitarianism is neither possible nor desirable.

As to the first, Confucius abhors dogmatism:

> The Master said, The gentleman is fair-minded and not partisan. The petty man is partisan and not fair-minded. (Watson, 2.14)

> The Master said, To delve into strange doctrines can bring only harm. (Watson, 2.16)

His concern about holding fast to certain doctrines, when particular circumstances might warrant flexible adaptation, reflects his understanding of moral complexity. Rigid application of unchanging rules is deeply unwise. The best decisions are made, and the best outcomes achieved, when all of the unique aspects of a specific social moment are taken into account. Confucius would certainly agree with Emerson that "a foolish consistency is the hobgoblin of little minds."

There are, of course, general ethical guidelines that should be kept in mind when determining the right course of action. As *Analects* 12.19, quoted above, implies, killing should be avoided. Mencius adds to this when he says that great men of the past, including Confucius, would never have killed a single innocent person (Bloom, 2A2). But Mencius also accepts the killing of tyrants. In most situations we should not kill but there are conditions that could make killing acceptable. Knowing how to creatively apply ethical guidelines to complex social realities is the work of the exemplary leader. He or she, through the conscientious development of his or her faculties of discernment and wisdom, will come to know the best course of action in each unique situation.[9] We should not look to such a person for unbending uniformity in weighing principle against circumstance. Ethical standardization is a recipe for harm and injustice.

Mencius gives us a poignant example of creative Confucian ethical deliberation in the story of Shun disobeying his father (Bloom, 5A2), which we encountered in the last chapter. Recall that Shun's father forbade him to marry. And since Shun was, above all, a filial son, he initially felt that he had to obey this paternal preference. But if he did not marry he would not be carrying on the project of humanity into the future, thus ending what his ancestors had started and, ultimately, depriving his own father of heirs, male or female, to remember and venerate him in time to come. In the end, when Yao offered his two daughters to him, Shun did decide to marry, but he did not tell his parents, for fear they would somehow thwart what he believed to be the best outcome.

Obeying one's parents is generally understood to be the first rule of filiality. But here, given the circumstances, the most filial course of action was to disobey his parents. When they discovered he had gone ahead and done what they had forbidden, Shun's parents were, no doubt, antagonized. Mencius, however, is suggesting here this immediate antagonism is less bad than the longer term antagonism that would have existed had Shun not married. Shun, in his wisdom, was able to understand and calculate all of these moral factors in making the ironic, yet correct, Confucian decision to disobey his parents in the name of filiality.

The story ends well. After Yao dies and Shun becomes king, Shun's father is said to have changed for the better (Bloom, 5A4). Though physically blind, the mean old man came to see the virtue and wisdom of his son's ways. The ultimate moral: thoughtful, undogmatic, and creative ethical action, which sometimes might appear to contradict key principles (i.e. disobeying parents can be filial), produces morally charismatic leadership that transforms those who witness and experience it.

Confucianism also encourages leaders to work to ameliorate extreme socio-economic inequality. In the Mencian vein, there is an initial equality across humankind. We might call it "original goodness," as opposed to original sin: all people start their lives with an inherent capacity for proper behavior. Confucius himself hints at this in *Analects* 17.2:

> The Master said: "We're all the same by nature. It's living that makes us so different." (Hinton)

Although we start out essentially the same, the living we do, the way we behave toward others, makes a difference. Some develop habits of right action; others deviate and fail to make the most of their inherent moral capabilities. We all begin with similar potential, but diverge because of circumstances we face and choices we make. While there is a suggestion of pessimism here – some, perhaps many, people will not realize the goodness within themselves – there is also a more optimistic possibility: we can all learn to be good again. The moral hierarchy of human society is not fixed and unchanging. Improvement is always possible.

Mencius tells us more. He makes a strong assertion of the inherent goodness of human nature, and he argues that education and training can better just about anyone. Real recalcitrants are rare. But we cannot conclude from this that "all men are created equal." No claims are made about rights. As mentioned above, Confucius and Mencius both recognize that some people are just born with a more mature moral sense than others. Some just have it; others have to work to develop their potential. Yet while all men may not be created equal, in the Mencian–Confucian worldview, virtually all can move their lives toward something better. And the key to maximizing society-wide moral accomplishment, which itself should be the goal of political leadership, is the provision of economic subsistence.

Mencius gets rather specific in outlining what is necessary to facilitate the broadest possible social good. Environmental factors are crucial. People must have a constant means of livelihood – employment, income, provisions – in order to carry out their familial and social duties with requisite dignity. If the economy is bad, and people have to struggle to survive materially, they could then be distracted by dire competition for food and shelter, and selfishness could come to the fore. He feared this in his own time:

> At present, the regulation of the people's livelihood is such that, above, they do not have enough to serve their parents and, below, they do not have enough to support their wives and children. Even in years of prosperity their lives are bitter, while in years of dearth they are unable to escape starvation. Under these circumstances they only try to save themselves from death, fearful that they will not succeed. How could they spare time for the practice of rites and rightness? (Bloom, 1A7)

A callous struggle for the means of life does not yield the survival of the fittest but, rather, the creation and reproduction of selfishness and inhumanity. Too much competition is a bad thing. Political leaders, therefore, should take responsibility for ensuring that all people have sufficient economic security. Mencius frames the issues in terms of his own historical context:

> When every five-acre farm has mulberry trees around the farmhouse, people wear silk at fifty. And when the proper seasons of chickens and pigs and dogs are not neglected, people eat meat at seventy. When hundred-acre farms never violate their proper seasons, even large families don't go hungry. Pay close attention to the teaching in village schools, and extend it to the child's family responsibilities – then, when their silver hair glistens, people won't be out on the roads and paths hauling heavy loads. Our black-haired people free of hunger and cold, wearing silk and eating meat at seventy – there have never been such times without a true emperor. (Hinton, 1.3)

This almost has the ring of the apocryphal Herbert Hoover formulation of "a chicken in every pot, and two cars in every garage." But the purpose here is different from the prosperity of the American Dream. Economic well-being is required not for its own good, nor for the wide array of possibilities for the "pursuit of happiness," but for much more specific moral ends. People need material security so that they can fulfill their familial and social duties, which will yield them more meaningful, good lives. If prosperity merely finances individual interest, disconnected from family and social networks, Confucians would demur. The Confucian Dream is more ethically specific than the American Dream.

Clearly, however, Mencius presses against acute economic inequalities. He makes the point above, suggesting that the government of a "true emperor" would fashion policies to ensure that people below the poverty line be provided the means to improve their circumstances. The modern analogues of mulberry trees might include: unemployment insurance; housing subsidies; food stamps; job training – programs that would facilitate economic security and, therefore, make possible the fulfillment of familial and social duties.

It would seem that, in the contemporary United States, policies espoused by the Democratic Party come closer to this Confucian ideal than the positions taken by the current Republican Party. The latter, in its zeal to reduce the presence of government in the economy, attaches too much emphasis on self-reliance and market competition for Confucian sensibilities. Mencius would be sympathetic to universal health insurance, for example, if that helped to avoid family crises brought on by crushing medical expenses. Political leadership, from his perspective, does have a responsibility for creating an economic environment that helps people do right by their families and communities.

The decision by Chief Justice John Roberts in the Affordable Care Act case would thus seem to satisfy several Confucian principles. In that ruling, Roberts appeared to resist calls from other conservatives to impose an ideologically pleasing outcome. He did not overturn the Act, much hated by Republicans, but found a doctrinally creative way of maintaining a Confucian-like humane policy. And he did so in a legally creative manner, hewing to certain precedents while developing a new basis for future policy. That he has a reputation as a good family man with high ethical standards simply makes the exemplary quality of the decision all the more notable.

Roberts also would agree with the Confucian expectation of individual responsibility. Government has a duty to make sure people have constant livelihoods, but, beyond that, individuals must follow through and do the right thing. If some persons benefit from the economically effective policies of a "true king," but then fail to perform their duties to others, they would be condemned by Confucians. However, harsh punishment would generally be avoided in favor of continued moral instruction. If Shun's wicked father could be transformed by repeatedly witnessing his son's virtue, others should, from the Confucian point of view, surely be similarly salvable.

Mencius, it should be emphasized, does not aim for absolute egalitarianism. Although he assumes that all people, within their being, have hearts that cannot bear to see others suffer and, thus, are capable of moral improvement, he knows that, ultimately, some will be better than others. And those who are better should rule. He rather famously – infamously for Chinese socialists and communists – quotes with approval an old adage:

> Some labor with their minds, while others labor with their strength. Those who labor with their minds govern others, while those who labor with their strength are governed by others. Those who are governed by others support them; those who govern others are supported by them. (Bloom, 3A4)

He thus justifies an economic and moral division of labor. Exemplary leadership is difficult, especially when it extends to higher political office. Leaders, therefore, should not be burdened with other tasks beyond the duties of their leadership. They should not, as the passage above suggests, be expected to work in the fields or factories. Others, whose moral accomplishments are of lesser significance, should continue to do the best they can in whatever social and economic positions they occupy, and accept the leadership of those who have refined their capacities of judgment and ethical behavior. Mencius does not mean for this division of labor to be unchanging. Shun was, after all, plucked from agricultural labor and elevated to king. But, generally, there should be a correlation between rectitude and political-economic function: the very good should rule and the less good should toil.

Many contemporary Americans would be repelled by the brains versus brawn distinction drawn by Mencius. Surely, intellectuals are not, simply by fact of their "labor with their minds," necessarily better than manual workers. But that is not the point. Rather, whomever it is that uses "mind" – and we must always remember that, in Chinese, we are referring to *xin*, 心, which connotes "heart" as well as "mind" – is exercising reflective moral judgment. They are thinking carefully about how to do the right thing. And if a person is not doing that, even a king or queen, then he or she does not really deserve the office, and may be better suited to some more physical labor.

In the end, Confucian leadership always comes back to character. A ruler must be honest and conscientious, must fulfill familial and social duties, and strive to create conditions that allow others to do the same. A leader is a person who advances humanity in his or her own life, and seeks to advance humanity in the lives of others.

Daoist leadership

Daoists would care little for either Bill Clinton or John Roberts. The personal faults of the former president would not surprise the writers of the *Daodejing* or *Zhuangzi*. They would see him as just another example of an individual who adores "tortuous paths," becoming obsessed with certain desires which then become barriers to the unencumbered unfolding of *Dao*. Indeed, Clinton's problem, from a Daoist perspective, might be more his desire to hold onto political power than his fancy for extramarital trysts. Nor would the rectitude and pragmatism of the Chief Justice impress Daoist thinkers and writers, who would question whether even the smartest policy compromises will actually achieve the ends for which they are designed.

Leadership, for Daoists, is not a morally necessary means for improving society, as it is for Confucians. It is, rather, an insecure inevitability of humankind. In any grouping of people – communities, provinces, nations – leaders will arise and politics, the struggle for power, will ensue. But the world is not, ultimately, governed by what leaders say and do. No one, even those with seemingly great political power, can control the course of *Dao*. Leadership, when it is premeditated and carefully planned, is folly, though a folly that seems inescapable for human society.

Daoism is not entirely anarchistic, though it recognizes the virtue of less government. The *Daodejing*, in particular, but also *Zhuangzi*, has much to say about leadership. Both texts recognize that rulers and sages are naturally a part of human experience. They take that observation, however, and push it in a direction that runs counter to Confucian standards, encouraging a minimalist, non-interventionist approach to leadership.

Chapter 7 of *Zhuangzi* offers a pointed assault on Confucian exemplary leadership:

> Jian Wu went to see the madman Jie Yu. Jie Yu said, "What was Zhong Shi telling you the other day?"
>
> Jian Wu said, "He told me that the ruler of men should devise his own principles, standards, ceremonies, and regulations, and then there will be no one who will fail to obey him and be transformed by him."
>
> The madman Jie Yu said, "This is bogus virtue! To try to govern the world like this is like trying to walk the ocean, to drill through a river, or to make a mosquito shoulder a mountain! When the sage governs, does he govern what is on the outside? He makes sure of himself first, and then he acts. He makes absolutely certain that things can do what they are supposed to do, that is all. The bird flies high in the sky where it can escape the danger of stringed arrows. The field mouse burrows deep down under the sacred hill where it won't have to worry about men digging and smoking it out. Have you got less sense than these two little creatures?" (Watson, 92–93).

The first image of the ruler here – a leader who devises his own principles and transforms others – is the Confucian ideal: the articulation of guiding moral standards that are reflected in the behavior of the leader himself. This is then rejected. That it is a madman that is doing the rejecting is a classic bit of Zhuangzi irony – only the crazy and outcast can truly see the failure of social and political conventions. Confucianism is a "bogus" or deceitful virtue that will ultimately fail because the world is impervious to human control. The text then reclaims the notion of "sage" from Confucianism, redefining it in Daoist terms. A person wise to the intricacies of *Dao* first considers his or her unique position in the totality of all things and then acts minimally to facilitate others to "do what they are supposed to do." The point is to not impose moral guidance, but to permit natural unfolding.

Conventional leadership, which attempts to intervene more systematically and implement predetermined plans, is something to be avoided. We should run from it like birds and mice escaping harm. As another passage suggests, it doesn't matter if typical leaders are good or bad, they should all be eluded:

> If springs dry up, leaving fish stranded together on dry ground, they may keep each other moist with misty breath and frothy spit – but that's nothing like forgetting each other in the depths of rivers and lakes. We can praise Emperor Yao and condemn Jie the tyrant – but that's nothing like forgetting them both and dwelling in the transformations of *Dao*. (Hinton, 86)

Yao is a Confucian paragon, Jie an archetypical villain: best to stay clear of both. In contemporary American terms, it doesn't matter if Clinton acted badly and Roberts behaved admirably, both of them are men of purposive action designed to bend *Dao* in a particular direction. In that, they are each reproducing a Confucian-esque futility.

Although the passages above would seem to warn any particular individual away from a position of authority, Daoism recognizes that some sort of leadership will emerge. Indeed, in facing this inevitability, Zhuangzi turns the idea of a moral exemplar on its head. He does not reject exemplary leadership but creates an anti-leader as exemplar. Take this passage:

> In Lu there was a man named Wang Tai who had had his foot cut off. He had as many followers gathered around him as Confucius.
>
> Chang Ji asked Confucius, "This Wang Tai who's lost a foot – how does he get to divide up Lu with you, Master, and make half of it his disciples? He doesn't stand up and teach, he doesn't sit down and discuss, yet they go to him empty and come home full. Does he really have some wordless teaching, some formless way of bringing the mind to completion? What sort of man is he?"
>
> Confucius said, "This gentleman is a sage. It's just that I've been tardy and haven't gone to see him yet. But if I go to him as my teacher, how much more should those who are not my equals! Why only the state of Lu? I'll bring the whole world along and we'll all become his followers!" (Hinton, 68)

Again, we can see Zhuangzi's humor here, having Confucius recognize that this man is a better leader than he. Wang Tai is an outcast, likely a criminal of some sort, as implied by his amputated foot, a common punishment then. But whatever he had done wrong, he has overcome it to become an inspiration of sorts. Unlike Confucius he does not teach explicitly. His wordless presence does not provide a clear set of guidelines for ethical behavior. He just is: a minimal existence in an immediate moment of *Dao*. And Confucius calls him a "sage."

There are other examples in *Zhuangzi* of such anti-leaders: men punished with amputation; ugly men; inarticulate men. Yet these are the ones that attract a following. In one case (5.4), a ruler is entranced by an unsightly man, who has nothing interesting to say, and offers him the position of prime minister. Even though the man ultimately rejects the office, the point is clear: good leadership is to be found at the margins of society because people there – outcasts, rejects, failures – inherently understand that conventional standards of accomplishment and virtue are meaningless in the vastness and complexity and disorder of Way.

Zhuangzi also provides some insight into the best sort of advice a close confidant or counselor might give to a ruler. Once more, he makes Confucius his foil. In this parable, Yan Hui, the most conscientious and respected of Confucius's disciples, seeks out The Master for guidance. Yan wants to go off and try to improve a ruler known to be a "reckless and self-indulgent young man," who is "careless about ruling his kingdom and blind to his own faults." (Hinton, 47). Confucius, in a most un-Confucian manner, wards him off this project, saying, in effect, that counseling rulers is futile. Giving advice requires analysis, breaking apart the constituents of a unique situation. When we engage in this kind of intellectual fragmentation, we lose sight of the larger picture. And that thought is consistent with the words that Zhuangzi scripts for Confucius in response to Yan Hui:

> *Dao* can't be unraveled. With unraveling comes multiplicity. With multiplicity comes trouble. With trouble comes grief. And once you've come to grief, nothing can save you. In ancient times, sages established *Dao* in themselves first. Only then did they establish it among the people. If you aren't sure about *Dao* in yourself, you don't have time to worry about the ways of some tyrant. (Hinton, 47)

The very act of offering advice requires a kind of distortion of *Dao*. We can't really capture the fullness of *Dao* in words and logic and analysis. When we attempt to describe it, in order to act upon it, we create a partial, inadequate account, one that then stands against other partial, inadequate accounts. In contemporary American terms, we create a liberal analysis and a conservative analysis and variations on those themes. Each asserts that it holds the key to the larger truth, but each is, necessarily, partial and inadequate. This is the kind of "multiplicity" of which Zhuangzi writes. Offering advice casts us into this irresolvable contest of deficient assertions. Best just to stay out of it.

The theme of self-preservation is important here as well. We cannot really know the circumstances and conditions of others, and we cannot understand the unfolding of Way. Thus, we should simply attend to what is immediately before us and open ourselves to *Dao* as we experience it in our own lives: establish *Dao* in ourselves first and then establish it among the people. This sounds like it could be consistent with Confucianism, which would tell us to rectify ourselves first before we attempt to rectify others. But the difference is great. Daoism takes a much more passive approach, one that does not rely on a pre-established set of principles that might define rectification. In Zhuangzi's rendition of the discussion between Confucius and Yan Hui, The Master ultimately tells the adept to meditate:

> Gaze into the cloistered calm, that chamber of emptiness where light is born. To rest in stillness is great good fortune. If we don't rest there, we keep racing around even when we're sitting quietly. Follow sight and sound deep inside, and keep the knowing mind outside. Even ghosts and spirits will come to dwell with you there – so how could humans fail to do the same? (Hinton, 52)

This is how we should advise rulers. Doing nothing, simply attending to one's immediate moment in *Dao*, sitting quietly and emptying the mind of preconceived expectations and beliefs, is presented here as a technique of leadership. Humans will "come and dwell with you there." They will look to your behavior as a model of sorts, an example of how one should exist in *Dao*. If people do that, rulers will eventually take notice as well. A minimalist – *wuwei* – approach to human action will take hold.

Zhuangzi's Confucius also says:

> You've heard of using wings to fly, but have you heard of using no-wings to fly? You've heard of using knowing to know, but have you heard of using no-knowing to know? (Hinton, 52)

This fairly well summarizes Zhuangzi's approach to leadership. Instead of valuing and seeking out the usual qualities of "leadership" – especially the virtues associated with Confucian sagehood – we should embrace the possibilities of "no-leadership" as a means of leadership. Don't place yourself out front; don't consciously cultivate public virtues; don't pass judgment on the actions of others. Just sit and act minimally and that will give you a path through *Dao* that allows for self-preservation, which in turn will become a kind of model for others. There's no need to fret about achieving particular goals; all that needs to happen will happen:

> When he governs, the sage emperor
> fills all beneath heaven with bounty,
> and yet he's nowhere to be found.
>
> He transforms the ten thousand things,
> and yet no one thinks to rely on him:
>
> People never even mention his name,
> for he lets things find their own joy.

He stands firm in the immeasurable
and wanders free in realms where there's nothing at all.

(Hinton, 107–108).

The *Daodejing* makes the same points.[10] The best leader, it tells us, is one that is hardly noticeable: "The loftiest ruler is barely known among those below" (Hinton, 17). And it goes on to provide somewhat more specific suggestions for how to embrace anti-leadership:

Stretch onto tiptoes and you never stand firm.
Hurry long strides and you never travel far.

Keep up self-reflection and you'll never be enlightened.
Keep up self-definition and you'll never be apparent.
Keep up self-promotion and you'll never be proverbial.
Keep up self-esteem and you'll never be perennial.

Travelers of the Way call such striving too much food and baggage.
Things may not all despise such striving, but a master of Way stays clear of it.

(Hinton, 24)

The ideas of the second stanza are presented a bit earlier in the *Daodejing* (Hinton, 22) in negative terms: "give up self-reflection and you're soon enlightened," etc. But the concept is the same. If you consciously strive to achieve certain leadership qualities, you will not succeed. It is only by letting go of such expectations, thus avoiding impediments produced by self-centeredness, that a kind of success can be reached.

On the face of it, applying these ideas of anti-leadership in a modern context seems far-fetched. Can we really expect a president of the United States or a senator or governor or mayor to "give up self-promotion"? Government or corporate decision-makers could hardly abandon the very idea of setting goals. How would he or she ever be nominated or elected or promoted? If a public figure advocated doing nothing when faced with serious social problems, it would likely be the end of a political or professional career.

But just as *wuwei* need not literally mean "doing nothing," Daoist leadership ideas could suggest a certain humility and modesty, not simply a complete absence of action. The thinking is cautionary. If you are overly concerned with self-promotion, or create plans that ignore the possibility of unexpected events and unintended consequences, your best laid leadership plans could well go awry. Action may indeed be possible, but it must be approached and performed with care and sensitivity. Daoism would counsel a ruler or manager to resist imposing "solutions" from the top down. It is better to allow circumstances to develop, to permit those involved to work on their own terms, and discover the best course of action *within the particular context*. There would be no prior assumption that a "model" derived from some remote experience might be appropriate in the unique conditions of different times and places. A kind of contextual pragmatism, a sensibility of discovering what is possible in a given moment, would be encouraged.

We can see some of this sensibility in the notion of "leading from behind." Commentators have noted that President Obama, by restraining American power in response to events in Iran and Libya, not intervening militarily when others urged immediate forceful action, was, in effect, leading from behind in his foreign policy.[11] In this he was moving in consonance with passage 66 of the *Daodejing*:

> Oceans and rivers become emperors of the hundred valleys because they stay so perfectly below them. This alone makes them emperors of the hundred valleys.

> So, wanting to rule over people a sage speaks from below them, and wanting to lead the people he follows along behind them,

> Then he can reign above without weighing the people down and stay ahead without leading the people to ruin.

> All beneath heaven rejoices in its tireless praise of such a sage. And because he's given up contention, nothing in all beneath heaven contends with him.
>
> (Hinton)

Notice: there is a prospect of success here. Leading from behind allows a ruler to "reign from above" and "stay ahead" and win "tireless praise." The leader is not doing nothing to no effect at all; rather, she is creating certain outcomes from the possibilities of a particular context. Things are happening; goals are being attained. This is taking place not as a result of a pre-formulated plan sprung from the mind of an all-knowing leader, but from an organic process of community-generated understanding of what can and should be done. A leader needs to facilitate this sort of indigenous and deliberative activity.

There is always a possibility of disagreement and dissent. In such cases, Daoism would generally agree with Confucians that coercion should not be used to force a decision or outcome. For Daoists, if people don't agree, they don't agree; that is a facet of that particular moment of *Dao*. Any attempt to unnaturally concoct a favored result or construct a false consensus will likely fail on its own terms, since it does not reflect circumstantial realities. And the use of violence will ultimately prove ineffective:

> In their misery, the people no longer fear death,
> so how can you threaten them even with death?
>
> Let the people fear death always,
> then if we seize those who follow sinister ways
> and put them to death,
> no one will dare live such lives.
>
> The Executioner's killing is perennial, it's true.
> But to undertake the killing yourself –
> that's like trying to carve lumber for a master carpenter.
> Try and carve lumber for a master carpenter
> and you'll soon have blood on your hands.
>
> (Hinton, 74)

In this passage the author seems to be in self-dialogue, at first raising the possibility of using violence against those who "follow sinister ways," but then pressing back against that idea with an assertion that if you "undertake the killing yourself," as opposed to letting the spontaneous course of events unfold, then negative consequences will ensue. The "executioner" here, it must be noted, is the natural ebb and flow of all life forms. All living things will have their ends, and we, as humans with an impulse to control, should restrain ourselves from interfering in that natural process.

Moreover, passage 74 suggests that bad leadership creates its own limitations. The idea that "people no longer fear death" suggests that basic life necessities – food, clothing, shelter – are in such short supply or poor quality that living no longer seems valuable. Elsewhere in the *Daodejing* the causes of poverty and privation are identified as the greed and power of leaders and elites:

> The people are starving, and it's only because you leaders feast on
> taxes that they're starving.

The people are impossible to rule, and it's only because you leaders are masters of extenuation that they're impossible to rule.

The people take death lightly, and it's only because you leaders crave life's pleasures that they take death lightly, they who act without concern for life: it's a wisdom far beyond treasuring life.

(Hinton, 75)

There is a libertarian tone here. If people are free from undue burdens of taxation and bureaucracy, they will find their own ways of flourishing. In regard to leadership, it suggests that leading from behind is likely to be more effective, in terms of creating relatively self-sufficient and sustainable living conditions in smaller-scale communities. If rulers live closely among the people, if they are neither shielded by Byzantine administrative structures and nor isolated in gated compounds, they will have a harder time feasting on taxes and craving life's pleasures. The penultimate passage of the *Daodejing* paints a rather idyllic picture of self-government and simple living in ordinary localities:

> Let nations grow smaller and smaller
> and people fewer and fewer,
>
> let weapons become rare and superfluous,
> let people feel death's gravity again
> and never wander far from home.
> Then boat and carriage will sit unused
> and shield and sword lie unnoticed.
>
> Let people knot ropes for notation again
> and never need anything more,
>
> let them find pleasure in their food
> and beauty in their clothes,
> peace in their homes
> and joy in their ancestral ways.
>
> The people in neighboring nations will look
> across to each other,
> their chickens and dogs calling back and forth,
> and yet they'll grow old and die
> without bothering to exchange visits.
>
> (Hinton, 80)

We might take this as an ideal of sorts, an outcome to which leadership of all sorts should be oriented. Large governing structures are absent, rulers are not mentioned, people live in self-sufficiency and simplicity, and coercion is not necessary. Happiness and satisfaction thrive. Of course, Daoist thinkers would warn us not to make this a concrete Goal that requires a Plan to Accomplish; that is, we should not consciously strive for such results. Rather, a content and peaceful community can be created without extensive government policy and expert guidance. It will emerge, locally and effortlessly, if people have a chance to follow their instincts for subsistence and sociality.

Optimism pervades this vision. The *Daodejing* assumes that, liberated from oppressive political power, enough people will focus on satisfying their basic needs in a constructive and convivial manner within their immediate social settings, that a community-wide comity will take shape. Perfect harmony is not the objective. Selfish and hurtful individuals will always press against the collective good and cause trouble. But the belief here is that there will not be so many bad apples that the whole crop is spoiled. In passage 80 above, weapons exist, but they are "rare and superfluous" because coercion is not necessary to suppress antisocial behavior. Bad things will happen, but the persons who are responsible for them will face the natural consequences of their actions.

Weapons are mentioned in other passages of the *Daodejing*, some of which raise troubling questions about Daoist leadership. Sinister implications arise in this excerpt:

> The submissive and weak conquer the strong.
> Fish should not be taken out of the depths;
> The state's sharp weapons should not be shown to the people.
>
> (Henricks, 36).

These lines are generally consistent with the vision of leadership and society described above: a soft, non-interventionist approach is better than a hard, coercive method. But that last line about "sharp instruments of the state" could be taken in a different direction. Does it suggest a more cynical understanding of power and politics? That leaders should have access to weapons, if they need them, but should hide them from the populace, so as not to reveal the full extent of their might? An ominous reading of the text might also be promoted by this passage:

> Never bestow honors and people won't quarrel.
> Never prize rare treasures and people won't steal.
> Never flaunt alluring things and people won't be confused.

This is how a sage governs.
Fill bellies and empty minds,
strengthen bones and weaken ambition,
always keep people from knowing and wanting,
then those who know are those who never presume to act.

If you're nothing doing what you do
all things will be governed well.

(Hinton, 3)

Taken in context of the book as a whole, this passage is telling us that a leader has no need of humanly created "knowledge," which here we might take as theories and plans about how to effect change in the world, and, therefore, should not encourage followers to pursue that same sort of knowledge. Moreover, as is made plain throughout the text, the *Daodejing* encourages a certain materialist simplicity. People, generally, should be satisfied with a basic level of physical comfort. Fancy food and clothes and possessions are unnecessary and diverting, taking us away from the task of opening ourselves honestly and uninhibitedly to Way. Indeed, it is precisely the people who are able to do this – do with less – that should lead.

When this stanza, therefore, instructs us to "fill bellies and empty minds" and "always keep people from knowing and wanting," it is simply suggesting that others should simply follow the leader, whose mind should already be empty and who has already abandoned wanting. But it can be read, and has been read historically, in a more manipulative manner. It could suggest that a select few need to control power and knowledge and resources because people, generally, must be kept down. It sounds like a strategy for authoritarianism, a means of concentrating and preserving the power of an elite. The Legalist writer Han Feizi appropriates Daoist ideas – importing the notion of a detached and unknowable ruler – with this more instrumentalist function in mind.[12]

But I don't think this power mongering interpretation is in keeping with the spirit of the text or the philosophy more broadly. When we consider other passages, we can see that the best course for a Daoist leader is to let go of power, not hold fast to it. The ideal is to minimize the structures and functions of administration and government, to let circumstances unfold unobstructed. The sinister reading contradicts this. Overall, suggestions for leadership in the *Daodejing* are not about preserving power but about transforming power by diffusing and de-centering it, allowing each thing to express its own power, based on its unique qualities within the context of all things simultaneously.

Thus, when the text tells us, "the sage is not humane; he regards the common people as straw dogs" (Hendricks, 5), it is a reminder that letting people determine their own lives will sometimes result in bad choices and tragedy. Yet even in these moments a leader should not intervene, but allow the misfortune to progress and dissipate on its own accord, and attendant lessons to be learned. The larger Daoist message is: " . . . in putting himself last the sage puts himself first, and in giving himself up he preserves himself" (Hinton, 7).

In sum, the *wuwei*, minimal action outlook of Daoism does not obviate the reality of leadership. In any human grouping, large and small, some individuals will gravitate into leading positions. What matters, for Daoism, is not so much how or why someone gains such a standing but, rather, how one behaves from there. The *Daodeijing* and *Zhuangzi* suggest that a leader should not consciously plan and strive to "lead." He or she should not impose a preferred result or force a specified option. Rather, the leader's role is to facilitate whatever possibilities inhere in a specific context. There is no need for a moral paragon, as in Confucianism, because purposeful principles invariably harden into dogma, detached from and irrelevant to actual circumstances. Character matters only to the extent that it allows a person to remain open to *Dao*, sensitive to the particulars of the moment and able to lead from behind.

The question of democracy

Daoism and Confucianism provide very different views on who should lead and how leaders should perform. The more activist Confucian ideal of an exemplary leader, living a morally good life and acting to make it possible for others to do the same, stands in stark contrast to the Daoist anti-leader, situated below and behind followers, doing as little as possible to facilitate what would have happened anyway. The two disparate perspectives, however, do share a key similarity: neither has much to say about how individuals ought to be placed in leadership positions.

Daoism, in warding individuals away from actively working to gain leadership roles, is indifferent on this central question of politics. Leadership will happen. It would be good if it worked to keep self-interested and grasping persons from gaining power, which would only be abused. However, the possibilities of either an open and competitive election for office, as is commonly the case in the United States, or a carefully orchestrated elite process of selection, currently the practice in China, would be anathema to the Daoist sense of minimal action and mental detachment. The *Daodejing* and *Zhuangzi* are not guidebooks for how to manage political selection and succession; they are sources of critique, a reservoir of skepticism inundating those in power.

As was mentioned above, the relativist and nonjudgmental quality of Daoist thought has allowed it, historically, to be appropriated by Han Feizi in the service of a decidedly authoritarian Legalism. With no moral foundation, Daoism offers no grounds to resist any particular political application of its ideas. Thus, even though the Legalist manipulation of Daoism might strike many casual readers as violating its philosophical spirit, there is really no basis, from within Daoist thought, to refute categorically such misuse. Be that as it may, it is wrong to assume that authoritarianism is somehow the only appropriate political expression of Daoism. It is not.

There is no singular political form of Daoism. Its ideas can have meaning in either an authoritarian or a democratic context. What is important to keep in mind in regard to contemporary America is that Daoism is certainly adaptable to democracy. Indeed, if democratic politics are structured in a way that empowers local decision making, allowing people in tight-knit communities to manage the conditions of their daily lives, then it would be consonant with the ideals of passage 80 of the *Daodejing*, where people find " . . . peace in their homes and joy in their ancestral ways." Moreover, the centrality of political equality to democracy is also consistent with Daoist suspicion of any sort of moral or power hierarchies. Democracy, when it functions as it should, creates channels of popular influence that limit the power of the centralized state. Daoists would appreciate this. And if democracy works to maximize individual freedom, facilitating each individual to find the fullest natural development of his or her innate capacities and proclivities, then that, too, would be welcomed by Daoists.

Daoist anti-leadership creates an anti-politics of sorts, focusing more on civil society than state power. In many ways this might have more in common with democracy than with authoritarianism, but Daoism does not encourage electoral competition or policy planning or judicial review. It is unconcerned with the structure and functioning of political institutions. While it can be adapted to modern democratic life, it is not a theory of modern democratic politics.

Confucianism, in its classical pre-Qin expressions, is not particularly democratic either. And we shouldn't expect it to be. The politics of the

Warring States period was aristocratic and authoritarian. While Confucius and Mencius struggled against the idea of hereditary succession, they did not succeed in changing many minds. Virtually all of the states of their time practiced hereditary transfers of power. There was no sense of popular sovereignty and no system of electoral choice. The people did not vote. Thus, Confucius and Mencius assumed that a socio-economic elite would dominate politics. Decisions about who should rule would be made among lords and nobles. Neither of these thinkers, then, advanced a fully formed argument for something like democracy.

Moreover, Confucian ideas, especially notions of filial obedience and moral hierarchy, were used throughout Chinese history to justify authoritarian imperial rule. Wouldn't any autocrat be happy with a system of thought that asserted that the morally good should rule? It was only a simple step from that assertion to the conclusion that any particular tyrant was good and, therefore, had an entitlement to rule. What became a long tradition of Chinese statecraft was based on a Confucian–Legalist synthesis – founded on the draconian penal system of the Legalists and veiled by an ideology of exemplary leadership – that would have likely distressed both Confucius and Mencius.[13]

Thus, today we are told that China cannot democratize because its "Confucian tradition" has not bequeathed it a democratic practice and culture. And from that it might be presumed that Confucianism has little to contribute to discussions about democracy in America. Both these contentions are not true.

Regarding contemporary China, or any other country in the world, the potential for democratization is not determined by history and culture. Other political factors – the mobilization of civil society; the strength of state institutions; the strategic orientation of the political elite – can create transitions to democracy in places with little or no prior experience of electoral competition or constitutional government.[14] This has already happened in Confucian cultural contexts. Taiwan, South Korea, and Japan all have moved from Confucian-inflected forms of authoritarianism to vibrant democracies. The reason why democratization is obstructed in the People's Republic of China is not the Confucian past but the powerfully entrenched ruling party.

Furthermore, when we look at Confucian thought itself we can see that it can be made compatible with democracy, even if that was not the thinking of its earliest originators. Mencius, who has been used by various East Asian democrats to further their cause, opens the door for the people to play a part in politics.[15] In a well-known statement on the Mandate of Heaven and political succession, we read:

> Wan Zhang said, "Did it happen that Yao gave the realm to Shun?"
>   Mencius said: "No. The Son of Heaven cannot give the realm to someone."
>   "But Shun did possess the realm. Who gave it to him?"
>   "Heaven gave it to him."
>   "When Heaven gave it to him, did it ordain this through repeated instructions?"
>   "No. Heaven does not speak. This was manifested simply through Shun's actions and his conduct of affairs."
>   "The Son of Heaven can present a man to Heaven, but he cannot cause Heaven to give him the realm. The lords can present a man to the Son of Heaven, but they cannot cause the Son of Heaven to make him a lord. A great officer can present a man to the lords, but he cannot cause the lords to make him a great officer. In antiquity Yao presented Shun to Heaven, and it was Heaven who accepted him. He displayed him to the people, and the people accepted him. This is why I said that 'Heaven does not speak.' This was manifested solely through his actions and his conduct of affairs." (Bloom, *Mencius*, 5A5)

"Heaven" here suggests a general sense of fate and destiny; not a strict predestination but a somewhat more open-ended evocation of legitimacy. If a ruler does not rule well he could lose the Mandate of Heaven and that could raise questions of abdication or removal from office. The process is focused on the elite. In the passage above, the practice is modeled on how lords and officers were appointed. But in the case of the top ruler, the Son of Heaven, we notice a role for "the people." They, like "Heaven," must accept the candidate. Further along in the same passage, Mencius goes on to describe how it works:

> When he put Shun in charge of the sacrifices, the spirits welcomed them. This is how Heaven accepted him. When he put Shun in charge of the nation's affairs, they were all ordered and the people were at peace. This is how the people accepted him. So Heaven gave it to him, and the people gave it to him. This is what I mean when I say the Son of Heaven cannot give all beneath Heaven to another. (Hinton, 9.5)

The people, their experience and reaction, are a measure of whether a ruler is doing the right thing. If the people are not at peace, if they are resisting or rejecting a ruler's policies, the legitimacy of that ruler is called into question. Mencius sums up this dynamic succinctly:

Heaven sees as my people see, Heaven hears as my people hear. (Bloom, 5A5)

The people are a vehicle for the expression of the Mandate of Heaven, the basis of political legitimation.

Now, it must be said, in his own time, and for centuries of Chinese history, Mencius's ideas on the role of the people in politics did not develop into a fully formed account of democratic politics. The people were not the source of sovereignty. Their role was largely reactive; they did not have agency. Now, however, when the idea of popular sovereignty is widespread across the globe, and embraced by the People's Republic of China (it purports to be a "People's Republic," after all), the rudimentary democratic-like suggestions of Mencius can take on a new meaning. Consulting the people is necessary to any process of leadership transition. And how might we best gauge the feelings of the people toward a particular candidate? Although Confucians might have the same concerns that the framers of the US Constitution had about the "rule of the mob," elections could be a means of discovering what the people see and hear.

And in modern democratic systems, Confucianism could serve at least two purposes, as suggested above: as a framework for assessing whether candidates maintain high ethical standards in fulfilling their family and social duties and thus being suitable exemplars; and as a guide for public policy to ensure that as many people as possible can carry out their duties with the dignity they deserve. It is not hard to conceive of a Confucian Party that would espouse those values and goals in a democratic political system.

Confucianism, like Daoism, does not have to be confined to any particular form of political regime. Neither is necessarily authoritarian nor democratic. And both can be adapted politically to an American democratic context.

Notes

1. Benjamin G. Bishin *et al.*, "Character Counts: Honesty and Fairness in Election 2000," *Public Opinion Quarterly*, 70 (2) (Summer 2006), pp. 235–248; Charles Prysby, "Perceptions of Candidate Character Traits and the Presidential Vote in 2004," *PS: Political Science and Politics*, 40 (January 2008), pp. 115–133.
2. Thomas E. Mann and Norman J. Ornstein, "Let's just say it: the Republicans are the problem," *The Washington Post*, April 27, 2012.

3. Adam Liptak, "After Ruling, Roberts Makes a Getaway From the Scorn," *New York Times*, July 2, 2012, p. A10; Dan Eggen, "Roberts health-care decision stuns many but is in line with his outlook," *The Washington Post*, June 28, 2012.

4. He is ambivalent on this point, however. He generally assumes that hereditary succession will produce humane leaders, but successors must still live up to and perform humanity. See: A.C. Graham, *Disputers of the Tao: Philosophical Argument in Ancient China* (Chicago, IL: Open Court Publishing, 1989), pp. 292–299.

5. William Nienhauser, ed. *The Grand Scribe's Records* (Bloomington, IN: Indiana University Press, 1994), vol. 1, pp. 11–12.

6. Yuk Wong, "Legalism," in Antonio S. Cua, ed., *Encyclopedia of Chinese Philosophy* (New York: Routledge, 2003), pp. 361–364.

7. A good starting point for learning about Xunzi is Paul R. Goldin, *The Confucians* (Berkeley, CA: University of California Press, 2011), Chapter 4, "Xunzi."

8. Justin Tiwald, "A Right of Rebellion in the *Mengzi*?" *Dao*, 7 (3) (September 2008), pp. 269–282.

9. The similarities between Confucianism and virtue ethics are explored in Bryan Van Norden, *Virtue Ethics and Consequentialism in Early Chinese Philosophy* (Cambridge: Cambridge University Press, 2007).

10. Hans-Georg Moeller, *The Philosophy of the Daodejing* (New York: Columbia University Press, 2006), Chapter 4, "Paradox Politics."

11. Ryan Lizza, "The Consequentialist: How the Arab Spring remade Obama's foreign policy," *The New Yorker*, May 2, 2011.

12. A.C. Graham, *Disputers of the Tao: Philosophical Argument in Ancient China* (Chicago, IL: Open Court Publishing, 1989), "Legalism and Lao-tsu," pp. 285–292.

13. Victoria Tin-Bor Hui, "How China Was Ruled," *The American Interest*, 3 (4) (March/April 2008).

14. Larry Diamond, *The Spirit of Democracy: The Struggle to Build Free Societies Throughout the World* (New York: Times Books, 2008).

15. For a rigorous analysis of how Confucian thought can authorize a more participatory politics, see Stephen C. Angle, *Contemporary Confucian Political Philosophy* (Cambridge, MA: Polity Press, 2012), especially Chapter 3, "Rethinking Authority and Rejecting Authoritarianism: Giving the People their Voice," pp. 36–57.

7

End of Life

> The prospect of death, for Confucians, creates particular social and famil-
> ial duties. If a terminally infirm parent asks for extraordinary medical
> intervention, children should generally comply. Conversely, should a par-
> ent ask that treatment be halted, a child should give that request serious
> consideration, but an ultimate decision must be based on the totality of
> circumstances. Similarly, when conditions warrant, parents must attend
> conscientiously to their children's end-of-life circumstances. Daoism in its
> philosophical expression, following its usual wuwei minimalism, is more
> skeptical of efforts to intervene medically at the end of life. When death is
> at hand, acceptance is Daoism's natural response.

It came unexpectedly. Aidan had experienced many medical difficulties in
his fourteen years; he had at least two near-death crises. His disabilities
were profound but he, and we, had always found a way to manage. The
thing that ultimately took his life was a common virus.

The ending began on a typical day. I was up early, ready to wash him
and dress him before heading out to work. He had not slept well the night
before, a bit of a cold was bothering him. When I peeked in to see how he
was doing, he was sleeping so soundly and comfortably that I decided to
forgo the morning ablutions and let him rest. Maureen could take care of
him a little later.

I was in the midst of lecturing to a class when my cellphone rang. It was
not my custom then to use a phone, much less bring it to class and leave it

Life, Liberty, and the Pursuit of Dao: Ancient Chinese Thought in Modern American Life,
First Edition. Sam Crane.
© 2013 John Wiley & Sons, Inc. Published 2013 by John Wiley & Sons, Inc.

on. But something had prompted me that morning to take it with me. As I raised the receiver to my ear, I could hear Maureen's distraught voice: "I'm taking him to the emergency room." She didn't have to say much more than that. We had been through upheavals before and I knew I had to get there immediately.

His cold had exploded into a extreme fever: 107.8 °F. Some of the doctors had never seen a fever so high. With his underlying seizure condition he was in severe danger. After a move to a larger medical center and a harrowing series of interventions over the next ten days, the final verdict came down on us: multiple organ failure. Aidan was dying. He had been placed on a respirator to assist with his breathing during the most aggressive period of treatment. At this point, however, further action was useless. One of the doctors came in and discussed taking him off the breathing apparatus.

Maureen and I were prepared for this eventuality, though the moment itself still came as a shock. We had seen Aidan slip to the edge of existence at least twice before. We understood the intricacies of a "do not resuscitate" order. He was leaving us and our job was to make him as comfortable as possible. We told the doctors to turn off the machines and we took him home.

Aidan died in his own bed in his own room, resting peacefully, with his parents by his side, on March 19, 2006, the last day of winter.

* * *

The Terri Schiavo story, which came to a crescendo and conclusion in 2005, riveted America's attention on the ethics of end-of-life issues. To review the most basic facts of the case: Terri had been profoundly disabled by a cardiac arrest in 1990 and lived in what some doctors termed a "persistent vegetative state" for many years. Her husband contended she had stated to him that she did not want to remain alive under such circumstances; her parents argued that she would have wanted to be kept alive. The courts consistently found her husband to be in the right. The battle focused on whether or not a feeding tube, which was her sole source of nutrition and hydration, should be taken out. It was removed on three occasions, restored twice, and the last removal resulted in her death by dehydration.[1]

The case garnered extensive media attention. It became a daily television drama; every aspect of the case was endlessly analyzed. The Florida legislature and courts, the US Congress and the president all intervened. The pope was invoked in a court filing. Its ultimate resolution, centered on the question of personal autonomy. Here is a strikingly clear statement from the Florida Court of Appeals, Second District:

> But in the end, this case is not about the aspirations that loving parents have for their children. It is about Theresa Schiavo's right to make her own decision, independent of her parents and independent of her husband.[2]

Although the evidence for establishing Terri's wishes seemed rather thin – several oral statements to her husband, his brother and sister-in-law – it was judged to be sufficient under Florida law.[3] Once her preferences were established, the legal system was destined to carry them out. The ruling assumption was that a person possesses his or her own body and, therefore, has clear and irrevocable authority over any medical interventions into that body.

There is a limit, however, under US law, for how far people can control their own bodies. While it is fairly well established that an individual can refuse medical treatment, such as a feeding tube, for oneself, it is also true that the Supreme Court has rejected the claim that there is a constitutional right to die, which would allow wider practice of doctor-assisted suicide. Euthanasia, actively causing the death of a person who may or may not be able to state his or her preferences, is illegal. However, assisted suicide, in which a physician or third party provides a person the means to end his or her life, is legal in Oregon and Washington (and Montana courts have accepted the idea but the legislature has not produced enabling laws).

A key distinction in working through questions of end-of-life care, assisted suicide, and euthanasia is, on the one hand, allowing a person to die, by withholding certain treatment, versus actively causing a death, usually by administering certain drugs.[4] Generally, we are allowed to let ourselves and others die; we cannot kill; and, outside of Oregon and Washington, we cannot assist in causing someone's death.

For classical liberals the Schiavo case fell in the "let her die" category. Once her preferences were determined, the courts allowed her, through the agency of her husband, to refuse treatment. From a liberal perspective, this is all well and good: personal autonomy ought to rule end-of-life decisions. The pain and suffering of spouses or parents or children are not sufficient to deny an individual's right to die passively from refusing medical treatment. Also, for liberals, claims that others might make about the sanctity of every individual life should not obstruct the will of an individual who has decided to forgo medical care. From this perspective, Terri Schiavo's death was not problematic, only its intense publicity was.

For sanctity of life advocates, the Schiavo case was more controversial. Some would look at her medical condition and agree that removing her feeding tube was a matter of letting her die. The cause of her death would be her inability to ingest food and water, brought on by her "persistent vegetative state." The liberal Catholic journal, *Commonweal* argued in an editorial:

> To insist that Schiavo be kept alive indefinitely because technology enables us to do so is to embrace vitalism; it is to elevate mere physical existence over all other values. The questions Schiavo's guardians must answer are, What benefit will she gain, and what burdens is she being subjected to, in being kept alive in her condition? Is the preservation of the life of someone in a permanent vegetative state actually a benefit to that person? Is it a just allocation of limited resources? Traditionally, Catholicism has answered no. Nothing in Schiavo's case presents a persuasive reason for thinking that teaching is erroneous[5]

But Pope John Paul II, in an address to a meeting of physicians and ethicists in March 2005 – at the denouement of the Schiavo affair and shortly before his own death – argued quite the opposite: the "administration of food and water, even when provided by artificial means, always represents a natural means of preserving life, not a medical act." Providing food and water, even through a tube, is "in principle, ordinary and proportionate, and as such, morally obligatory."[6] From this point of view the withholding of food and water is itself the cause of death.

One implication of the pope's position is that the suffering of the individual is not sufficient to override the sanctity of that individual's life. Indeed, it is in suffering that sanctity is realized. If one is suffering, one cannot invoke a right to be allowed to die; rather, one must bear the suffering and accept even unwanted provision of food and water.

Interestingly, a similar argument is advanced in a somewhat more secular form, centering on the inherent dignity and rights of every person, by conservatives.[7] By this account, personal autonomy does not allow us to control our end-of-life circumstances. An individual, invested with a universal dignity and rights, cannot contradict an objective standard of "worthy care" even if he or she wants to. The inviolability of the human dignity natural to all persons trumps any personal calculations of what may or may not be dignified.

These, then, are two prominent arguments that slug it out when controversial end-of-life cases come along: *personal autonomy* that empowers individuals to determine when and how they should be allowed to die versus *universal duty* that strives to preserve every life, even against the wishes of an individual facing death.

Confucianism on death and dying

A modern day Confucian would sympathize with Terri Schiavo's parents. That understanding, however, would be based on reasons other than those put forth by the parents themselves. Confucians would not expend as much energy on the struggle to interpret Terri's final wishes, because they would hold that other factors must also be weighed. Personal autonomy is not inviolable to a Confucian. Neither is Confucianism as concerned about a universalized sanctity of life or dignity. The particularistic quality of Confucian ethics would keep open a variety of acceptable outcomes, depending on the circumstances involved. In some cases, contingent upon the cast of relevant familial and social actors, a Confucian outlook might agree with letting a person die; in other cases, it might advocate keeping a person alive. Moreover, the conditionality of a Confucian moral calculus might also come to the conclusion that assisted suicide or even euthanasia could be appropriate. It is the social context of the Schiavo case, particularly the fact that her parents attached so much value to keeping her alive and seemed willing to participate in her care, that would lead a Confucian to assign greater significance to their claims than did the US legal system.

Confucius leavens the grim inevitability of death with a hope for moral fulfillment. On the one hand, he is accepting of mortality when it comes at the end of a long life well lived, or when traded for an advance of humanity. But he is saddened and shocked, and perhaps might be moved to intervene to prolong a life, when death comes too soon, robbing the world of a person who is conscientiously fulfilling familial and social duties.

In the *Analects*, Confucius asserts that moral purposes can take precedence over the defense of an individual life:

The Master said, The man of high ideals, the humane person, never tries to go on living if it is harmful to humaneness. There are times when he sacrifices his life to preserve humaneness. (Watson, 15.9)

If an ethical objective requires death, then death should be accepted. Of course, the moral aims that might take precedence over life are clear to Confucians: they would emanate primarily from filial and familial responsibilities. Mencius echoes this idea in his famous comparison of fish and bear paws, both considered culinary delicacies:

> Mencius said: "I want fish, and I also want bear paws. If I can't have both, I'll give up fish and take bear paws. I want life, and I also want duty. If I can't have both, I'll give up life and take duty. I want life – but there's something I want more than life, so I won't do wrong just to stay alive. I loathe death – but there's something I loathe more than death, so there are disasters I won't avoid." (Hinton, 11.10)

The implications of "duty" – *yi* – or "rightness" or "moral appropriateness" are that we should attend to our parents and siblings and spouses, and when those duties are accomplished we can then extend our obligations to friends and neighbors and acquaintances. And that graduated series of relationships should shape our responses to end-of-life questions.

In the first instance, this seems to suggest that children should be willing to face death in order to fulfill their filial obligations. That might be a bit extreme, but certainly children should be prepared to endure hardship in serving their parents. More generally, the idea here is that the value of any life is determined by its moral accomplishment, or the experience of conscientiously performing one's obligations. One who is willing to give up life in the name of duty comes closer to the ideal of humanity than one who is unwilling. Living a morally appropriate life is a greater good than just living life. Some lives, those that have come closer to perfecting humanity, could therefore be more valuable than others. In terms of end-of-life care, it would thus be justifiable to consider the moral standing of a patient in determining the extent to which life saving or preserving care is provided.

On the other side of the equation, some lives, for Confucius, are rather less valuable, as is intimated here:

> Yuan Rang sat waiting on his haunches.
> When he arrived, the Master said: "Showing no deference or respect when young, accomplishing nothing worth handing down when grown, and refusing to die when old – such people are nothing but pests."
> At that, flicking his walking-stick, the Master cracked Yuan on the shin. (Hinton, 14.43)

People who have lived morally deficient lives – "accomplishing nothing worth handing down when grown" – should not refuse to die. Of course, there is no implication here that they should be killed. Confucianism is generally averse to killing. Rather, this sort of person, if facing a terminal medical condition, would seem to have less of a claim to being kept alive by extraordinary means, especially if such action would take resources away from keeping other, more deserving, people alive. This is not an absolute restriction, however. Moral judgment, for Confucianism, depends on the standpoint of the individual making a decision about right action. The son or daughter of a dissolute father or mother, bound by filial obligation, might need to work to keep a parent alive, if that is the parent's wish. He or she might dutifully seek the help of others in this task. Those others, however, not beholden by filiality, could respond based on the moral reckoning suggested in *Analects* 14.43. They would not be categorically obligated to help, but they could be moved by the opportunity of preserving a particularly honorable life or repelled by prospect of saving someone undeserving.

Such calculations are not wholly individualistic. A person's moral worth is established within a social context. If a depraved father has an exceptionally filial son, then the moral value of that relationship, and other relationships that it intersects, is greater than a bond of bad father with a bad son. This was the case with the legendary sage-king Shun. His father was infamously immoral, but Shun consistently maintained the highest standard of filial respect and care. Ultimately, after much turmoil, the father was transformed, coming to appreciate his son's extraordinary virtue. This story suggests that an apparently bad person who is embedded in a positive familial relationship could be worthy of preservation. Moreover, the mere existence of the father, regardless of his deplorable acts, was central to Shun's perfection of humanity. Shun would not have been the exemplary leader he was without his relationship with his father. If his father had fallen gravely ill, Shun would have extended life-saving care to him and he might have argued that hospital staff and others should participate in that care in order to preserve the humanity-generating father–son relationship. This is not a defense for being a bad father; Confucians would urge all fathers to be better than Shun's. But it does indicate that determining whether a person's life should be saved requires, for a Confucian, consideration of the moral quality of the familial relationships and social networks in which that person is embedded.

Children, of course, have a primary Confucian obligation to care for their parents. There is, however, no absolute rule on how exactly this is to be done. A child's response to a parent's demise should take into account a parent's wishes, as suggested in *Analects* 2.5:

> Meng Yizi asked about filial conduct. The Master replied: "Do not act contrary." Fan Chi was driving the Master's chariot, and the Master informed him further: "Meng Yizi asked me about filial conduct, and I replied: 'Do not act contrary.'" Fan Chi asked: "What did you mean by that?" The Master replied: "While they are living, serve them according to the observances of ritual propriety; when they are dead, bury them and sacrifice to them according to the observances of ritual propriety." (Ames and Rosemont).

Thus, if a parent has a living will that directly states that no efforts at resuscitation should be attempted in the event of cardiac arrest, a filial child would be bound to take that into account. The parent's wishes should be given significant consideration, but they are not necessarily conclusive. A conscientious child will weigh all of the contextual variables – the age of the parent, the moral accomplishment of the parent, the views of other family members – to make a final decision. It might be that, as with Shun and his decision to marry without telling his parents, filiality might best be realized in disobeying parents, keeping them alive even when they say they want to die. The correct outcome will emerge from the moral discernment of the child, and will become a reflection of his or her ethical accomplishment.

Short of end-of-life issues, children, as a matter of general filial duty, certainly have a duty to provide care and comfort for parents as they experience the limitations of old age. This responsibility may be carried out in a variety of ways. There is no fixed Confucian requirement that a parent live in a child's house or that the child personally perform the parent's intimate health care. But neither should children pack off parents to substandard nursing homes and forget about them. Children must be engaged with their parents' care; they must take responsibility for the provision of high-quality care; and they must be continually and regularly involved, emotionally and rationally, in their parents' care. Otherwise, as *Analects* 2.7 states: " . . . they may as well be feeding animals" (Hinton). If a child cannot be there, due to conflicting obligations to his own children or spouse, he should make sure compassionate and capable people are providing the care. If a child can be there, he should oversee or even take on the care duties himself. The closer and more involved, the better.

Conversely, parents also have a responsibility to care for their children. Although Confucius and Mencius do not say much about this parental duty, *Analects* 17.21 links the care parents give to children to the mourning children owe their parents when they die, a fundamental filial obligation:

> It is only after being tended by his parents for three years that an infant can finally leave their bosom. The ritual of a three-year mourning period for one's parents is practiced throughout the empire. Certainly Zaiwo received this three years of loving care from his parents. (Ames and Rosemont, 17.21)

The parental role here seems to be stated in empirical terms, while the children's response is normative: parents *do* care for children, therefore, children *should* mourn for parents. But Mencius puts more of a normative gloss on parental care of children when he presents it as a moral equivalent of filial duty:

> Therefore, an enlightened ruler will regulate the people's livelihood so as to ensure that, above, they have enough to serve their parents and, below, they have enough to support their wives and children. (Bloom, 1A7)

A person should care for his children just as he cares for his parents. Thus, if a child is critically ill or near death, parents are obliged to care for them. Indeed, if caring for children is an ethical counterpart to caring for parents, then caring for a sick or dying child is a fundamental means of creating and reproducing humanity in the world. That is why Confucians would sympathize with Terri Schiavo's parents.

In the Schiavo case, a Confucian would push against the Florida Court of Appeals, especially the first line of statement quoted above: "But in the end, this case is not about the aspirations that loving parents have for their children." Quite to the contrary, Confucianism would have demanded that Terri's personal preference not be wholly determinative. Her preferences should have been considered in relation to the views of her parents, her husband, her siblings, even her closest friends. Any disagreement among these various parties should have been settled through evaluation of the *social value* of continuing her life. If her family members had shown that their own progress toward humanity would have been enhanced by keeping her alive, then, for a Confucian, it would have been better to maintain her care, especially if the family members themselves are performing the care in an immediate and loving way, and she herself was in no pain, even if that violated her wishes. Had her parents and siblings taken up the daily work of her care – washing her, dressing her, sitting her up, lying her down, changing her diapers – the routine performance of these loving relationships would have been a moral benefit for all involved, Terri included. It would have been what Confucius meant by ritual: the regular enactment, in actions large and small, of our social duties. The ritual purpose and meaning of her life would be enough to justify the food flowing through the tube.

In other circumstance a different outcome might be warranted. If Terri's parents had not argued for the moral benefits of continuing her life, there would have been no Confucian grounds to keep her alive. Had they decided that she had lived a good life but it was now at an end, or that they simply could not take on the continuing obligation of her care, given her precarious medical condition, Confucianism would not demand that they keep her alive. Confucians would resist the notion that there is a universal dignity or sanctity of every life that might somehow override the decisions reached by the social network of the person facing death. The pope's argument and the secular conservative contention would both be rejected.

Removing the feeding tube, in and of itself, would not have had as much significance to a Confucian as it had for the pope. Terri was in dire straits and would have died much earlier if aggressive medical interventions had not been performed (she had initially collapsed fifteen years before, in 1990, and would have passed away then but for heroic treatment). Her parents were thus faced with a highly unusual situation, well beyond customary parental obligations. Had they felt that they could not maintain the feeding tube, that it was beyond what they believed reasonable or was obstructing their capacity to carry out other family duties, then they could rightfully let her die.

Confucius recognizes the inevitability of death. Heaven – in the ancient Chinese sense of fate or destiny – governs life's end and when the time comes there is nothing we can do but lament, as he himself did for two of his followers:

> Boniu was very ill, and the Master went to visit him. Grasping his hand through the portal he said, "We are losing him, and there is nothing we can do. But that this man should have this illness, and there is nothing we can do! That this man should have such an illness!" (Ames and Rosemont, 6.10)

> When Yan Hui died, the Master cried: "Oh my! Tian [heaven] is the ruin of me! Tian [heaven] is the ruin of me!" (Ames and Rosemont, 11.9)

These were good men, especially Yan Hui, his most loyal and virtuous disciple who died young. Presumably, had the technology been available,

Confucius would have wanted to preserve their lives. He may have argued in favor of a feeding tube for each of them.

Confucius, however, would not have created a universal rule that would apply to all cases. The idea of legislating regulations for end-of-life situations would be abhorrent to him. Whether or not care is continued should rest upon those who are involved in the patient's closest social circle and the totality of the circumstances surrounding the case. It would be impossible to attempt to predict and prejudge all the possible situations and reasons for withdrawing a feeding tube and create some sort of general law. What would matter to a Confucian would be adherence to the core value of humane action. As long as the people involved in the decision were carefully considering the best outcome for all concerned, then a tube could be removed or left alone, depending on particular conditions. Intention and sincerity are what matter for a Confucian: if those are genuine, then the result will be morally acceptable.

As a practical matter, in the contemporary United States, it would be virtually impossible, politically and legally, to deny individual rights in end-of-life cases. A modified Confucian view, therefore, could only expect a procedural change: that the views of relevant social participants be solicited and weighed and, perhaps, a period of time be set aside before treatment is withheld, to allow for all concerned to find their peace.

Ironically, Confucianism would agree with liberals on keeping open the possibility of assisted suicide or even euthanasia. Again, the grounds for such decision would not be a liberal assertion of personal autonomy and control over one's body. Rather, the rationale would be rooted in the deliberation of the key members of relevant relationships, and the immediate circumstances. If an elderly parent with a late-stage terminal illness stated a clear preference for assisted suicide, and conscientious children accepted that this would be a humane action, then Confucians would not want the state to stand in the way of that action. It is a matter for those immediately concerned. Obviously, children should not kill their parents, but if a father or mother faces a painful end-of-life condition and seeks aid in reaching a near and inevitable death, then sons and daughters can rightfully provide that aid.

In the end, the Schiavo case would have posed some difficulties for a Confucian. On the one hand, the claims of the parents would be apposite. The prospect of their continuing involvement in her care, and the humanity-generating possibilities of that outcome, could have been a good result. But the objections of the husband, another moral agent in the case, weakened the social basis for keeping her alive. In a perfect Confucian world perhaps the claim of the parents would supersede that of the husband. He could have gone his way and permitted the feeding tube to remain; they could have stayed and looked after her. That this might have violated Terri's own preferences would not have made the difference: the social value of keeping her alive might have been greater than her apparent desire to die.

But the parents would eventually die, and what then? Would there be people in close enough relationship with Terri to maintain conscientious attention to her needs? There is nothing worse in a Confucian moral universe than social abandonment. We cannot find our humanity in isolation. Maybe, in a somewhat different way, that is what Terri herself feared. She might have anticipated that a "persistent vegetative state" would undermine her capacity for social reciprocity, which is needed for the realization of humanity. Even with her parents' care, she may not have been able to do what she needed to do to fulfill her own familial and social duties. If she had argued that she should not be kept alive because, under the circumstances, she would be "accomplishing nothing worth handing down," then perhaps a Confucian could not refuse to let her die.

Daoism on death and dying

Death is a major theme of *Zhuangzi*. At various points in the text, we are counseled to embrace the inevitable, to detach ourselves from the desire to preserve life beyond its natural bounds. The *Daodejing* (Hinton, 50), too, tells us that those who are preoccupied with staying alive in effect move themselves inexorably into the place of death: "People born into life enter death." There is no escape; acceptance is the only real option; anything else is distraction that can undermine our experience of life. Philosophical Daoists would thus be firmly in the "let her die" camp in the Schiavo case. Indeed, a Daoist may have resisted the earliest efforts to aggressively treat her cardiac arrest. Her life had naturally ended that day, and subsequent efforts produced more heartbreak and suffering than anything else.

Zhuangzi tells a story in Chapter 6 that speaks to many of issues of the Schiavo case, about four friends who share with each other their feelings about physical demise and death. This excerpt, which bears quotation at length, instructs the reader to get free from the fear of death and be open to the transformations of the end of life:

> All at once Master Yu fell ill. Master Si went to ask how he was. "Amazing!" said Master Yu. "The Creator is making me all crookedy like this! My back sticks up like a hunchback and my vital organs are on top of me. My chin is hidden in my navel, my shoulders are up above my head, and my pigtail points to the sky. It must be some dislocation of the yin and yang!"
>
> Yet he seemed calm at heart and unconcerned. Dragging himself haltingly to the well, he looked at his reflection and said, "My, my! So the Creator is making me all crookedy like this!"
>
> "Do you resent it?" asked Master Si.
>
> "Why, no, what would I resent?" If the process continues, perhaps in time he'll transform my left arm into a rooster. In that case I'll keep watch on the night. Or perhaps in time he'll transform my right arm into a crossbow pellet and I'll shoot down an owl for roasting. Or perhaps in time he'll transform my buttocks into cartwheels. Then, with my spirit for a horse, I'll climb up and go for a ride. What need will I ever have for a carriage?
>
> "I received life because the time had come; I will lose it because the order of things passes on. Be content with this time and dwell in this order and then neither sorrow nor joy can touch you. In ancient times this was called the "freeing of the bound." There are those who cannot free themselves, because they are bound by things. But nothing can ever win against Heaven – that's the way it's always been. What would I have to resent?" (Watson 84–85)

This is more than simple acceptance; it is irreverent celebration of bodily collapse. Master Yu is dying, his form disfiguring, but in the face of anatomical breakdown, he marvels at the changes he is experiencing. He pointedly rejects resentment. Not only will he bear what others might interpret as misfortune, he will make fun of it. If his left arm is disabled, he will use it in a whimsical manner. Zhuangzi here fundamentally shifts the discourse on death and dying. The Confucian mood of tragedy and ethical evaluation are cast aside. Death, for Zhuangzi, is not something to mourn and resist. There is no need to search for moral meaning. Mortality is a certainty that should be recognized and appreciated, perhaps like a beautiful summer sunset or a colorful autumn forest.

The reference to a "Creator" should not be taken as a nod toward theism, mono- or otherwise. For philosophical Daoists, there are no creator-gods or god overseeing the processes of life and death in the universe. There is only *Dao*, a never-ending and never-beginning totality of all things unfolding together now and for ever. And in that all-inclusive sense *Dao* is the creator of all things and the killer of all things; but it is not a "god" in the usual sense of that word.

It must be noted, however, that religious Daoism takes a rather different view on death, one that places greater value on naturalistic strategies for prolonging life. This view can lead to a sort of resistance against death, or at least an aversion to mortality.[8] Indeed, within the totality of Daoist thought, philosophical and religious together, this may be one of the most conspicuous disparities: the texts of the *Daodejing* and *Zhuangzi* convey a strong philosophic sense of acceptance of death, but religious interpreters and practitioners have found there justifications for immortality. Since our focus is philosophic, we will continue in that vein, noting, however, that even religious Daoists would likely reject much modern medical technology surrounding the Schiavo case as "unnatural."

In the final paragraph of the passage above we can see that philosophic sense of morality. Life and death come in their own time, on their own terms. We are merely transient recipients. And if we understand that, and don't attempt to defy the routine movement from life to death, we can free ourselves of the bonds of sorrow and resentment. Further on in this same section Zhuangzi recapitulates this idea:

> This Mighty Mudball of a world burdens us with a body, troubles us with life, eases us with old age, and with death gives us rest. We call our life a blessing, so our death must be a blessing too. (Hinton, 93)

These same lines are repeated in *Zhuangzi*, Chapter 6, suggesting the author wants to draw special attention to them. We should neither fear death nor worship life. Worldly immortality, in the sense of extending the physical life of the body, is impossible. Existence is shaped by forces beyond our control: fate, destiny, chance, "Heaven." No one can ultimately direct the course of his or her life. Zhuangzi is fairly clear on this point:

> Life and death are fated – constant as the succession of dark and dawn, a matter of Heaven. There are some things which man can do nothing about – all are a matter of the nature of creatures. (Watson, 80)

From this perspective, defining end-of-life issues in terms of individual autonomy or universal duty makes little sense. Daoists would not recognize personal autonomy to the extent that is common in the United States today.

They would acknowledge the unique character of each living thing and the equal value of all things, but they would place each individual in a broader natural context shaped by complex webs of interdependence. This is what is meant by *Dao*, as in this passage from *Zhuangzi*:

> So the real is originally there in things, and the sufficient is originally there in things. There's nothing that is not real, and nothing that is not sufficient.
>
> Hence, the blade of grass and the pillar, the leper and the ravishing Xi Shi, the noble, the sniveling, the disingenuous, the strange – in Dao they all move as one and the same. In difference is the whole; in wholeness is the broken. Once they are neither whole nor broken, all things move freely as one and the same again. (Hinton, 23)

Individuals are distinct, each with its own character and prospects and story; but none can be separated from its context. Property cannot be alienated. Self-possession cannot be sustained. We come to believe that we are independent but we never really are. It is *in Dao* – embedded in the totality of all things existing together – that "all move as one and the same."

This identity of all things – moving as one and the same – vitiates autonomy. We usually think of autonomy as freedom from external influence that distinguishes us from others. For Zhuangzi, this is simply a matter of perspective: if we look for difference, we will see it; but if we look for sameness, we will see that as well. Both sameness and difference exist simultaneously. We can never wholly escape sameness to establish a unique difference that would authorize something like individual autonomy. In the passage below, Zhuangzi again impersonates Confucius and talks about how it is that a man who has had his foot cut off has come to be a respected teacher:

> "If you see the world in terms of difference," replied Confucius, "there are liver and gallbladder, there are Ch'u lands and Yueh lands. But seen in terms of sameness, the ten thousand things are all one. If you understand this, you forget how eye and ear could love this and hate that. Then the mind wanders the accord of Integrity. And if you see the identity of things, you see there can be no loss. So it is that he saw nothing more in a lost foot than a clump of dirt tossed aside." (Hinton, 68)

Modern Americans might worry about a loss of autonomy, an idea that Zhuangzi would find amusing, since there was nothing to lose in the first place. We might also think of autonomy as enabling us to exercise our free will and do something significant in the world. But Daoists hold that we depend on nature for our survival; we are tossed by fate and forces beyond our reach. We cannot control our surroundings. So, it is better that we do nothing, or little. The fatalism and minimalism of *wuwei* suggest that we cannot break free from and master our circumstances. *Daodejing* 23 reads in part:

> Fierce winds don't last the whole morning;
> Torrential rains don't last the whole day.
> Who makes these things?
> If even Heaven and Earth can't make them last long –
> How much the more is this true for man?!
> (Henricks)

There is a sense of freedom here. Burton Watson, in his Introduction, suggests that freedom is the one word that might best summarize Zhuangzi's thought.[9] But this is a freedom not of an individual at liberty to do whatever he or she wants, but a freedom rooted in a recognition of dependence. It is a selfless freedom, not a selfish freedom:

> If you serve your own mind, joy and sorrow rarely appear. If you know what's beyond your control, if you know it follows its own inevitable nature and you live at peace – that is Integrity perfected. Children and ministers inevitably find that much is beyond them. But if you forget about yourself and always do what circumstances require of you, there's no time to cherish life and despise death. Then you do what you can, and whatever happens is fine. (Hinton, 54)

In order to "serve your own mind" you must "forget about yourself." The only way to realize something close to independence, then, is to accept your dependence on circumstance and what is beyond your control. While this may well be a form of freedom, a kind of extensive negative liberty freeing us from the social obstacles that block our direct experience of dependence within *Dao*, it is not the autonomy of Western liberalism.

Turning back to the Schiavo case, it is obvious that appeals to Terri's autonomy would not be recognized by Daoists. Terri did not control her fate; none of us do. Death was upon her and trying to avoid that stark reality was futile. While her parents may have wanted to prolong her life, their desires were destined to fail since "... nothing can ever win against Heaven."

Regarding the appeal to universal dignity, Daoists are more radical than Confucians in their rejection of the sanctity of life in general or any one life in particular. For Daoists, each thing in the universe has a unique integrity unto itself and a destiny of its own. Destiny, here, is not predestined by some suprahuman god; it is immanent in each particular thing. All things are flowing in Way and "move as one and the same," but each is sufficient and real unto itself. While there is a basic sameness of all things in their coincidence in Way, there is also is a fundamental incommensurability of things. The experience of one cannot be used to understand or judge the experience of another. This is the message of the first chapter of *Zhuangzi*, which starts out describing enormous mythical animals:

> In Northern Darkness there lives a fish called Kun. This Kun is so huge that it stretches who knows how many thousand miles. When it changes into a bird it's called Peng. This Peng has a back spreading who knows how many thousand miles, and when it thunders up into flight its wings are like clouds hung clear across the sky. (Hinton, 3)

But when a small quail hears this story it makes no sense:

> A quail laughs and says: "It's setting out for where? I bound into flight, and before I've soared a dozen yards I'm fluttering around in the brush again. Surely that's the limit of flight. It's setting out for where?" (Hinton, 6)

Small cannot comprehend or assess large; nor large small. There is no point outside of any particular individual's context that would allow for objective observation and evaluation. And, therefore, there is no possibility for an enforceable universal moral standard. Good and bad, right and wrong inhere in the constitution of each particular thing. Bad things will happen, and really cannot be stopped from happening – the indifference of *wuwei* stretches into the realm of morality:

> Way is the mystery of these ten thousand things.
> It's a good person's treasure
> And an evil person's refuge.
> Its beautiful words are bought and sold
> And its noble deeds are gifts enriching people.
> It never abandons even the evil among us.
> (Hinton, *Daodejing*, 62)

This is not really nihilism. While evil continues to exist, it, too, is limited within its own particularities. Moreover, there is a "harm principle" of sorts in Daoism. One should generally not infringe upon the life's course of other things. Killing is generally prohibited. Even if Daoists recognize that people adore "tortuous paths" (i.e., actions that might lead them away from their natural integrity within Way), there is a clear preference for pacifistic, simplistic, ascetic, yielding, and accepting behavior. To the extent to which people are free to choose one action over another, and such choice is obviously limited by circumstance, they should choose the good over the bad. For some, however, their inevitable natures will drive them toward hurtful or selfish acts. These people will meet their ultimate fate, their lives will end as all do, but we should not believe that we can extinguish all evil or create a legal framework that will effectively and extensively counteract or prevent bad behavior or enforce some understanding of the good.

So where does this leave us with the Schiavo case? The very idea that a law covering such intensely personal affairs could be drafted and impersonally applied to a wide array of diverse individuals would be anathema to Daoists. The actions of the Florida legislature and the United States Congress, futile as they were, would clearly be beyond the pale of reasonable behavior for Zhuangzi and the authors of the *Daodejing*.

Although they would not be absolute in their thinking, Daoists would have counseled those involved to let Terri die. Yielding to Terri's death would be in keeping with the general Daoist aversion to purposive human action aimed at changing the course of nature. Ironically, philosophical Daoists would agree with the liberal Catholic position that it was her underlying inability to eat or drink that would be the cause of her death. The extent of her initial injuries and the great efforts that the family originally made to try to improve her situation would have been deemed more than enough justification for allowing her life to end. It was her fate; cruel, perhaps, but unalterable. Better to find joy in the life she had than to try to deny the inevitable finish she faced.

Whereas "letting die" is acceptable, "causing death," as in assisted suicide or euthanasia, would, at first, seem to run counter to Daoist ideas. A final determination on any specific case, however, would depend upon the severity of the intervention required. If a person was in the early stages of a terminal illness and wanted to be shot in the head, a Daoist would likely recoil. The timing and quality of such action would violate the general *wuwei* ethic of not taking action that runs counter to the natural unfolding of things. The patient might want to argue that the "natural course" in this instance inevitably results in death, but the Daoist response would be: every life faces a similar fate; why intervene so abruptly in this one as opposed to any other? Alternatively, were an individual closer to the end, suffering from intense pain, and asking for drugs that would bring death, a Daoist might see this as more justifiable. After all, that person is not trying to contradict Heaven, and he might be seen as being true to his inevitable nature by simply finishing what has already begun. In any event, Daoism would not create any hard and fast rules. It would simply offer some general judgments without demanding absolute adherence.

As to suffering, Daoists would not find in it the sanctifying virtue that Pope John Paul II did. In the story of the four friends, Zhaungzi does not mention pain. If, however, a physical condition became truly unbearable, the tenets of Daoism, which tells us to look forward to death as a blessing, would tolerate the hastening of an end, should the sufferer so desire.

Mourning

When a loved one dies, however he or she has died, feelings of loss and grief naturally arise in those closest to the deceased. Confucianism believes that these emotions are the deepest wellsprings of humanity, the most fundamental sentiments of human love. Instead of denying grief, Confucius and Mencius tell us to cultivate it, to bring it into the center of our daily lives through conscientious mourning. Thoughtful practices of bereavement are central to the Confucian idea of ritual. We need to think carefully about how best to commemorate family members and others worthy of remembrance, and we need to consistently carry out those rites.

In their own time, Confucius and Mencius held to a tradition of a "three year" mourning period for parents. In practice, this was not thirty-six months; the idea was to extend mourning into the third year, something along the lines of twenty-five to twenty-seven months.[10] The main point is to take a significant amount of time, step back from other responsibilities, especially from the mundane demands of work, and find a way of integrating mourning into daily life. And people, Confucius assumed, would want to do this, because the emotional impact of death is so profound it can only be absorbed and diffused over an extended period of time. A lack of profound grief was abnormal, a sign of moral degeneration to Confucius:

> The Master said, "What could I see in a person who in holding a position of influence is not tolerant, who in observing ritual propriety is not respectful, and who in overseeing the mourning rites does not grieve!" (Ames and Rosemont, *Analects*, 3.26)

The purpose of Confucian mourning is not only to facilitate emotional catharsis; it also heightens our ethical awareness in other aspects of our lives going forward. The loss of a loved one shocks us into self-revelation:

> Master Zeng said, I have heard our Master say, People never fully express what is in them. If one had to cite an exception, it would be when they are mourning a parent. (Watson, 19.17)

In fully expressing our true selves, we are more able to engage in self-examination. We reflect upon our responsibilities and obligations. That process of turning inward to scrutinize the conscience is fundamental to the more general Confucian practice of enacting duty through ritual to progress toward humanity. Mencius picks up this same theme with a story about a prince whose father has died.

The prince inquires of Mencius, through an intermediary, how best to ritualize mourning for his father, and Mencius sends back fairly standard Confucian advice:

> ... in the three years' mourning, the garments of coarse cloth and the diet of rice gruel were shared in common by the three dynasties and extended to everyone from the Son of Heaven to the common people. (Bloom, 3A2)

Notice how daily life is affected: dress and diet are changed to convey the inner sense of loss. The prince, who admits he was never good at attending to such matters, decides he will follow the Confucian way and undertake an abstinent and austere three year mourning. But he runs into a dilemma with his local advisers:

> The family elders and the high officials did not concur in this and said: "None of the former princes of our ancestral house of Lu practices this, nor did any of our former princes. For you to take it upon yourself to contravene what they did is unacceptable. Moreover, the Record says, 'In the observance of mourning and sacrifice, one follows the elders.'" They said, "We have a source for this." (Bloom, 3A2)

Here we have a conundrum rather like Shun's problem of marrying but not informing his parents: two competing moral directives, each with its own basis in Confucian ethics. Should he follow the general prescription of a three year mourning period or should he listen to his elders and follow the ritual traditions of his people? For the prince this in not merely an intellectual question. He is grieving the loss of his father and needs to find for himself the best way to settle that deep sorrow. Indeed, Mencius, in this same passage, reminds him that, in working through these sorts of problems, " . . . he cannot turn to anyone outside himself." Only the prince knows how best to tap into his emotions and connect them with a social practice that expresses, in a manner appropriate to his cultural context, the moral significance of his father's life.

Ultimately, the prince decides to enact Confucian mourning practices, which involve moving into a modest hut as well as other abstemious behavior, but only for a period of five months. The local elders find this proper and, presumably, since his final decision was the result of conscientious self-reflection, it would meet with Mencius's approval.

The prince's experience provides a model for applying Confucian principles of mourning to modern circumstances. First, and most importantly, we must mourn and we must find a means of mourning that allows for both personal catharsis and social commemoration. Second, while established rituals for mourning within particular cultural or religious communities should be recognized and respected, they need not harden into absolute and unvarying standards. Genuine bereavement, like other forms of Confucian ritual, must reflect the particular moral character of the mourner. It must come from the inside out and express the emotional disposition of the individuals involved. Mencius says: "Weeping for the dead should be out of grief and not for the sake of the living" (Bloom, 7B33). It is not a show for others but a manifestation of one's self. And when it is done right it not only eases the pain and sadness of those left; it also adds to the moral achievement of the compassionate and introspective mourners.

Zhuangzi is having none of this. For him, while there certainly is an emotional sense of loss when a loved one dies, there is no good reason to expand upon that feeling and build it into something so conspicuous as Confucian mourning. He tells a story about two men who are happily singing over their dead friend's corpse, in obvious contravention of ritual propriety. And, just to leave no doubt that this is a better response to death than a more elaborate funeral service, Zhuangzi sarcastically ventriloquizes Confucius to approve of their behavior:

> [Adept Kung asks:] "Can you explain such strange men?"
> [Confucius answers:] "They may be strange to people but they are kindred to heaven"(Hinton, 96)

This Confucius-against-Confucius trope is used again in another *Zhuangzi* passage recounting a son's sorrowless response to his mother's death. Here, we have the sage instructing his most virtuous student, Yan Hui, on the wisdom of not grieving, pointing out that the apparently wayward son, "... has mastered it all... He's stepped beyond mere understanding" (Hinton, 96). This invokes the Daoist idea that conscious human thought and planning, as opposed to unmediated acquiescence, are meaningless in the vast unruliness of Dao. If the son knows that death is inevitable, and that his mother has fulfilled her time of life, and thus his grief is limited and comforted by that awareness; he has, in a sense, stepped "beyond mere understanding" to perceive that elaborate mourning accomplishes nothing. This may sound harsh, but in Zhuangzi's eccentric response to the death of his wife, we can see compassion at work:

> Zhuangzi's wife died. When Huizi went to convey his condolences, he found Zhuangzi sitting with his legs sprawled out, pounding on a tub and singing. "You lived with her, she brought up your children and grew old," said Huizi. "It should be enough simply not to weep at her death. But pounding on a tub and singing – this is going too far, isn't it?"
>
> Zhuangzi said: "You're wrong. When she first died, do you think I didn't grieve like anyone else? But I looked back to her beginning and the time before she was born. Not only the time before she was born, but the time before she had a body. Not only the time before she had a body, but the time before she had a spirit. In the midst of the jumble of wonder and mystery a change took place and she had a spirit. Another change and she had a body. Another change and she was born. Now there's been another change and she's dead. It's just like the progression of the four seasons, spring, summer, fall, winter."
>
> "Now she's going to lie down peacefully in a vast room. If I were to follow after her bawling and sobbing, it would show that I don't understand anything about fate. So I stopped." (Watson, 191–192)

Zhuangzi loved his wife. When she died, he lamented "like anyone else." But that initial sadness gave way to the realization that she had simply experienced a transformation that all will move through. She was gone from his life. There was nothing he could do about that. Fate had taken her and he could not know what the afterlife was like. So, he imagined her lying down peacefully in a vast room, no longer beset by the travails of human existence, resting in peace – a solace common to many different times and places.

The peace of death is linked here to the peace that precedes life. Zhuangzi looks back to the time before she was born, which, of course, is infinite. There he finds a perspective, a long, long view, that allows him to marvel at the mere fact of her existence. It seems a fleeting moment in forever. How extraordinary that it happened just as it did, how she emerged in the world as a beautiful child, grew into a loving wife and mother, and finally lay down serenely and died. There is in it a sense of chance, randomness even, but a wonderful fortune nonetheless.

That may seem an unusual source of consolation. Many religions make much more grandiose promises: an omniscient god, or gods, responsible for bringing you forth into life and embracing you into eternity at the end. Meaning is transcendently imparted. Life is not pointless and death is not lonely. There seems to be a powerful human desire for such beliefs, for the comfort of a supernatural and sacred controlling force that determines our fate, and providentially moves with a sense of justice. Many Americans embrace that faith. In contrast, philosophical Daoism offers thin gruel. Indeed, it promises only that Way is "the thinnest of bland flavors" (Hinton, *Daodejing*, 35): no god, no heaven, no redemption, no immortality – just "a vast room." It's a hard sell to convince devout Americans that Daoism might relieve their grief.

But it helped me. When Aidan died, I did not sing and pound on a tub like Zhuangzi. I cried and ached. With some foreknowledge that his end was upon us, I sat with my wife and designed his funeral service, picking out readings and songs. I delivered a eulogy. In short, we did what Confucius would want us to do: we thought carefully about how best to express our grief and commemorate Aidan's life, and we enacted those intentions ritually. But afterwards, when the relatives had gone home and I found myself alone, in darkness, facing an absence where his presence had once been, then the Daoism helped.

I thought back to the time before Aidan was born, before he had a spirit. And the sheer wonder of his being cascaded down upon me. His time of life was short, but in the vastness of Way all life is short. His disabilities had limited his experience, but in the narrow confines of time and knowledge and circumstance, we are all limited. His years had been remarkable, a marvel of integrity (*de*) unfolding in a singular and unique manner. Why not celebrate his presence rather than grieve his absence? Like Zhuangzi, I had to let go of my desire that he live, relinquish my claim to his life, and simply revel in the moment he had provided. Love cannot demand eternity but must accept impermanence. And in that knowledge is a kind of liberation. We'll give Zhuangzi the last words:

> Joy and anger, sorrow and delight, hope and regret, doubt and ardor, diffidence and abandon, candor and reserve: it's all music rising out of emptiness, mushrooms appearing out of mist. Day and night come and go, but who knows where it all begins? It is! It just is! If you understand this day in and day out, you inhabit the very source of it all. (Hinton, 19)

Notes

1. The single best source for documents and a timeline on the Schiavo case is a website, Abstract Appeal, maintained by Matt Conigliaro, especially the "Terri Schiavo Infopage": http://abstractappeal.com/schiavo/infopage.html, accessed March 5, 2013. For overviews, see: Timothy E. Quill, M.D.,, "Terri Schiavo – A Tragedy Compounded," *The New England Journal of Medicine*, 352 (April 21, 2005), pp. 1630–1633; Joan Didion, "The Case of Theresa Schiavo," *The New York Review of Books*, 52 (10) (June 9, 2005).

2. "In re: Guardianship of: Theresa Marie Schiavo, Incapacitated," District Court of Appeal of Florida, Second District, Case No. 2D02-5394, opinion filed June 6, 2003, p. 10. Available at: http://statecasefiles.justia .com/documents/florida/second-district-court-of-appeal/2D02-5394.pdf?ts =1323891584, accessed March 5, 2013.

3. "In re: Guardianship of: Theresa Marie Schiavo, Incapacitated," Circuit Court for Pinellas County, Florida, Probate Division, file number 90-2908GD-003, ordered February 11, 2000, pp. 9–10. Available at: http:// abstractappeal.com/schiavo/trialctorder02-00.pdf, accessed March 5, 2013.

4. Daniel Callahan, "Can we return death to disease?" *The Hastings Center Report*, 19 (1) (January–February, 1989), pp. 4-6.

5. "Allowing to Die," *Commonweal*, CXXX (19) (November 7, 2003), p. 7.

6. "Allowing to Die II," *Commonweal*, CXXXI (8) (April 23, 2004), p. 5.

7. "But the real lesson of the Schiavo case is not that we all need living wills; it is that our dignity does not reside in our will alone, and that it is foolish to believe that the competent person I am now can establish, in advance, how I should be cared for if I become incapacitated and incompetent. The real lesson is that we are not mere creatures of the will: we still possess dignity and rights even when our capacity to make free choices is gone; and we do not possess the right to demand that others treat us as less worthy of care than we really are." Eric Cohen, "How Liberalism Failed Terri Schiavo," *The Weekly Standard*, April 4, 2005. Available at: http://www.weeklystandard.com/Content/Public /Articles/000/000/005/408ytxle.asp, accessed March 5, 2013.

8. Ying-Shih Yu, "Life and Immortality in the Mind of Han China," *Harvard Journal of Asiatic Studies*, 25 (1964–1965), pp. 80–122.

9. "The central theme of the Chuang Tzu may be summed up in a single word: freedom. Essentially, all the philosophers of ancient China addressed themselves to the same problem: how is man to live in a world dominated by chaos, suffering, and absurdity? . . . Chuang Tzu's answer to the question is: free yourself from the world." Burton Watson, *The Complete Works of Chuang Tzu* (New York: Columbia University Press, 1968), p. 3.

10. Norman Kutcher, *Mourning in Late Imperial China: Filial Piety and the State* (Cambridge: Cambridge University Press, 1999), pp. 15–16.

Index

Life, Liberty, and the Pursuit of Dao: Ancient Chinese Thought in Modern American Life,
First Edition. Sam Crane.
© 2013 John Wiley & Sons, Inc. Published 2013 by John Wiley & Sons, Inc.